AS Psychology for AQA (A)

Jean-Marc Lawton, Richard Gross, Geoff Rolls

DYNAMIC LEARNING

HODDER EDUCATION
AN HACHETTE UK COMPANY

Photo credits

The authors and publishers would like to thank the following for the use of photographs in this volume:

p.2 © Hulton-Deutsch Collection/Corbis; p.4 © Photosani – Fotolia (top); p. 4 © Lindsey Bowes (bottom); p.8 © Joanna Zielinska – Fotolia; p.9 © Gideon Mendel/In Pictures /Corbis; p.11 © Topham Picturepoint/Press Association Images; p.17 © picsfive – Fotolia; p.20 © Kris Krug; p.21 © AP/Press Association Images; p.22 © Dron – Fotolia; p.30 © schmecko – Fotolia; p.31 © PA Archive/ Press Association Images; p.32 © Ingram Publishing Ltd (top); p.32 © Yuri Arcurs – Fotolia (bottom); p.37 © Luciana Bueno – Fotolia; p.39 © Martin Rogers / Stone / Getty Images; p.41 © Nina Leen//Time Life Pictures/Getty Images; p.44 Photo Courtesy U.Va. Public Affairs; p.47 © Simone van den Berg – Fotolia; p.48 © Eleanor Bentall/Corbis; p.49 © John Warburton-Lee Photography / Alamy; p.61 © Lagui – Fotolia; p.64 © Jennie Hart / Alamy; p.68 © Vlad – Fotolia; p.73 © Andres Rodriguez – Fotolia; p.81 © Still Representation - Fotolia (top); p.81 © Paul Hebditch – Fotolia (bottom); p.78 © Ror – Fotolia; p.80 © Monika Adamczyk - Fotolia. com (top); p.80 © Stockbyte / Getty Images (bottom); p.81 © Christian Schwier – Germany; p.84 © AP/Press Association Images; p.88 © cphoto – Fotolia; p.90 © Mi.Schneidmiller – Fotolia; p.99 ©.Anke van Wyk – Fotolia; p.102 © Liv Friis-larsen – Fotolia; p.115 © Marzanna Syncerz – Fotolia; p.120 Courtesy Professor Janice Kiecolt-Glaser (left); p.120 © 2009 Robert Byron – Fotolia (right); p.121 © MICHELE S. GRAHAM / SCIENCE PHOTO LIBRARY; p.125 © Stephen Finn – Fotolia; p.127 Courtesy of UZ Leuven; p.128 © 2006 Daryl Marquardt – Fotolia; p.136 © Elenathewise – Fotolia; p.139 © Image State Media; p.140 © Matthias Lenke – Fotolia; p.142 Courtesy Professor Randy Sansone; p.144 © 2007 Ron Chapple Stock – Fotolia; p.145 © Stockbyte / Getty Images; p.146 © Fantasista – Fotolia; p.147 © PATRICK BAZ/AFP/Getty Images; p.153 © TIM SLOAN/AFP/Getty Images; p.154 © DOMINIQUE FAGET/AFP/Getty Images (top); p.154 © cphoto – Fotolia (bottom); p.156 Reproduced with permission. Copyright © 2011 Scientific American, a division of Nature America, Inc. All rights reserved; p.159 © Pascal Eisenschmidt – Fotolia (left); p.159 © Jana Lumley – Fotolia (right); p.160 © Nash Photos / Photographer's Choice RF / Getty Images (top); p.160 © AndersonRise – Fotolia; p.161 © Hulton-Deutsch Collection/Corbis; p.163 © AP/Press Association Images (top); p.163 © Courtesy of the American Psychological Association Archives (bottom); p.165 From the film Obedience © 1968 by Stanley Milgram, © renewed 1993 by Alexandra Milgram; p.166 © APIC / Hulton Archive / Getty Images; p.168 © Paylessimages – Fotolia; p.169 © TopFoto / Photo News; p.171 © 8899 – Fotolia; p.175 © lightpoet – Fotolia; p.178 © YOSHIKAZU TSUNO/AFP/Getty Images; p.182 © Jon Jones/Sygma/Corbis; p.186 © PA Archive/Press Association Images; p.188 © PA Archive/Press Association Images (left); p.188 © epa/Corbis; p.192 © ODETTE M. RIGAUD / SCIENCE PHOTO LIBRARY (right); p.193 © SCIENCE PHOTO LIBRARY; p.194 © Gary Woodard – Fotolia; p.197 © AP/Press Association Images; p.200 © Archives of the History of American Psychology, the Center for the History of Psychology – The University of Akron; p.201 © Ana Blazic – Fotolia; p.205 © stuchin – Fotolia; p.208 © Andrzej Tokarski – Fotolia.

Every effort has been made to trace and acknowledge ownership of copyright. The publishers will be glad to make suitable arrangements with any copyright holders whom it has not been possible to contact.

Orders: please contact Bookpoint Ltd, 130 Milton Park, Abingdon, Oxon OX14 4SB. Telephone: (44) 01235 827720. Fax: (44) 01235 400454. Lines are open from 9.00 – 5.00, Monday to Saturday, with a 24-hour message answering service. You can also order through our website www.hoddereducation.co.uk

If you have any comments to make about this, or any of our other titles, please send them to educationenquiries@hodder.co.uk

British Library Cataloguing in Publication Data
A catalogue record for this title is available from the British Library

ISBN: 978 1 444 12334 0

First Published 2011
Impression number 10 9 8 7 6 5 4
Year 2015, 2014, 2013, 2012

Cover photo © Vit Kovalcik – Fotolia.com
Illustrations by Barking Dog Art
Typeset by DC Graphic Design Ltd, Swanley Village, Kent.
Printed in Dubai for Hodder Education, an Hachette UK Company.

Contents

Introduction

This text is aimed specifically at those students studying the AQA (A) Psychology AS specification, though it will also prove useful to any students of psychology.

The book describes the course content as outlined by the AQA specification, but it is hoped that it will also be used as a learning aid in itself and not just as a basic textbook. There is a standard format throughout the book and the features are designed specifically to help students get the most out of their studies and achieve the best possible grade at final examinations.

The book is divided into six chapters, which reflect the six topics that make up Units 1 and 2 of the AQA (A) AS course. What you will find within these chapters is basic text describing the relevant theories and explanations required for study, as well as the following regular features, which need some explanation in order for you to understand and get the most from them.

Understanding the specification

Found at the beginning of each chapter, the Understanding the specification section details the specific elements of topics that need to be studied in order to guarantee being able to answer any possible examination question you may face.

In the news

This feature will highlight topical news items which illustrate central themes of the topics being discussed.

Key terms

Concise and clear explanations of significant words and phrases associated with each topic. The key terms will be highlighted within the text and then fully explained in the associated text box feature.

Evaluation

This feature tends to occur after a research section or at the conclusion of an explanation/theory and consists of general evaluative and analytical points that could be used as AO2 material in exam answers.

Research in focus

Using examples from the text, this feature gets students to focus on methodological aspects of research studies (how studies are carried out) and asks relevant questions to assist learning and understanding. Knowledge of research methods is examined directly in the Unit 1 paper and can help form evaluative material for longer answer questions. This knowledge is essential for those hoping to progress to A2. It is often a good idea to reference material in Chapter 3 (Research methods) to get the most out of this feature.

You are the researcher

This feature again focuses on research methods, but this time from the viewpoint of the design of psychological studies. This helps to foster a greater understanding of why and how psychologists conduct research and helps students to develop the necessary skills to plan research themselves.

Web support

For those interested and motivated enough to take their learning further, this feature directs students to websites that provide a wealth of further information not located in the text.

Classic research

As the title suggests, this feature focuses on famous psychological studies, taking you in some detail through the thinking behind such studies, as well as the aims, procedure, findings, conclusions and evaluation.

Contemporary research

Similar in focus and presentation to the classic research feature, but this time featuring more recent cutting-edge research, providing an up-to-date account of the subject and an opportunity for students to include more modern material in their exam answers.

Supplementary learning

This feature provides extra learning material to form a useful and relevant source of elaboration for exam answers. This information is aimed at those who wish to take their learning further.

Psychology in action

This is an occasional feature which focuses on practical applications of psychological research. It will help to form a valuable source of AO2 evaluative material.

Strengthen your learning

Generally found at the end of each element of a topic, this feature has been designed to help students to focus on and appraise the material covered in the previous section. Acting as a form of comprehension exercise, the questions can be used as a means of revision before attempting the exam-based assessment questions that tend to follow this feature. Some detailed suggestions for answers are provided on the free-access part of the online dynamic learning platform.

Assessment check

These are genuine exam-type questions covering just about every type of exam question that students can expect to be confronted with in their AS Unit 1 and 2 papers. The feature includes some helpful examination guidance, highlighting what is required in an answer, as well as pointing out pitfalls to avoid.

End of chapter review

Each chapter concludes with a review of the main points covered in bullet-point form.

Examination skills

The AQA (A) AS examination papers assess two examination skills. These are Assessment Objective 1, more commonly known as AO1, and Assessment Objective 2 or AO2.

AO1 assesses level of knowledge and understanding by asking candidates to outline and describe relevant theories/explanations and research studies.

AO2 takes this further by assessing candidates' ability to analyse and evaluate such material, in other words consider its meaning and worth. This could be achieved through a consideration of what research findings suggest, support/lack of support from other research sources, methodological criticisms, relevant ethical points, as well as practical applications and implications of research.

Acknowledgements

JML would like to thank Tim Lloyd for his friendship and encouragement over so many years, peace, love and Northern Soul.

1 Cognitive psychology

Introduction

Cognitive psychology concerns the study of mental processes, with emphasis on information processing, for example, how people think and learn. The specific topic featured is memory, the retention of experience. The chapter will focus on three aspects of memory:

- how memory works
- factors affecting the accuracy of memory
- strategies for memory improvement.

Understanding the specification

- You must have knowledge of the multi-store and working memory models, including their strengths and weaknesses, as they are directly referred to in the specification and could be included explicitly in the wording of examination questions.
- Eyewitness testimony and factors affecting it must also be studied, especially anxiety and age, as they are directly referred to and could feature specifically in examination questions.
- There is a requirement for misleading information and the use of the cognitive interview to be included in your studies, as this is stated clearly in the specification and could again form the basis of examination questions.
- The same is true of strategies for memory improvement; you could be asked specific questions about them in your AS Paper 1. However, no specific strategies are listed, so any relevant ones would be creditworthy.
- These are the basic requirements to ensure you can answer any examination question, however other relevant material is included in this chapter, to provide depth and detail to your understanding and hopefully help to maximise marks gained in your AS examinations.

Models of memory

The multi-store model

The **multi-store model** (MSM), developed by Atkinson and Shiffrin in 1968, explains how information flows from one storage system to another, with three permanent structures in memory: sensory memory (SM), short-term memory (STM) and long-term memory (LTM). Each memory stage differs in terms of:

- capacity – how much information can be stored
- duration – how long information can be stored
- encoding – the form in which information is stored.

Information received through the senses enters SM. A small fraction is attended to and selected for further processing in STM. If not attended to, sensory information is immediately forgotten or not even processed in the first place. If information is actively processed, mainly through rehearsal, then it may be transferred to LTM for more permanent storage.

IN THE NEWS

Memories of D-Day, 6 June 1944 from a BBC Two programme, *The Mind Machine* shown in 1988

Ken Jones had always possessed a good memory, but then a viral infection robbed him of the ability to recall recent events. He could still talk, read and walk normally, indeed do everything he had before his illness, but he could not retrace a route of just seven destinations, laid out for him by Professor Barbara Wilson of Southampton University ten minutes before. Ken thought years had passed in seconds and couldn't recall the date, but when told it was 6 June, instantly remembered in vivid detail his involvement in the D-Day landings on the beaches of Normandy on that date in 1944. He could recall the girl he loved, his marriage to her for three decades, but not her death a year ago.

Figure 1.1 Allied troops on D-Day, 6 June 1944

Ken's illness prevented him from transferring short-term memories to long-term memories. This case study is strong evidence that memory has two parts, a short-term and a long-term component, and that without normal memory capabilities, the quality of life is severely diminished.

Sensory memory

Sensory memory is a short-duration store retaining unprocessed impressions of information received through the senses, with a separate sensory store for each sensory input, such as the **iconic store** for visual information and the **echoic store** for auditory information. **Trace decay** results in information being lost rapidly from SM, though information paid attention to passes to the STM for a more lasting representation.

Research studies into SM

Crowder (2003) found that SM retains information for a few milliseconds within the iconic store but about 2–3 seconds within the echoic store, supporting the idea of a separate sensory store for each sensory input.

Treisman (1964) presented identical auditory messages to both ears of participants, with a slight delay between presentations. Participants noticed the messages were identical if the delay was two seconds or less, implying that the echoic store has a duration of up to two seconds and is longer than the iconic store.

Haber (1969) found about five per cent of children have **eidetic memory** (photographic memory) and can hold visual images for up to several minutes. Such children can answer accurately questions about the image, which suggests that for some individuals, the iconic SM is relatively long lasting.

Figure 1.2 Five per cent of children have a photographic memory

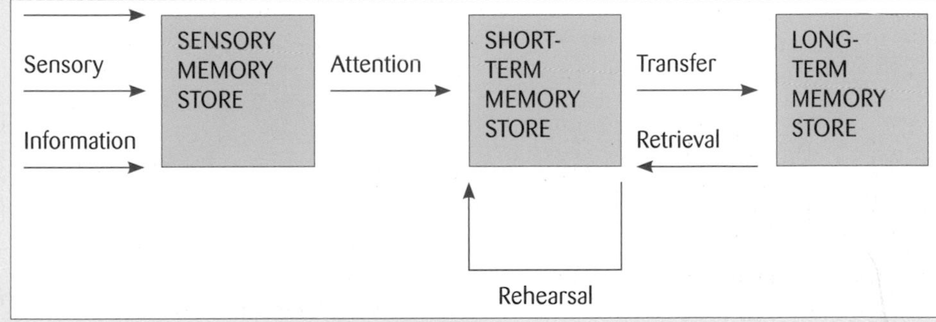

Figure 1.3 The multi-store model

Short-term memory

Short-term memory is an active memory system containing information currently being thought about. STM is a temporary storage of information received from the SM. STM differs from LTM in terms of duration, capacity, encoding and how information is forgotten.

Key terms

Encoding – the means by which information is represented in memory

Storage – the retention of information in memory

Capacity – the amount of information that can be stored at a given time

Sensory memory – a short-duration store holding the impressions of sensory information

Short-term memory – a temporary store holding small amounts of information for brief periods

Duration – the length of time information remains within storage

Long-term memory – a permanent store holding limitless amounts of information for long periods

Figure 1.4 A banana can be encoded in STM in several ways

Encoding in short-term memory

Information arrives in the SM in its original form, such as sound or vision. This is encoded in a form the STM can deal with. If the input into SM is the word 'banana', this could be encoded in one of three ways:

- **visually** by thinking of an image of a banana
- **acoustically** by saying 'banana' repeatedly
- **semantically** (through meaning) by using your knowledge of bananas – for example, they are yellow, curved and edible.

The dominant form of encoding in STM is acoustic.

Classic research

Encoding in STM – Alan Baddeley, 1966

Professor Alan Baddeley of York University is best known for helping develop the working memory model (1974), but he also carried out lots of other memory research, including the following experiment into encoding in STM.

Figure 1.5 Alan Baddeley

Aim: To examine whether encoding in STM is primarily acoustic or semantic.

Procedure: 75 participants were presented with one of four word lists repeated four times.

List A – acoustically similar words ('cat', 'mat', 'sat')

List B – acoustically dissimilar words ('pit', 'day', 'cow')

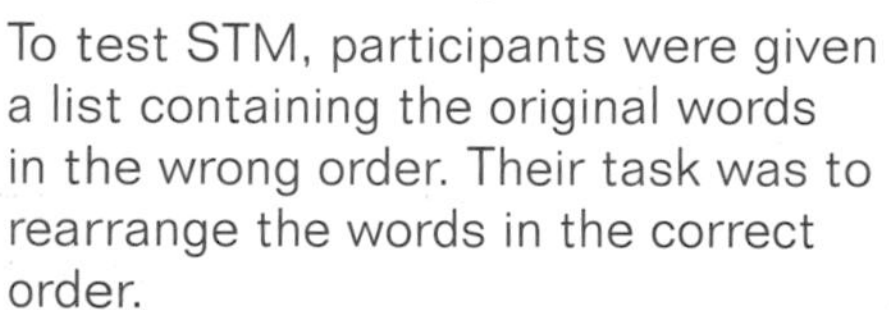

List C – semantically similar words ('big', 'huge', 'tall')

List D – semantically dissimilar words ('hot', 'safe', 'foul')

To test STM, participants were given a list containing the original words in the wrong order. Their task was to rearrange the words in the correct order.

Findings: Participants given List A (acoustically similar words) performed the worst, with a recall of only 10 per cent. They confused similar sounding words, such as recalling 'cap' instead of 'cat'. Recall for the other lists was comparatively good at between 60 to 80 per cent.

Conclusions: Since List A was recalled the least efficiently, it seems there is acoustic confusion in STM, suggesting STM is encoded on an acoustic basis.

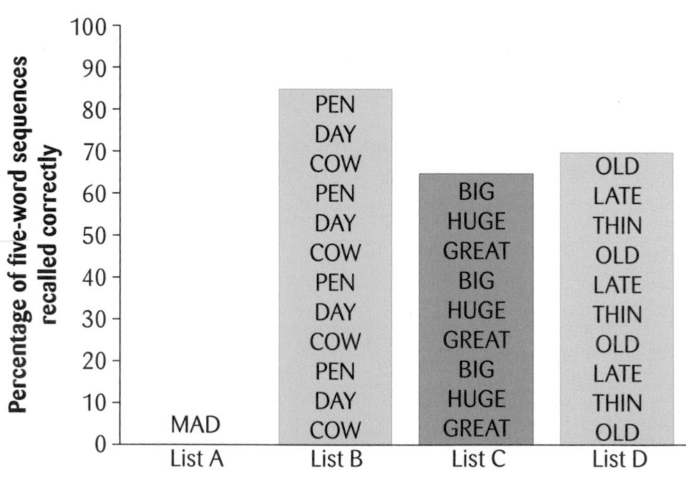

Figure 1.6 Baddeley's 1966 acoustic/semantic study findings

continued ...

...continued

Evaluation:

- Baddeley's findings make 'cognitive sense'. For example, if you had to remember a shopping list, you'd probably repeat it aloud (acoustic rehearsal) walking to the shops.
- This was a laboratory study and therefore shows **causality** (cause and effect relationships), but may lack **ecological validity** (not representative of real life activities).
- As a laboratory study it can be **replicated** (repeated) exactly to check the results.

Research in focus

Baddeley's (1966) study into encoding in STM was an experiment, but what type of experiment was it?

Give a strength and a weakness of this type of experiment.

What were the independent variable (IV) and the dependent variable (DV) in Baddeley's study?

What is a DV always a type of?

(See Chapter 3, Research methods, for more information about IVs and DVs.)

Other research studies of encoding in STM

- Conrad (1964) presented participants with visual strings of letters for three-quarters of a second. He found that V and B often got confused with P, while S did not. This type of error suggests that visual information is converted to acoustic information, implying that encoding in STM is primarily acoustic.
- Posner and Keele (1967) found participants were faster in deciding 'A' followed by 'A' was the same letter than when 'A' was followed by 'a'. As the visual code differs for the second letter when 'A' is followed by 'a', the findings suggest visual encoding also occurs in STM.
- Wickens *et al.* (1976) gave participants three successive trials of different words from the same semantic category (types of fruit). Participants had to count backwards to prevent rehearsal. On the fourth trial the semantic category was changed, for example to professions. Recall decreased on the first three trials, as it became increasingly difficult to recall which specific fruits were presented. However, recall improved on the fourth trial, suggesting semantic encoding was occurring.

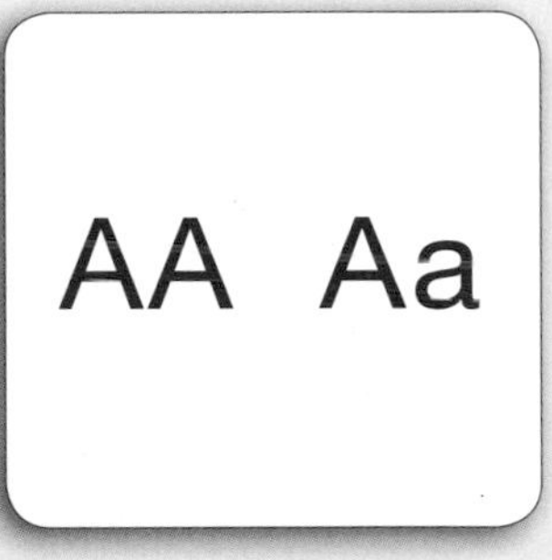

AA Aa

Figure 1.7 It is easier to decide that AA are the same letters than Aa

Evaluation

Evaluation of encoding in STM

- STM is not restricted to acoustic coding. The small difference in recall between semantically similar (64 per cent) and semantically dissimilar (71 per cent) lists suggests there is some semantic coding in STM. We also remember visual images, such as faces, in STM that would be difficult to encode acoustically.
- Overall research suggests that encoding in STM is predominately acoustic, but that other sensory codes, such as visual codes, are also used.

Capacity of STM

STM has a limited capacity; we can hold only a small amount of information before it is forgotten. This can be investigated with the **digit span technique**, where participants are presented with increasingly long sequences of digits, to be recalled in the correct order (e.g. 26478, 968423, 2975841 and so on). When participants fail on 50 per cent of the trials, it is said that they have reached their digit span capacity. Research indicates a STM capacity of five to nine items. Capacity is increased through chunking where the size of the units of information in memory is increased.

> **Key terms**
>
> **Chunking** – grouping information in short-term memory into larger units to increase capacity

Research studies of capacity in STM

- Jacobs (1887) gave participants increasingly longer lists of either letters or numbers, finding capacity for numbers was nine items and for letters was seven items.
- Baddeley (1999) found that capacity for numbers increased if the numbers were read aloud rather than sub-vocally, possibly because the memory trace was strengthened through using the echoic store.
- Miller (1956) concluded from reviewing research that the capacity of STM was between five and nine items, but that the 'chunk' (grouping information into meaningful bits) was the basic unit of STM. This meant that between five and nine chunks could be contained within STM, effectively increasing its capacity.

SHOPPING LIST
Jar of honey
Bag of haycorns
Bale of thistles
Tin of condensed milk
Extract of malt

Figure 1.8 The best way to remember a shopping list is to repeat it aloud

Duration of STM

The duration of STM is fairly limited – less than 30 seconds. Research also indicates that information is lost rapidly from STM if it is not rehearsed. Repetition retains material within the STM loop, until eventually it becomes a permanent feature within LTM.

Evaluation

Evaluation of capacity in STM

- Numbers may be easier to recall as there are only nine of them, compared to 26 letters in the English language.
- Other factors, like age and amount of practice, also influence STM capacity. Nowadays, STM limitations are considered mostly to be limitations on processing associated with attention.
- Simon (1974) found that although STM capacity should be measured in terms of chunks, this varies with the type of material being recalled and the amount of information contained within the chunks.
- Experimental tasks that participants are required to perform, like recalling lists of letters, often have little relevance to everyday activities and so may lack mundane realism.
- There may be individual differences in STM capacity. Daneman and Carpenter (1980) found capacity ranged from 5 to 20 items between those with advanced and poor reading comprehension.

Research studies of duration of STM

- Peterson and Peterson (1959) read nonsense trigrams (such as XQF) to participants and then got them to count backwards in threes from a large three-digit number for between 3 and 18 seconds to prevent rehearsal. About 90 per cent of trigrams were recalled after a 3-second retention interval, but only around five per cent after 18 seconds, suggesting that STM duration is about 20 to 30 seconds.
- Healy *et al.* (1993) presented participants with two four-consonant segments, separated by an exclamation mark, with the same four items occurring in each segment across all trials. Participants were required to recall the order of one of the two segments. Decline in recall was as little as seven per cent, suggesting that the duration of STM is longer than first thought.
- Marsh *et al.* (1997) found that if participants were not expecting to have to recall information, then STM duration was brief, at between 2 to 4 seconds, suggesting duration of STM is related to the amount of processing of information.

Figure 1.9 90 per cent of trigrams are recalled after a 3-second retention interval, but only five per cent are recalled after 18 seconds

Evaluation

Evaluation of duration of STM

- Reitman (1974) suggested that the brief duration of STM is due to displacement; as new information comes into STM, the existing information is kicked out due to its limited capacity.
- Peterson and Peterson's results may have occurred due to flawed methodology. Because different trigrams were used on each trial, this may have led to interference between items, leading to decreased recall.
- Recalling nonsense trigrams bares little relevance to STM tasks occurring in our everyday lives and therefore lacks mundane realism.
- There is little in the way of research evidence considering the STM duration of other forms of stimuli, like visual images.

Long-term memory

Long-term memory involves the storage of information over extended periods of time, potentially a whole lifetime. Forgetting from LTM may not occur due to loss of information, but rather to problems in retrieving memory traces. Storage of information longer than 30 seconds counts as LTM.

Encoding in long-term memory

With verbal material, it appears that coding in LTM is mainly semantic (based on meaning), although there is research to indicate a visual and an acoustic code.

Research studies into encoding in LTM

- Baddeley (1966) used the same procedure as in his STM study (see page 4), but with a 20-minute interval before recall, during which participants conducted another task. Participants with list C (semantically similar) had only 55 per cent recall, while recall for the other lists was comparatively good at 70–85 per cent. As list C was recalled with the least efficiency, it appears that there is semantic confusion in LTM, suggesting that LTM is encoded semantically.

- Frost (1972) gave participants 16 drawings in four categories (e.g. animals), differing in visual orientation, like angle of viewing perspective. The order of recall of items suggested participants used visual and semantic encoding, implying evidence for a visual code in LTM.
- Nelson and Rothbart (1972) demonstrated that acoustic encoding also occurs in LTM, as participants made recall errors involving homophones – words that are pronounced the same, but have different meanings – like 'night' and 'knight'.

Evaluation

Evaluation of encoding in LTM

- Semantic encoding makes 'cognitive sense'. Recall a TV programme you watched and you will remember the overall message (meaning), but not the actual words (acoustic).
- Different types of LTM, like **procedural memory** (how to perform tasks like riding a bike) and **episodic memory** (memories of events) are rarely researched and are arguably not encoded in the same way.
- It is difficult to see how smells and tastes could be encoded semantically and reason suggests that songs must be encoded acoustically, supporting the idea of several forms of encoding in LTM.

Capacity of long-term memory

The potential capacity of LTM is unlimited. No one has ever shown that their brain is full! Information may be lost due to decay and interference, but such losses do not occur due to limitation of capacity.

Research studies of capacity of LTM

Figure 1.10 Knowing how to ride a bike is part of our procedural memory

- Anokhin (1973) estimated that the number of possible neuronal connections in the human brain is 1 followed by 10.5 million kilometres of noughts. He concluded 'no human yet exists who can use all the potential of their brain', suggesting that the capacity of LTM is limitless.
- Linton (1975) spent six years creating a diary of 5,500 personal events. She tested herself for recognition of events each month and found she had excellent recall of dates, demonstrating the colossal potential capacity of LTM.
- Similarly, Wagenaar (1986) created a diary of 2,400 events over six years and tested himself on recall of events rather than dates. He found that he too had excellent recall, again suggesting that the capacity of LTM is extremely large.

Research in focus

Diary studies, like those of Linton and Wagenaar, are a type of case study. Why is it difficult to generalise from case studies?

Case studies often rely on retrospective memories. What kind of problems might this cause for researchers?

Diary studies can also be considered longitudinal studies. Explain what is meant by a longitudinal study. What is the main thing that such studies can show?

Evaluation

Evaluation of capacity of LTM

- Diary studies are a type of case study and are therefore not representative of the general population.
- There could also be an element of bias as people are testing themselves.
- The capacity of LTM is assumed to be limitless as research has not been able to determine a finite capacity.

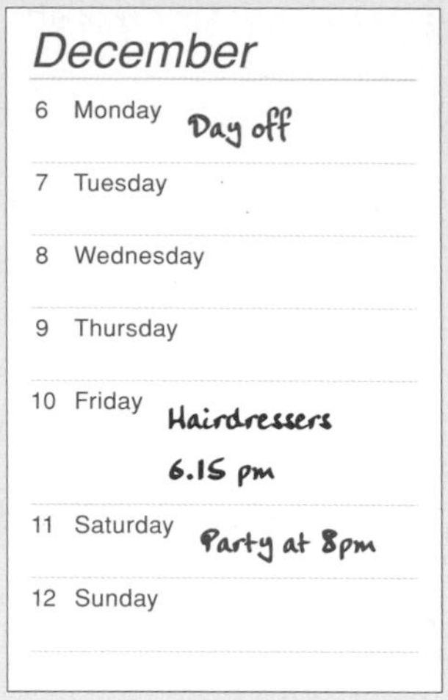

December
6 Monday Day off
7 Tuesday
8 Wednesday
9 Thursday
10 Friday Hairdressers 6.15 pm
11 Saturday Party at 8pm
12 Sunday

Figure 1.11 Diary studies permit us to study the capacity of LTM

Duration of long-term memory

Memories can last a lifetime, so the duration of LTM depends on an individual's lifespan. Older people often have very clear childhood memories. Items in LTM have a longer duration if originally well-learned. Certain forms of information have a longer duration, like information based on skills rather than just facts. Material in STM that is not rehearsed is quickly forgotten, but information in LTM does not have to be continually rehearsed to be retained.

Research studies of duration of LTM

- Bahrick *et al.*(1975) showed 400 participants aged 17–74 years a set of photos and a list of names, some of which were old school friends, and asked them to identify their old school friends in the photos. Those who had left high school in the last 15 years recalled 90 per cent of faces and names, while those who had left 48 years previously recalled 80 per cent of names and 70 per cent of faces, suggesting that memory for faces is long lasting.
- Goldman and Seamon (1992) asked participants to recognise odours of everyday products experienced in the last two years and odours not experienced since childhood. Although recognition (by name) was better for more-recent odours, there was significant recognition of less-recent odours, suggesting that duration of olfactory information in LTM is very enduring.
- Shephard (1967) found that participants were able to recognise pictures seen an hour earlier when viewed amongst other pictures and were still able to recall about 50 per cent of the photographs four months later, again suggesting duration of LTM to be long lasting.

Figure 1.12 Our memory for faces is long lasting

Evaluation

Evaluation of duration of LTM

- It is difficult to ascertain whether information is actually lost from LTM; it may just get increasingly difficult to access.
- The type of testing techniques used may affect research findings from studies of duration of LTM. For instance, recall is better when done by recognition, rather than free recall.
- Certain forms of information may have a longer duration than others. Conway *et al.* (1991) found that statistical information is retained longer, possibly as it involves the learning of skills, rather than just plain facts.

Table 1.1 Summary of STM/LTM differences

	STM		LTM	
Encoding	Mainly acoustic (sound)	Baddeley (1966) – immediate recall study	Mainly semantic (meaning)	Baddeley (1966) – delayed recall study
Capacity	Small (7 +/– 2 chunks of information)	Jacobs (1887) – digit span	Unlimited	Wagenaar (1986) – diary study
Duration	Short (<30 seconds)	Peterson and Peterson (1959) – trigrams retention experiment	30 seconds to a lifetime	Bahrick *et al.* (1975) – high school study

Evaluation

Evaluation of the multi-store model

- The MSM was influential, inspiring interest and research and paving the way for subsequent models, like the Working Memory Model, leading to a greater understanding of how memory works.
- There is considerable evidence for the existence of distinct types of memory stores – namely SM, STM and LTM.
- Shallice and Warrington (1970) reported the case study of K.F. who as a result of an accident had a reduced STM of only one or two digits and a recency effect (see Supplementary learning section on page 11) of one item. Yet his LTM for events after the accident was normal, supporting the idea of separate short- and long-term memory stores as proposed by the MSM.
- Scoville (1957) attempted to treat patient H.M.'s epilepsy by removing his hippocampus, amygdala and entorhinal and perirhinal cortices. This resulted in the patient being unable to encode new long-term memories, although his STM seemed unaffected, again supporting the idea of separate memory stores.
- Bekerian and Baddeley (1980) found that people were unaware of changes to BBC radio wavelengths despite hearing the information, on average, over a thousand times. This suggests that rehearsal is not the only factor in the transfer of STM to LTM, which contradicts the MSM.
- The multi-store model is over-simplified in assuming that there is a single STM and a single LTM. Research indicates several types of STM, such as one for verbal and one for non-verbal sounds, and different types of LTM, like procedural, episodic and semantic memories.
- Cohen (1990) believes memory capacity cannot be measured purely in terms of the amount of information, but rather by the nature of the information to be recalled. Some things are easier to recall, regardless of the amount to be learned, and the MSM doesn't consider this.
- MSM describes memory in terms of structure, namely the three memory stores and the processes of attention and verbal rehearsal. However, MSM focuses too much on structure and not enough on processes.

Figure 1.13 Clive Wearing

A famous case study is that of Clive Wearing, who through illness suffered damage to his STM, but not his LTM, providing a degree of support for the MSM. An illuminating video clip can be seen at http://www.youtube.com/watch?v=wDNDRDJy-vo

Supplementary learning

Serial position effect

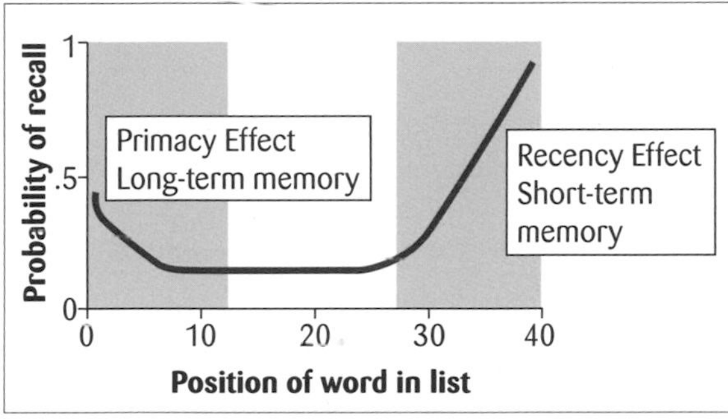

Figure 1.14 Results from free recall experiment. The probability of recall varies with an item's position in a list

- Murdock (1962) presented participants with a list of words to be recalled in any order (free recall). Words at the beginning and the end of the lists were recalled better than those in the middle. This is the **serial position effect**. Words at the beginning of the list are recalled because they have been constantly rehearsed and transferred to LTM (the **primacy effect**), while words from the end of the list are recalled as they are still in STM (the **recency effect**), supporting the idea of separate STM and LTM.
- Glanzer and Cunitz (1966) introduced an **interference task** in the form of participants counting backwards in threes for ten seconds at the end of the list and before recall, in order to eliminate the recency effect. Recall was good of earlier items, which had been rehearsed and were in LTM, but not of the last few items, which had not. This further supports the idea of a separate STM and LTM, suggesting one can be altered without affecting the other.
- Glanzer (1972) subsequently found that other factors affect the primacy effect but not the recency effect. For example, the slower items were presented, the better they were recalled, younger people recalled more items and well-known words were remembered better. This again suggests the existence of a separate STM and LTM.

You are the researcher

A lot of research has been done into the serial position effect which involves both the primacy and recency effects. Read the text in the Supplementary learning feature above which details such research and then see if you can design a simple study using a list of about 15 unconnected words which investigates this effect. How many participants would you need to use to ensure a fairly representative sample?

Previous research indicates that more words from the beginning and the end of the list will be recalled, so what kind of hypothesis would you use?

If you wished to perform subsequent research that only investigated the recency effect, how could you prevent the primacy effect from occurring?

Strengthen your learning

1. Explain what is meant by a) encoding, b) capacity and c) duration.
2. Outline what is meant by STM and LTM.
3. Describe in no more than 50 words the MSM. Although brief, your answer should be accurate and detailed.
4. What is the difference between the echoic and the iconic stores in SM?
5. Outline the differences in encoding, capacity and duration between STM and LTM.
6. Outline one research study into a) encoding, b) capacity and c) duration of STM. Repeat this for LTM.
7. Explain two evaluative points each for encoding, capacity and duration of STM. Repeat this for LTM.
8. Make a list of evaluative points, both positive and negative, relating to the MSM. Also list any research evidence supporting these points. (This could form the basis of an answer for a 12-mark question asking you to outline and evaluate the MSM.)

Assessment Check

1 The following are concepts relating to memory.

A	Duration	**C**	Capacity
B	Retrieval	**D**	Encoding

Copy and complete the table by writing which concept (A, B, C or D) matches which definition. [3 marks]

Definition	Concept
The length of time information remains in storage	
The amount of information that can be stored at a given time	
The means by which information is represented in memory	

2 A case study on Elidh, whose brain was damaged in a car crash, revealed that she could recall a maximum of three numbers in her short-term memory, but that her long-term memory was unaffected.

a) In what way did Elidh's short-term memory differ from that of a normal adult? [2 marks]

b) In what way do the results of the case study support the multi-store model? [4 marks]

c) Give one strength and one weakness of a case study [2 + 2 marks]

3 Explain two weaknesses of the multi-store model of memory. [3 + 3 marks]

4 Outline and evaluate the multi-store model of memory. [12 marks]

Examination guidance:

1 This is a selection question, where the answers are provided, but have to be inserted correctly into the table. One concept will be left over.

2 In this question, information in the scenario has to be used to form an answer. Part c) requires knowledge of research methods, namely case studies.

3 This question focuses on weaknesses of the MSM. Advantages earn no credit and if more than two weaknesses were provided, all are marked, but only the best two will be credited.

4 This is a long-answer question, where six marks are available for outlining the MSM and six marks for evaluating it.

The working memory model

In 1974, Baddeley and Hitch questioned the existence of a single STM store (they weren't concerned with LTM), arguing that STM was more complex than being just a temporary store for transferring information to LTM. They instead saw STM as an 'active' store, holding several pieces of information while they are being worked on (hence 'working' memory). Cohen (1990) described working memory (WM) as: 'the focus of consciousness – it holds information consciously thought about now'.

Replacing the single STM, Baddeley and Hitch proposed a multi-component WM comprising three components based on the form of processing each carried out. A fourth component was added later by Baddeley and Lewis (1982).

The central executive

The central executive (CE) is the filter that determines which information is and is not attended to. It processes information in all sensory forms, directs information to other 'slave' systems and collects responses. It is limited in capacity and can only cope effectively with one 'strand' of information at a time. It therefore selectively attends to particular types of information, attaining a balance between tasks when attention needs to be divided between them, for example, talking while driving. It also permits us to switch attention between different inputs of information.

Key terms

Central executive – oversees and coordinates the components of working memory

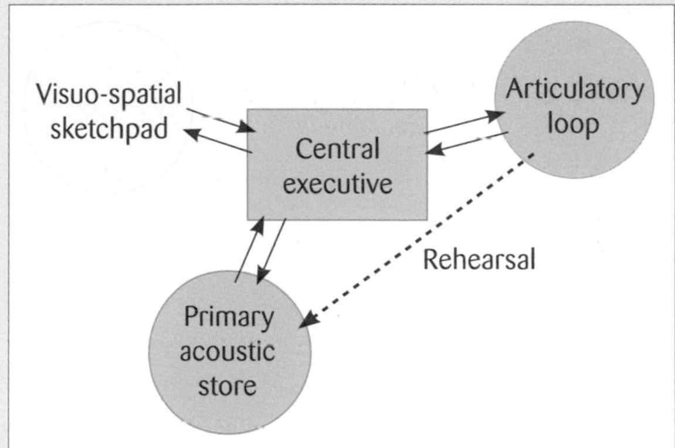

Figure 1.15

Research studies of the CE

- Eslinger and Damasio (1985) studied a patient who, after the removal of a brain tumour, could still perform well on tasks requiring reasoning, but not tasks requiring decision-making, implying that there is more than one component to the CE.
- Baddeley (1996) discovered that participants found it difficult to generate lists of random numbers while simultaneously switching between numbers and letters, suggesting that the two tasks were competing for CE resources. This supports the idea of the CE being limited in capacity and only being able to cope with one type of information at a time.
- D'Esposito *et al.* (1995) found using fMRI (functional magnetic resonance imaging) scans that the pre-frontal cortex was activated when verbal and spatial tasks were performed simultaneously, but not when performed separately, suggesting that this brain area is associated with the workings of the CE.

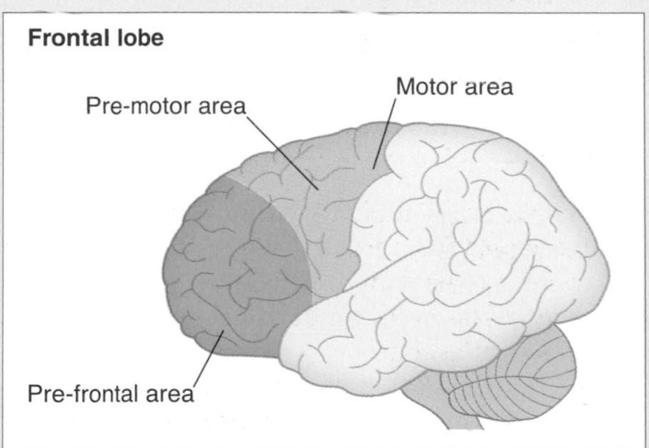

Figure 1.16 Research has shown that the pre-frontal cortex is associated with the workings of the CE

Research in focus

Research into the working memory model (WMM) tends to use laboratory-based experiments. This permits *confounding variables* to be kept to a minimum. What are **confounding variables** and why is it important to try and limit their influence?

Key terms

Phonological loop – deals with auditory information

Visuo–spatial sketchpad – deals with visual and spatial items

Phonological store – stores words heard

Articulatory process – allows sub-vocal repetition of information in the phonological loop

Primary acoustic store – stores recently heard speech or sound

The phonological loop and visuo–spatial sketchpad

The phonological loops (PL) and visuo–spatial sketchpad (VSS) are two 'slave' systems – temporary stores dealing with different kinds of incoming sensory information.

The PL is similar to the rehearsal system of the MSM with a limited capacity determined by the amount of information spoken out loud in about two seconds. It deals with auditory information and the order of information. As it is primarily an acoustic store, confusions occur with similar-sounding words.

Baddeley (1986) divided the PL into two sub-parts: the phonological store (PS) and the articulatory process (AP). The PS, or **inner ear**, stores words heard, while the AP, or **inner voice**, allows sub-vocal repetition of information stored in the PL.

Research studies of the PL

- Trojani and Grossi (1995) reported a case study of S.C. who had brain damage affecting the functioning of his PL, but not his VSS, suggesting the PL to be a separate system.
- Baddeley *et al.* (1975) reported on the **word length effect**, where participants recalled more short words in serial order than longer words, suggesting that the capacity of the PL is set by how long it takes to say words, rather than the actual number of words.
- Baddeley *et al.* (1975) found that the word length effect could be suppressed if participants had to say a word repeatedly while reading short and long words, supporting the idea of a separate AP.
- Eysenck (1995) reported on the case study of P.V. whose memory span was not affected by articulatory suppression (see below), presumably because information was going straight into the PS and missing out the AP. This suggests the existence of a separate PS.

The primary acoustic store (PAS) was added to the model by Baddeley and Lewis in 1981 after it was found that memory of nonsense words was not affected by **articulatory suppression**, where learned words are prevented from being spoken out loud. Memory for nonsense words must therefore be reliant upon a memory component other than the AP. This is the PAS, which is believed to hold recently heard speech or sound.

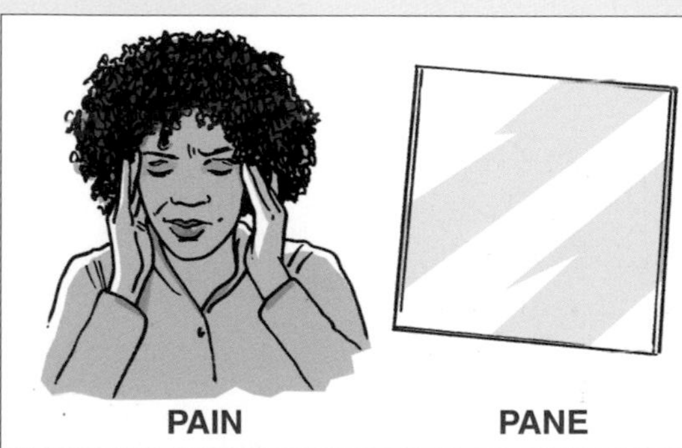

Figure 1.17 Homophones are words pronounced the same, but with different meanings

Research studies of the PAS

- Levy (1971) found that if participants were given concurrent auditory and visual material, then articulatory suppression did not affect recall, supporting the existence of the PAS.
- Baddeley and Lewis (1982) found that participants could identify which nonsense words were **homophones** (words pronounced the same, but with different meanings, like 'pain' and 'pane'), even when using their PL for a different task, suggesting that the PAS is separate from the PL.

Research in focus

The **dual-task technique** is used to perform research into the WMM. It involves participants simultaneously performing two tasks. According to the WMM, should it be easier, more difficult or as equally difficult to perform a visual and a verbal task, rather than two visual (or verbal) tasks? Explain your answer.

The VSS, or **inner eye**, handles non-phonological information and is a temporary store for visual and spatial items and the relationships between them; essentially, it is a store for what items are and where they are located. The VSS therefore helps individuals to navigate and interact with their physical environment, with information being rehearsed and encoded through the use of 'mental pictures'.

Logie (1995) suggests sub-dividing the store further into a visual cache, which stores visual material about form and colour, and an inner scribe, which handles spatial relationships and rehearses and transfers information in the visual cache to the CE.

Key terms

Visual cache – stores visual material about form and colour

Inner scribe – stores information about spatial relationships

Episodic buffer – stores integrated information from the central executive, phonological loop, visuo–spatial sketchpad and long-term memory

Research studies into the VSS

- Gathercole and Baddeley (1993) found participants had difficulty simultaneously following a moving point of light and describing the angles on a hollow letter 'F', because both tasks involved using the VSS. Other participants had little difficulty in following the light and performing a simultaneous verbal task, as they involve using the VSS and the PL, indicating the VSS to be a separate slave system.
- Quinn (1996) found that dynamic visual noise caused interference to a word list learned under visual conditions, but not to one learned under verbal conditions, again suggesting the VSS is separate from the PL.
- Klauer and Zhao (2004) suggested that there is more interference between two visual tasks than between a visual and a spatial task, implying the existence of a separate visual cache and inner scribe.
- Smith and Jonides (1999) found that PET scans showed brain activation in the left hemisphere with visual tasks, but activation in the right hemisphere with spatial information, supporting the idea of a separate visual cache and inner scribe.

The episodic buffer

In 2000, Baddeley added a third slave system, the episodic buffer (EB), as the model needs a general store to operate properly. The slave systems deal with processing and temporary storage of specific types of information. The CE has no storage capacity and so cannot contain items relating to visual and acoustic properties. Thus the EB is a limited capacity store, integrating information from the CE, the PL and the VSS, as well as from LTM.

Research studies into the EB

- Prabhakaran *et al.* (2000) used fMRI scans to find greater right frontal brain activation for integrated verbal and spatial information, but greater posterior activation for unintegrated information, suggesting evidence for an EB that allows temporary retention of integrated information.
- Alkhalifa (2009) reported on a patient with severely impaired LTM who demonstrated STM capacity of up to 25 prose items, far exceeding the capacity of both the PL and the VSS. This suggests the existence of an EB, which holds items in working memory until they are recalled.

Contemporary research

Exhibiting the effects of the episodic buffer on learning with serial and parallel presentations of materials – Ashaa Alkhalifa, 2009

Ashaa Alkhalifa is a member of the royal family of Bahrain, and has devised a method of testing for the existence of the episodic buffer.

Aim: To determine the existence of the EB by seeing if parallel presented information overwhelms both the PL and the VSS, causing a reduction in learning, while the same information presented sequentially results in improved learning, as information is stored firstly in the PL and the VSS and then filtered to the EB which should have a larger capacity.

Procedure: Forty-eight university students were presented with numerical information on a screen in either a sequential fashion (such as 1, 2, 3, 4) or a parallel fashion (where participants compare information in different parts of the screen simultaneously). Numbers of sufficient complexity were used to overwhelm the capacities of both the phonological loop and the visuo–spatial sketchpad. Participants were required to answer a number of problem-solving questions concerning the numerical information presented.

Findings: Problem-solvers using sequentially presented information were superior to those using information presented in parallel fashion.

Conclusions: A limitation exists on information passing from perception to learning, as parallel processing caused a hindrance in learning.

As sequential processing was more effective, it suggests that the total capacity of WM is larger than that determined by the capacity of the phonological loop and the visuo–spatial sketchpad, implying the existence of the EB.

Evaluation:

- The findings suggest practical applications in the designing of educational systems.
- As a laboratory study, the findings may lack **external validity** – they cannot necessarily be generalised to other settings.

An internet site documenting the development of the WMM, including some useful evaluative points, can be found at http://en.wikipedia.org/wiki/Baddeley's_model_of_working_memory

Evaluation

Evaluation of the WMM

- In contrast to the MSM, the WM model does not over-emphasise the importance of rehearsal for STM retention.
- PET scans indicate different brain areas are activated during undertaking of verbal and visual tasks, supporting the idea of a working memory involving separate components.
- The WMM is more plausible than the MSM as it demonstrates STM in terms of temporary storage and active processing.
- It may be that the EB provides the storage space and the CE the underlying processing of information that allows the separation of accurate recall from false memories and delusions.

continued ...

...continued

- WMM concerns itself only with STM and so is not a comprehensive model of memory.
- Many of the findings supporting the WMM come from laboratory studies and may lack mundane realism.
- Little is known about the central executive. It is not clear how it works or what it does. This vagueness means it can be used to explain almost any experimental results. If two tasks cannot be performed together, it is said that the two processing components are conflicting or that the tasks exceed the central executive's capacity. If two tasks can be done simultaneously, it is argued that they do not exceed the available resources – in essence a circular argument.
- The WMM does not explain changes in processing ability occurring as the result of practice or time.

Figure 1.18 The WMM has practical applications in the classroom

Psychology in action

Practical applications of the WMM

The WMM suggests practical applications, especially for children with learning difficulties relating to impairments of WM. There is little evidence that coaching WM in children with low WM abilities will lead to gains in academic performance. Instead Alloway (2006) recommends several methods to help children focus on the task at hand:

- Use brief and simple instructions so the child will not forget what they are doing.
- Break instructions down into individual steps.
- Repeat instructions frequently.
- Ask the child to repeat instructions periodically.

Recent research by Klingberg *et al.* (2002) has suggested computerised working memory training, which uses systematic exercises to produce cognitive gains, is beneficial to those with poor WM, for example sufferers of Attention Deficit Hyperactivity Disorder (ADHD).

Strengthen your learning

1. What are the four components of the WMM?
2. Outline the roles of the CE, the PL and the VSS and state what research has suggested about them.
3. What is the main criticism of the CE?
4. What is the PAS and what evidence is there for its existence?
5. What is the EB? Explain why it was added to the WMM and outline what research has told us about its role.
6. Give two positive and two negative points about the WMM.

Assessment Check

1 Below is a list of components that relate to the WMM.

- Central executive
- Visual cache
- Semantic memory
- Episodic buffer
- Articulatory process

Copy and complete the table by matching the component to the correct description. [4 marks]

Name of component	Description of component
	A filter determining which information is attended to
	Allows sub-vocal repetition of information stored in the phonological loop
	Stores information about form and colour
	A slave system dealing with processing and temporary storage of specific types of information

2 a) Outline key features of the WMM. [6 marks]

b) Explain one strength of the WMM. [4 marks]

3 Identify and explain one weakness of the WMM. [3 marks]

4 Gregor is in the habit of doing his homework while watching the TV. Explain using the WMM why this may not be a desirable practice. [4 marks]

5 Outline and evaluate the WMM. [12 marks]

Examination guidance:

1 This is a selection question, where the answers are provided, but have to be inserted correctly into the table. One option is left spare.

2 This is a parted question, so make sure your answer is too, with the outline in a) and the strength in b). No marks here for a weakness.

3 This question does require a weakness. One mark for identification with a further two marks for elaboration.

4 Information in the scenario is used to form an answer.

5 This is a long-answer question; six marks are available each for an outline and an evaluation of the WMM.

Memory in everyday life

Eyewitness testimony

Court cases often depend upon eyewitness testimony (EWT), with the guilt or innocence of people being decided on the accuracy of the memories of eyewitnesses. Juries can find EWT of overriding importance in their deliberations and yet in 75 per cent of cases where people have been found by DNA evidence to have been wrongly convicted, the original guilty verdict was formed on the basis of inaccurate EWT. Research into EWT helps further our understanding of how memory works and suggests practical applications in how court cases should be conducted and how testimonies are gathered.

As long ago as 1932, Bartlett stated that memories are not an accurate snapshot of an event, but are reconstructed over time, influenced by active **schemas**. Schemas are ready-made expectations based on previous experiences, moods, existing knowledge, contexts, attitudes and stereotypes. We use schemas to interpret the world. They help 'fill in the gaps' in our knowledge and simplify the processing of information. This has implications for the reliability of EWT, because witnesses are not merely recalling facts as they happened, instead they are reconstructing memories and these reconstructions are biased by schemas active at the time of recall.

Factors affecting the accuracy of recall

Several factors affect the accuracy of recall, such as misleading information, anxiety and the age of witnesses.

Misleading information

Key terms

Misleading information – information that suggests a desired answer

Retrieval – the extraction of stored information

Research consistently shows that EWT is affected by experiences occurring after the witnessed event. A key factor is the use of misleading information, particularly in the form of misleading questions. In courtroom dramas, barristers are often accused of 'leading the witness'.

There are two types of misleading questions:

- **leading questions** – questions that make it likely that a participant's schema will influence them to give a desired answer.
- **post-event information** – misleading information added to a question after the incident has occurred.

Research into the effect of leading questions on EWT

- Loftus and Palmer (1974) asked participants to estimate the speed of cars in a film concerning traffic accidents and found the estimated speed was affected by participants being asked how fast the cars were going when they either 'contacted', 'hit', 'bumped', 'collided' or 'smashed' into each other, implying that leading questions affected participants' schemas, influencing them to give the desired answer. The researchers also found that more participants mistakenly remembered a week later seeing non-existent broken glass if given the verb 'smashed' rather than 'hit', suggesting that at recall, misleading information is reconstructed with material from the original memory.

Key terms

Eyewitness testimony – evidence provided by witnesses to a crime

- Bekerian and Bowers (1983) showed slides of events leading up to a car crash and found that participants' memories remained intact despite being asked misleading questions, suggesting that post-event information affects the retrieval of memories rather than their storage.
- Loftus (1975) found that 17 per cent of participants who watched a film of a car ride and were asked 'how fast was the car going when it passed the white barn', when there was no barn, recalled seeing the barn one week later. This supports the idea of post-event information, where misleading information is added to the question after an incident has occurred.

IN THE NEWS

'I was certain, but I was wrong'

Figure 1.19 Ronald Cotton and Jennifer Thompson

Jennifer Thompson was a college student back in 1984. One night an intruder burst into her flat and held a knife against her throat. As he raped her Jennifer carefully memorised his appearance, studying every detail of his face, determined that if she lived her attacker would be caught and imprisoned. Later that day she worked with police officers in drawing up a sketch, looking through hundreds of images of facial features to ensure she got it right. It was just a few days later when she identified Ronald Cotton as the rapist. She was absolutely certain and picked him out again in a police identity parade. On the strength of Jennifer's eyewitness testimony Ronald was imprisoned – she declared it to be the happiest day of her life. Indeed she was so sure of his guilt that she wanted him electrocuted, desiring to flip the switch herself.

However, in 1995, after Ronald Cotton had been in prison for 11 years, DNA evidence proved it was another man who had raped Jennifer and Ronald was released. Ronald and Jennifer have become friends and Jennifer is now an outspoken opponent of the death penalty and a regular lecturer on the unreliability of eyewitness testimony (EWT). This was not an isolated case and there is every possibility that innocent people have been executed on the basis of incorrect EWT. The Innocence Project in the USA has facilitated the exoneration of 214 men convicted of crimes they did not commit as a result of faulty eyewitness evidence. It is therefore an important area for psychologists to investigate and one with serious implications, especially in courts of law.

You can read a fuller account of Jennifer Thompson's absorbing story at http://faculty.washington.edu/gloftus/Other_Information/Legal_Stuff/Articles/News_Articles/Thompson_NYT_6_18_2000.html

Figure 1.20 Misleading information can lead to false memories

Evaluation

Evaluation of the effect of leading questions on EWT

- It is unclear with leading questions whether inaccuracies in recall are due to demand characteristics or genuine changes in the memory of an event.
- The consequences of inaccurate memories are minimal in research settings compared to real-life incidents. Foster *et al.* (1994) showed EWT was more accurate for real-life crimes as opposed to simulations.
- Participants do not expect to be misled deliberately by researchers and therefore inaccurate recall should be expected since participants believe the researchers to be telling the truth.
- Misleading information affects only unimportant aspects of memory. Memory for important events is not easily distorted when the information is obviously misleading.

Contemporary research

'The advertisers are coming for your childhood' – Elizabeth Loftus and Jacqui Pickrell, 2003

Figure 1.21 Elizabeth Loftus

In this study, the researchers showed how it is possible to create false memories about events in a person's own life.

Aim: To investigate whether autobiographical advertising can make memories become more consistent with images evoked in advertising.

Procedure: 120 participants who had visited Disneyland in childhood were divided into four groups and instructed to evaluate advertising copy, fill out questionnaires and answer questions about a trip to Disneyland.

- **Group 1** read a fake Disneyland advert featuring no cartoon characters.
- **Group 2** read the fake advert featuring no cartoon characters and were exposed to a cardboard figure of Bugs Bunny placed in the interview room.
- **Group 3** read the fake Disneyland advert featuring Bugs Bunny.
- **Group 4** read the fake advert featuring Bugs Bunny and saw the cardboard rabbit.

Findings: 30 per cent of participants in group 3 and 40 per cent of participants in group 4 remembered or knew they had met Bugs Bunny when visiting Disneyland. A ripple effect occurred whereby those exposed to misleading information concerning Bugs Bunny were more likely to relate Bugs Bunny to other things at Disneyland not suggested in the ad, such as seeing Bugs and Mickey Mouse together. Of course they can't actually have seen Bugs at Disneyland as he isn't a Disney character.

Conclusions: Through the use of misleading information false memories can be created.

Evaluation: Memory is vulnerable and malleable. The study shows the power of subtle association changes on memory. A practical application is that of advertisers using nostalgic images to manufacture false positive memories of their products.

Anxiety

Anxiety is often associated with witnessing real-life crimes and can divert attention away from the important features of a situation. Deffenbacher (1983) used the Yerkes-Dodson inverted-U hypothesis to explain this phenomenon. The hypothesis states that moderate amounts of emotional arousal improve the detail and accuracy of memory recall up to an optimal point, after which further increases in emotional arousal leads to a decline in recall. This is shown graphically in Figure 1.22.

As long ago as 1894, Freud provided an alternative explanation of repression, suggesting that anxiety impairs the recall of memories. Forgetting is seen as being motivated by the traumatic content of memories, with access to memories denied in order to protect individuals from being emotionally distressed.

Key terms

Anxiety – an unpleasant state of emotional arousal

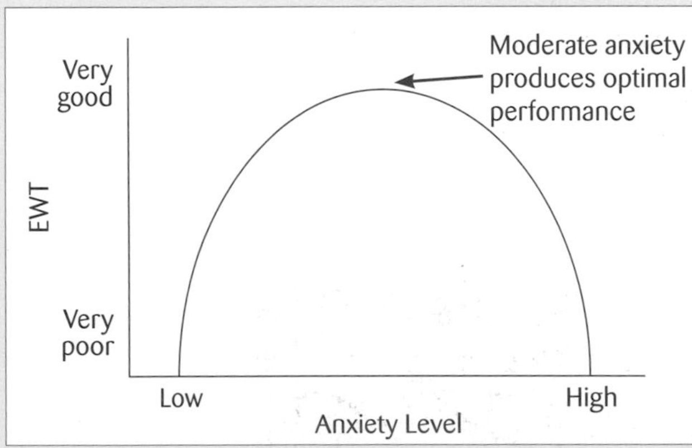

Figure 1.22 The Yerkes-Dodson inverted-U hypothesis

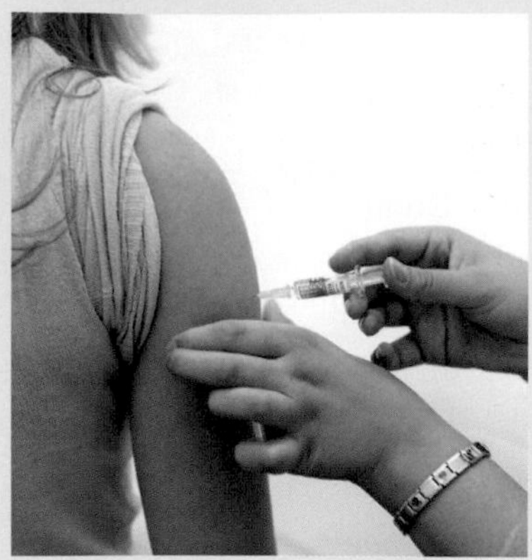

Figure 1.23 Anxiety-creating situations can affect recall

Research into anxiety factors

- Loftus *et al.* (1987) found that if a person is carrying a weapon, then a witness will focus on the weapon rather than the person's face, negatively affecting their ability to recall facial details of armed criminals and thus supporting the idea that anxiety can divert attention from important features of a situation.
- Deffenbacher (1983) performed a meta-analysis of 21 studies examining the role of anxiety in the accuracy of EWT, finding heightened anxiety tended to negatively affect the memory of eyewitnesses. This suggests anxiety can divert attention from the important features of a situation.
- Christianson and Hubinette (1993) studied the recall of witnesses to bank robberies. They found that increased arousal led to improvements in the accuracy of recall, suggesting that anxiety-creating situations do not always divert attention from the important features of a situation.
- Research suggests that anxiety reduces the field of view of a witness. Oue *et al.* (2001) found that participants who were anxious from viewing emotionally negative events recalled fewer details from the periphery of a scene than participants witnessing emotionally neutral events.
- Support for the Yerkes-Dodson inverted-U hypothesis comes from Ginet and Verkampt (2007). They produced moderate anxiety in participants by telling them that fake electrodes gave electric shocks. Such participants' recall of minor details of a traffic accident viewed on film was superior to that of participants with low arousal produced by being told the fake electrodes were purely for recording purposes. This implies moderate anxiety does facilitate EWT.
- Further support comes from Peters (1988) who tested people attending their local health clinic for an inoculation. During the visit, they met a nurse, who gave them an injection and a researcher for equal periods of time. Up to a week later, participants were asked to identify the nurse and the researcher from photographs. Identification of the researcher proved easier than the nurse, suggesting the heightened anxiety levels due to the injection led to a decrease in memory accuracy.
- Koehler *et al.* (2002) found participants less able to recall stressful words than non-stressful words, lending support to Freud's concept of repression. However, Hadley and MacKay (2006) found stressful words were better recalled, as they were more memorable, suggesting that repression may occur in some instances, but not all.

Evaluation

Evaluation of anxiety factors

- Much research into anxiety and EWT is laboratory based, raising the question of whether findings would be similar in real-life scenarios. Indeed Yuille and Cutshall (1986) who investigated the anxiety levels and accuracy of recall of 13 witnesses to a fatal shooting found that those with high arousal recalled fewer items correctly than those with lower levels, but that those witnesses with very high arousal had extremely accurate recall. However, Fruzetti *et al.* (1992) point out that those with the highest levels of stress were actually closer to events and suggest that this might have helped their accuracy recall.
- In 2004, Deffenbacher reviewed his earlier findings (see page 21) and found them over-simplistic. He performed a meta-analysis of 63 studies, finding that EWT performance increases gradually up to extremely high levels of anxiety and then there is a catastrophic drop in performance with a negative impact on both accuracy of eyewitness identification and accuracy of recall of crime-related details.

Age

There are indications that cognitive abilities diminish with age, suggesting that the accuracy of EWT decreases as people grow older. However, factors have been identified that moderate the effect of age upon the accuracy of recall.

Children appear more willing to accept inaccurate information provided by adults for fear of contradicting adult authority figures, but have more accurate and detailed memories when they identify an event as serious. In addition, the accuracy of children's answers can vary depending on how they are questioned. Younger children, in particular, are vulnerable to being misled by post-event information and leading questions.

Older people have less accurate and less detailed recall than young or middle-aged people and appear more prone to misleading information. However, research findings from all age groups are not always consistent, possibly due to methodological flaws.

Research into age factors

- Roberts and Lamb (1999) found that in 68 out of 161 interviews with children who made allegations of abuse, investigators misinterpreted or distorted children's reports, but that two-thirds of these inaccuracies went uncorrected by the children. This suggests that children do accept inaccurate information for fear of contradicting adult authority figures.
- Ochsner *et al.* (1999) found that children who watched a staged theft remembered more details than those who saw the same event without the theft. This may be because the theft caused children to consolidate memories by telling others about it or that the activity was taken more seriously due to the seriousness of the crime.
- Krackow and Lynn (2003) found that children aged between 4 and 6 years, who had been touched or not touched on various parts of their bodies, answered truthfully when asked directly, but wrongly half of the time when asked indirectly with a leading question. This emphasises the vulnerability of young children to being misled by leading questions.
- Poole and Lindsay (2001) found that children aged 3–8 years included a lot of post-event information in their recollections of a science demonstration, suggesting that young children are especially affected by such information and thus provide more inaccuracies in EWTs.
- Gordon *et al.* (2001) found that young children give accurate, detailed EWTs, but are prone to being affected by leading questions. As a consequence, there are direct implications for how children are questioned in legal settings.
- Brimacombe *et al.* (1997) found that the elderly gave less accurate EWTs of events viewed on video than young adults. This was backed up by Wright and Holiday (2007) who found that as participants aged, recall was less complete, with more inaccuracies, suggesting that recall deteriorates as a product of age.
- Cohen and Faulkner (1989) found that elderly participants gave more inaccurate responses than middle-aged participants when given misleading information, implying that the elderly are more susceptible to misleading information.
- Loftus *et al.* (1991) found that elderly people were more likely to make false identifications and were poorer at recalling specific details. In addition, elderly men in particular were prone to distortions through misleading post-event information, again suggesting accuracy of recall declines with age and that the elderly are susceptible to misleading information.

Evaluation

Evaluation of age factors

- Elias *et al*. (1990) states that it is unclear why age effects occur. The superior performance of younger adults may be simply that they are more used to tests or more motivated to achieve. The poor physical health of some elderly people may impact on their memory.
- One problem in the study of age factors and EWT is the type of research methods used. Older adults are often compared with college students, but on stimuli suited more to the college students. Anastasi and Rhodes (2006) tested participants' recall of photographs previously seen. They found that all age groups performed best with photographs of people from their own age group, suggesting that the stimuli used in research have an influence on findings.
- There are problems in controlling confounding variables when comparing different age groups. For example, the people tested may also differ in the amount and type of education received and such factors may affect results.
- Some studies use samples of elderly people from nursing homes, who may have reduced memory abilities anyway and thus do not form a representative sample.

Figure 1.24 Can age affect accuracy of recall?

Figure 1.25 Children can give accurate EWTs if certain procedures are followed

Psychology in action

The use of children as eyewitnesses

In recent years, there has been a rise in the number of children who are having to present court testimonies and participate in identification procedures, generally due to the rise in child abuse cases. Huneycutt (2004) reports that very young children do have the ability to provide accurate EWTs, but suggests that certain procedures should be followed to ensure that demand characteristics (see Chapter 3, Research methods), 'suggestibility' and guessing are eradicated.

- Those interacting with child witnesses should have training so that they are aware of children's development and capacities.
- Children should be familiarised with procedures they will be subjected to, for example what a 'don't know' response is and when to use it.
- Children who make line-up identifications should be provided with non-verbal response options, such as a picture of a person scratching his head to represent a lack of memory. They should also be given instructions and demonstrations of possible response options, in other words, the selection of a target person, an indication that the person is not there and a 'don't know' response.
- The person working with the child should not be involved in the investigation to protect against bias.
- The use of leading questions should not be permitted.
- Language appropriate to a child's age and development should be used.

Classic research

The effects of the age of eyewitnesses on the accuracy of their testimony – Pamela Coxon and Tim Valentine, 1997

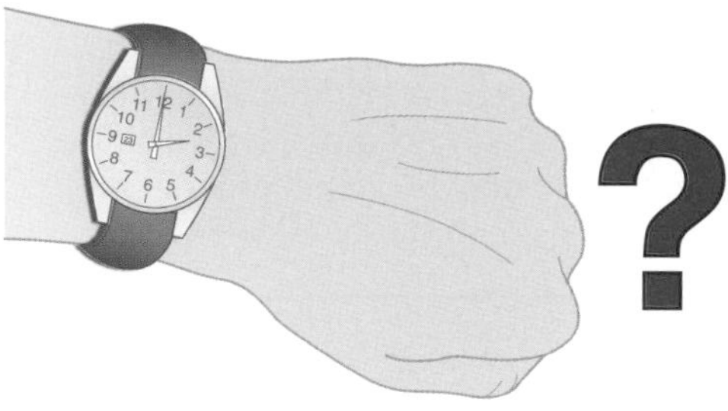

Figure 1.26

This classic study suggests that there are qualitative differences in recall between different age groups.

Aim: To test age differences in susceptibility to misleading information.

Procedure: 52 children with a mean age of 8 years, 53 young adults with a mean age of 17 years and 42 elderly participants with a mean age of 70 years were asked 17 questions after watching a video of a kidnapping. For half the participants in each age group, four of these questions contained misleading information, such as 'which arm did the kidnapper have her watch on', when there was no watch. The other (control) participants received no misleading information. All participants were then asked 20 questions, four of which tested for acceptance of misleading information.

Results: The total number of questions answered correctly was worse in both older adults and children than in young adults. However, on the questions testing for misinformation acceptance, the older adults were less suggestible than young adults and were the only age group not to show a statistically significant misinformation effect.

Conclusions: Young children and the elderly recall witnessed events less accurately than young adults and therefore make less reliable eyewitnesses. Elderly people provide less complete recall of events, but do not demonstrate susceptibility to misleading information. This suggests that the performance of different age groups is qualitatively different: elderly people remember less, but what they remember is more reliable.

Supplementary learning

Other factors affecting accuracy of recall

Police procedures

Various factors in how police officers collect eyewitness evidence can affect the reliability of EWT. Greathouse and Kovera (2008) found that line-up administrators can unconsciously bias the judgement of eyewitnesses. As a result, the researchers recommend the use of double-blind line-up administration, where police line-ups are conducted by someone not connected to the case and unaware of the identity of the suspect.

Personality factors

Some types of people seem more affected by misleading questions, demand characteristics and anxiety. Tomes and Katz (1997) proposed a personality type more likely to be affected – such individuals generally identify with the mood of others more easily, score highly on measures of imagery vividness and may have poor recall.

Consequences

Research has investigated the accuracy of EWT in situations where testimonies have real consequences. Foster *et al.* (1994) showed participants a video of a robbery and found that those who thought it was real and believed that their evidence could influence a court verdict produced more accurate testimonies than those who believed the video to be a simulation.

Figure 1.27 Line-up administrators can unconsciously bias the judgement of eyewitnesses

Research in focus

The Greathouse and Kovera study from 2008 focuses on the dangers of demand characteristics in real-life situations, though they are more commonly associated with affecting behaviour in experimental situations. What are demand characteristics and how may they affect experiments negatively?

How are filler questions used in questionnaires to try to reduce the impact of demand characteristics? (See Chapter 3, Research methods, for more information about demand characteristics.)

Strengthen your learning

1. What worrying fact has emerged about EWT in courts of law?
2. What are schemas and how can they affect EWT?
3. What two types of misleading information are there?
4. What have research studies told us about the effects of leading questions on EWT?
5. Give two evaluative points about the effect of leading questions on EWT.
6. How might advertisers create false memories?
7. How might the inverted-U hypothesis be used to explain how anxiety affects recall?
8. How can repression affect memory?
9. What has research told us about the effect of anxiety on EWT?
10. What have psychologists learned about how age affects recall?
11. Give two evaluative points about the effects of age on recall.

Assessment Check

1 Outline how one research study investigated the accuracy of EWT. [4 marks]

2 Bheilbheit works as a barrister and has noticed while questioning witnesses in court that their recall of events can be affected by how questions are put to them.
   a) Outline one way in which Bheilbheit could use misleading questions to affect the accuracy of EWTs. [2 marks]
   b) One reason for inaccuracies in EWTs could be the influence of demand characteristics. Explain what demand characteristics are and how they might affect EWTs. [3 marks]

3 Explain one way in which age may affect EWTs. [3 marks]

4 Outline and evaluate the effects of anxiety on the accuracy of EWTs. [12 marks]

Examination guidance:

1 A single mark is earned by identifying a relevant study, with further marks for elaboration. A popular choice would be the various studies by Loftus.

2 Part a) requires an answer where knowledge of misleading questions is focused on the scenario, while part b) requires application of knowledge of this particular element of research methods (demand characteristics) to EWTs.

3 Identification of a relevant way in which age affects EWT earns one mark, with another two marks available for elaboration. If more than one way is given, only the best one is credited.

4 This is a long-answer question, with six marks available for outlining the effects of anxiety on EWTs and six marks available for elaboration, such as the degree of research support and practical applications of such research, for example in a court of law.

Improving accuracy of EWT – the cognitive interview

One way of improving the accuracy of EWTs is the cognitive interview (CI) developed by Fisher and Geiselman (1992) to improve recall in police interviews.

The CI was based on Tulving's (1974) idea that there are several retrieval paths to each memory and information not available through one technique may be accessible through another. Two such strategies are the 'change of narrative order' and 'change of perspective' instructions, which encourage interviewees to recount events in a variety of orders and from different perspectives.

The second principle behind the CI involves Tulving and Thomson's Encoding Specificity Theory (1973). This theory suggests that memory traces are made up of several features and that as many retrieval cues as possible should be used to enhance recall. Context provides cues that increase feature overlap between initial witnessing and subsequent retrieval contexts. 'Context reinstatement' involves emotional elements (how an individual was feeling), which work via state-dependent effects (returning to the scene of the crime and picturing how it smelt or what could be heard) and sequencing elements (what you were doing at the time). The final element is 'reporting everything', as trivial incidents can trigger more important memories.

It is believed the change of narrative order and change of perspective strategies aid recall because they reduce witnesses' use of prior knowledge, expectations and schemas, increasing witness accuracy.

The four components of the cognitive interview are summarised below:

1. **Change of narrative order**: recount the scene in a variety of different chronological orders, for example, from the end to the beginning.
2. **Change of perspective**: recount the scene from different perspectives, for example, from the offender's point of view.
3. **Mental reinstatement of context**: return to both the environmental context (place, weather) and emotional context (feelings) of the crime scene.
4. **Report everything**: recall all information, even if it appears to have little relevance or is accorded a lower level of confidence.

Fisher *et al.* (1987) suggested an amended version of the CI known as the enhanced cognitive interview (ECI). Extra features include:

- minimisation of distractions
- reduction of anxiety
- getting the witness to speak slowly
- asking open-ended questions.

Research studies of the cognitive interview

- Geiselman and Fisher (1997) found that the CI works best when used within a short time following a crime rather than a long time afterwards.

Figure 1.28 The cognitive interview is designed to improve recall in police interviews

Key terms

Cognitive interview – a procedure for police interviews of witnesses to facilitate accurate, detailed recall

Enhanced cognitive interview – an advanced method of interviewing witnesses to overcome problems caused by inappropriate sequencing of questions

An audio presentation about the cognitive interview, given by Dr Becky Milne of Plymouth University, can be found at http://www.open2.net/eyewitness/becky_milne.html

The presentation lasts 15 minutes, giving an exceedingly clear, step-by-step breakdown of the procedure.

- Milne and Bull (2002) found the 'report everything' and 'context reinstatement' components of the CI to be the key techniques in gaining accurate, detailed recall.
- Ginet and Py (2001) found that using the CI resulted in a significant increase in the quantity of correct information remembered by witnesses without a comparable increase in the number of errors, suggesting that the CI is effective.
- Geiselman *et al.* (1985) found that the results of the CI procedure compared favourably with those from a standard interview technique and a hypnosis interview, suggesting that the technique is valid.
- Fisher *et al.* (1989) assessed the performance of police officers in gathering facts when using the ECI compared to a standard interview technique, and found the ECI to be superior.

Evaluation

Evaluation of the cognitive interview

- Although the ECI has proved a more effective technique, it is prone to producing **false positives**, where incorrect items are recalled.
- The CI is composed of several techniques and as different police forces use different versions, it makes comparisons difficult.
- The CI is recommended for use from 8 years upwards. Geiselman (1999) found that children younger than this recalled facts with less accuracy than with other interview techniques.
- A practical problem with the CI is that it is time consuming, often requiring more time than officers have operational time for.
- Memon *et al.* (1993) reported that police officers believe the 'change of perspective' component misleads witnesses into speculating about the event witnessed and due to this concern it is less frequently used.

Research in focus

Fisher *et al.* (1989) got police officers to compare the standard interview technique with the ECI by conducting a **field experiment**, a controlled experiment conducted outside the laboratory.

In what way do field experiments differ from natural experiments?

Field experiments have more **ecological validity** than laboratory experiments. What does this mean?

How might a field experiment be used to reduce **participant reactivity**?

Why might a field experiment have less **causality** than a laboratory experiment?

Strengthen your learning

1. What is the purpose of the CI?
2. Outline the two principles underpinning the CI.
3. Outline the components of the CI.
4. What extra features does the ECI contain?
5. What has research told us about the CI/ECI?
6. What criticisms of the CI are there?

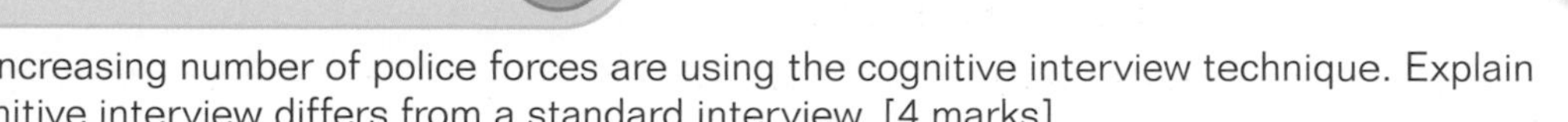

Assessment Check

1 An increasing number of police forces are using the cognitive interview technique. Explain cognitive interview differs from a standard interview. [4 marks]
2 The following are procedures of a cognitive interview:

A Change of narrative order
B Mental reinstatement of context
C Report everything
D Change of perspective

Copy and complete the table below by matching the procedure, A, B, C or D, with its description. [4 marks]

Type of procedure	Description
	Recount the scene in different chronological orders
	Recall the scene as written bullet points
	Return to the environmental and emotional context of the crime scene
	Recount the scene from different perspectives
	Recall all information even if it appears to have little relevance or is accorded a lower level of confidence

3 Identify and explain two techniques used in the cognitive interview. [3 marks + 3 marks]
4 Discuss the use of the cognitive interview. [12 marks]

Examination guidance:

1 Candidates who show some understanding of a cognitive interview, like naming/outlining techniques, receive a maximum of two marks. A difference must be given to access the full four marks, e.g. effectiveness/implications of cognitive interviews.
2 This question involves making choices from information supplied. There will be one descriptor left over that is not a procedure.
3 For both parts there is one mark for identifying a relevant procedure and two further marks for elaboration.
4 A description of the cognitive interview is required for six marks, with a further six marks available for evaluation, like the degree of research support, operational problems, etc.

Strategies for memory improvement

Psychological research has led to the creation of techniques designed to improve recall.

Retrieval cues

Retrieval cues act as prompts to trigger recall. There are two types – external (context-dependent) cues and internal (state-dependent) cues. These are discussed in more detailed below.

External (context-dependent) cues

The physical environment in which material is learnt can affect memory and research indicates that context-dependent cues facilitate recall.

Research into external retrieval cues

- Abernethy (1940) tested participants' recall using a mixture of familiar and unfamiliar instructors and teaching rooms. Participants tested by a familiar instructor in a familiar room performed best, suggesting familiar external cues are useful in improving recall.

Key terms

Retrieval cues – prompts that trigger recall

- Godden and Baddeley (1975) got divers to learn and recall word lists either on dry land or underwater. Results showed that words learnt and recalled in the same context were remembered better.

Internal (state-dependent cues)

An individual's physiological state can affect their memory. Research suggests that recall of information is facilitated if people have a similar internal environment at recall as when information was encoded.

Research into internal retrieval cues

- Overton (1972) got participants to learn material when either drunk or sober and found that material was recalled best when participants were in the same internal state (drunk or sober) as when they encoded the information. This suggests that state-dependent cues aid recall.
- Darley *et al.* (1973) found that participants who hid money while high on marijuana were more likely to recall the hiding place when in a similar drugged state, supporting the idea of state-dependent cues being an aid to recall.

Figure 1.29 Context-dependent cues aid recall

Evaluation

Evaluation of retrieval cues

- Students can make practical use of internal and external retrieval cues. Revision and examinations should be undertaken in circumstances as similar as possible to those experienced when the material was learned.
- Research evidence supports the idea of cue-dependent forgetting being the main reason for forgetting in LTM, demonstrating the importance of retrieval cues in memory recall.
- Fernandez and Glenberg (1985) tried to replicate studies of context-dependent forgetting, but found no consistent support for context-dependent effects. However, in practical terms it does seem useful to learn material in the same place it will be recalled.
- Studies have investigated the effect of mood on recall, with inconclusive results. Ucros (1989) performed a meta-analysis, finding a small state-dependent effect of mood.
- Many studies supporting cue-dependent recall are laboratory based and unlike everyday memory. For example, the ability to do things previously learned (procedural memory) like riding a bike is not affected by retrieval cues.

Research in focus

Ucros's (1989) study (see Evaluation box above) is an example of a meta-analysis, a research method which is becoming increasingly popular.

How is a meta-analysis performed?

What is the main advantage of carrying out a meta-analysis?

Are there any weaknesses of this method?

Psychology in action

Figure 1.30 The reconstruction of the last movements of Danielle Jones

Proving murder without a body

In addition to using cognitive interviews, the police also use **reconstructions** of unsolved crimes. The aim is to jog the memory of witnesses by reinstating the context of the incident through the use of retrieval cues. Participants wear identical clothes to those worn by the people involved, and the reconstruction takes place in the same location and at the same time as the original incident.

Danielle Jones was murdered in Essex in 2001, but her body was never found. Her uncle was eventually convicted, largely due to forensic evidence and witness testimony that emerged after a reconstruction of the crime. Witnesses recalled seeing Danielle arguing with a man and getting into a blue transit van, a vehicle owned by her uncle. He was sentenced to life imprisonment.

Chunking

The capacity of STM can be increased by grouping separate 'bits' of information into larger 'chunks'. The information is bound together using a common factor, making it more comprehensible, a process known as chunking. For example, the number 19391945 can be 'chunked' in such a way that it is seen as the start and end dates of the Second World War. Reading involves the chunking of letters into words and words into sentences.

Key terms

Chunking – combining items into meaningful units

Research studies into chunking

- Simon (1974) found that the size of chunks had an effect on recall. Participants recalled more small chunks with fewer amounts of items within them than large chunks with greater amounts of items within them.
- Baddeley *et al.* (1975) found that the length of words being chunked affected recall. Participants were better able to recall short words than long ones. This is the **word length effect**.

Evaluation

Evaluation of chunking

- Chunking is an effective learning strategy for those learning and recalling lots of information, such as students.
- The idea of 'chunking' shows that it makes sense to think of memory capacity in terms of units of organised information rather than individual pieces of information.

Mnemonics

Mnemonics assist memory recall, usually by organising information in some way. One proven method is to impose a structure upon material to be recalled.

Visual imagery mnemonics focus on visual images, such as a familiar route through the rooms of a house, whereby objects to be recalled are placed in each room. These objects are visualised within their visual settings and recall is facilitated by individuals imagining taking the familiar route.

Key terms

Mnemonics – various techniques facilitating recall

Figure 1.31 London cabbies have a huge spatial memory

Verbal mnemonics focus on words. Commonly, this involves using an **acronym** whereby the information to be recalled is formed from the first letters of other words. For example, **R**ichard **O**f **Y**ork **G**ave **B**attle **I**n **V**ain can be used to help remember the order of colours in a rainbow – **R**ed, **O**range, **Y**ellow, **G**reen, **B**lue, **I**ndigo, **V**iolet.

You are the researcher

All licensed London taxi drivers must pass a test before they can drive one of the city's famous black cabs. To achieve this they must do 'the knowledge', which consists of learning all the street names and locations of London off by heart.

Devise a study that tests the theory that using visual imagery mnemonics is the best method to employ. You will need a comparison group to set up your IV. You could use the streets in your location, but a map with street names would also suffice.

Research studies of mnemonics

Figure 1.32 Elderly people are better suited to using verbal mnemonics

- Bower and Clarke (1969) found that participants who used narrative stories to help recall lists of nouns in the correct order remembered 93 per cent compared to only 13 per cent for participants not using narrative stories. This suggests that verbal mnemonics are a powerful aid to memory.
- Marston and Young (1974) compared visual and verbal mnemonic techniques in remembering word lists. They found that verbal strategies produced equal recall of items classed as 'high imagery' and 'medium imagery', while visual strategies resulted in higher performance for 'high imagery' words, but lower performance for 'medium imagery' words. This suggests that the best strategy to use depends upon the type of information being recalled.
- Baltes and Kliegl (1992) found that older adults should use verbal mnemonics rather than visual ones, as they increasingly find it harder to produce and recall visual images. This suggests that the ability to use different forms of mnemonics changes throughout an individual's life.
- Herrmann (1987) found that interactive imagery, where two items are linked together, was the most effective strategy, but that the verbal mnemonic of creating a narrative story is most effective for recalling lists of items in any order. This implies different mnemonic techniques are more effective with particular types of memory tasks.

Evaluation

Evaluation of mnemonics

- People differ in their abilities to visualise and therefore the usefulness of visual imagery is dependent on how much an individual is a 'high-imager' or a 'low-imager'.
- Mnemonics work by allowing the storage of structured material, providing links to existing memories. Information becomes linked in an organised way, whereby retrieval of a familiar item leads to the recall of less familiar items.
- Visual imagery mnemonics often only work when trying to learn and recall actual objects rather than abstract concepts and ideas.

Active processing

Active processing refers to procedures in which a learner goes beyond mere passive, unthinking encoding of information and instead subjects material to deep and meaningful processing.

> **Key terms**
>
> **Active processing** – subjecting information to deep and meaningful analysis

Research into active processing

- Craik and Lockhart (1972) found that if participants analysed material by its meaning (semantics), recall was superior, suggesting that semantic processing draws upon many varied associations within LTM. Recall becomes easier as numerous recall pathways are established.
- Morris *et al.* (1985) found that football fans recalled more actual scores than non-fans, as they actively processed the information, for example by comparing actual scores to expected ones and calculating the impact upon league positions. This suggests active processing is a useful strategy for memory improvement.

Arsenal 0	vs	Port Vale 6
Manchester United 0	vs	Accrington Stanley 4
Exeter City 2	vs	Plymouth 1
Dagenham & Redbridge 3	vs	Barnet 0
Inverness CT 1	vs	Ross County 5

Figure 1.33 Active processing helps football fans to remember scores

> A BBC website focusing on ways of improving memory, but also providing links to other aspects of memory, with memory tests and interactive features, can be found at http://www.bbc.co.uk/sn/tvradio/programmes/memory/programme.shtml

Evaluation

Evaluation of active processing

- Active processing is a **circular concept**. Not only is strongly processed information seen as being recalled better, but it is also said that information that is well recalled must have been actively processed. This makes the concept untestable and unscientific.
- Active processing is a dynamic theory, seeing memory as a process, not a set of passive stores. It provides meaningful associations between memory and other cognitive areas.

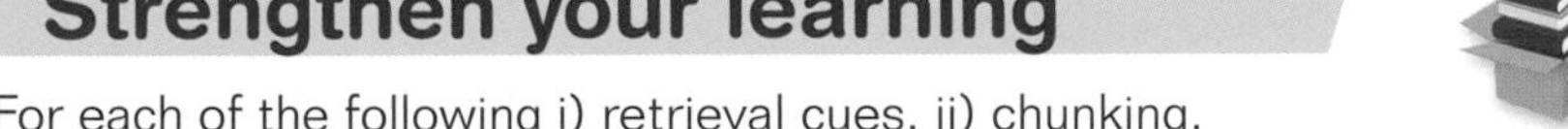

Strengthen your learning

1 For each of the following i) retrieval cues, ii) chunking, iii) mnemonics, iv) active processing
 a) give a concise, detailed outline.
 b) report on what research studies have revealed.
 c) provide a summarised evaluation.

Assessment Check

1 Derek finds it hard to remember things he has learned in class, so goes to see a psychology teacher to find some strategies for improving his recall.
Outline a strategy Derek could use and explain how it might improve his memory. [4 marks]
2 Outline and evaluate strategies for memory improvement. [12 marks]
3 Outline two strategies for memory improvement. [2 + 2 marks]
4 Some researchers test out the use of chunking, where items are grouped into meaningful units, by comparing one group who use chunking against another group using free recall on the same list of test items.
   a) What type of research design has been used? [1 mark]
   b) What would be the independent variable? [1 mark]
   c) What would be the dependent variable? [1 mark]
   d) Explain why the same list of test items is used with both groups. [4 marks]

Examination guidance:

1 One mark is earned by identifying a relevant strategy, e.g. deep processing, with three further marks available for elaboration.
2 Six marks are available for outlining relevant strategies. At least two must be included, with less detail expected if more than two were described. A further six marks are available for evaluation, like the degree of research support, strengths and weaknesses of such strategies, etc.
3 Unlike Question 1, no explanation is required, but two strategies are needed. If more are outlined, only the best two are credited.
4 This question presents a simple study into chunking and asks questions about research methods based on this material. (See Chapter 3, Research methods, for guidance.) In part d) one mark is available for a correct answer, with three further marks available for elaboration.

End of chapter review

- The multi-store model (MSM) explains how information flows between three storage systems: sensory memory (SM), short-term memory (STM) and long-term memory (LTM).
- STM is an active memory system containing information currently attended to. It differs from LTM in terms of duration, capacity, encoding and how information is forgotten.
- The dominant form of encoding in STM is acoustic, however, other codes are also used.
- Duration of STM is less than 30 seconds. Information is lost from STM if not rehearsed. Repetition retains material within the STM loop, until it becomes a permanent feature within LTM.
- LTM involves the storage of information over extended periods. Forgetting may be due to problems in retrieving memory traces.
- Coding in LTM is mainly semantic. Other codes also occur.
- The MSM is supported by research illustrating differences between STM and LTM in encoding, storage and capacity.
- The working memory model (WMM) regards STM as an 'active' store, holding several pieces of information being worked on.
- The central executive (CE) is a limited capacity filter. It determines which information is attended to, directs information to other 'slave' systems and collects their responses. It permits attention to be switched between different inputs of information.
- The phonological loop (PL) and visuo–spatial sketchpad (VSS) are 'slave' systems – temporary stores, dealing with different kinds of sensory information.
- A third slave system, the episodic buffer (EB) was added as the model needs a general store. The EB has limited capacity and integrates information from the CE, the PL, the VSS, as well as from LTM.
- Much evidence supports the existence of a working memory involving several components.
- The WMM only concerns STM and thus is not a comprehensive model of memory.
- Court cases often depend upon eyewitness testimonies (EWTs), but research suggests errors and inaccuracies occur, resulting in wrongful convictions.
- Memories are reconstructed over time due to active schemas – ready-made expectations based on previous experiences, moods, existing knowledge, contexts, attitudes and stereotypes.
- There are two types of misleading questions: leading questions, which increase the chances of schema creating a desired answer, and post-event information, misleading information added to questions after incidents have occurred.
- Anxiety affects recall by diverting attention away from important features of a situation.
- The Yerkes-Dodson inverted-U hypothesis is used to explain how moderate amounts of emotional arousal improve memory recall up to an optimal point, after which further increases lead to a decline.
- Repression suggests anxiety impairs recall, with forgetting being motivated by the traumatic content of memories. Access to such memories is denied to protect individuals from emotional distress.
- There is evidence that accuracy of EWTs decreases with age. But factors exist that moderate the effect of age upon recall.
- Personality factors and a consideration of the consequences of EWT have been shown to affect recall accuracy.
- The cognitive interview (CI), designed to improve recall in police interviews, is based on the idea of several retrieval paths for each memory, with recall being enhanced by using many retrieval cues.
- The CI has four components: 1) Change of narrative order, 2) Change of perspective, 3) Mental reinstatement context, 4) Report everything.
- The enhanced cognitive interview (ECI) includes extra features: minimising distractions, reducing anxiety, getting the witness to speak slowly and asking open-ended questions.
- The physical environment where material is learnt affects memory, with research indicating that context-dependent cues facilitate recall.
- The physiological state an individual is in affects memory. Research suggests that having a similar internal environment at recall as at encoding facilitates recall.
- Mnemonics assist memory recall by organising information – they impose a memorable structure upon material.

2 Developmental psychology

Introduction

Developmental psychology involves the study of how individuals change over time. Focus is placed upon developmental influences, both biological, like genetics, and environmental, like parenting. Attention centres on childhood and adolescence due to the high degree of development occurring during those years. An important feature of early development is attachment behaviour, where infants form close bonds with others. Several explanations of attachments exist and psychologists have studied types of attachments formed, whether these are cross-cultural and how they affect subsequent relationships, as well as investigating the effects of disrupting attachments. Another important feature is attachments in everyday life, like the impact of daycare on social development and its implications for childcare practices.

Understanding the specification

- You must have knowledge of two explanations of attachment, learning theory and Bowlby's theory, as they are directly referred to in the specification and could be explicitly included in the wording of examination questions.
- Secure and insecure attachment types, as well as the studies of Ainsworth and cultural variations in attachment, are also directly referred to and so could explicitly feature in examination questions.
- The specification also focuses on disruptions of attachment, failure to form attachments (privation) and the effects of institutionalisation, so again you may have to answer questions on these.
- There may be a question on the impact of different forms of day care on children's social development, including the effects on aggression and peer relations, as these too are specifically listed.
- Your studies must include implications of research into attachment and day care for childcare practices, as once again they are specified requirements, which means you may be examined on them.

Attachment

An attachment is an enduring, two-way, emotional tie to a specific other person, usually between a parent and a child, which develops in set stages within a fairly rigid timescale. Human babies are **altricial**, which means that they are born at a relatively early stage of development and need to form bonds with adults who will protect and nurture them.

> **Key terms**
>
> **Attachment** – a two-way, enduring, emotional tie to a specific other person

Several explanations of attachment have been formulated, but the two we are concerned with here focus on learning theory, where attachments are seen to form as a result of conditioning, and the evolutionary perspective, where attachment is seen as a biological device with a survival value.

IN THE NEWS

Lesbians make 'better parents'

Figure 2.1

Lesbians are better at raising children than conventional couples, a senior member of the Government's parenting academy has said. According to the annual British Social Attitudes Report, more than a third of people believe same-sex parents are as good as heterosexual couples.

Research shows that children from lesbian couples do better in life than the offspring of heterosexual couples and suggests that children with two female parents are more aspirational than those with opposite-sex parents. Some studies also show that children with lesbian parents are no more or less likely to have tendencies towards homosexuality.

Research at Birkbeck College, London, and Clark University in Massachusetts suggests that same-sex couples make good parents because children cannot be conceived accidentally – parents make an active decision to adopt or find a sperm donor.

Campaigners counter that fathers play an important part in family life and that children have a right to know both their biological parents.

Ann Widdecombe, MP for Maidstone and the Weald, said: 'This contradicts every other government study that has ever been done. These studies, which are quoted so often by the Government and the opposition, clearly show children do better when they have both a mother and a father figure.'

Source: adapted from the *Daily Telegraph*, 15 November 2009 © Telegraph Media Group Limited 2009

This article on homosexual adoption neatly sums up the controversy over what constitutes acceptable child-rearing practices, with opposing parties each claiming that research studies back up their viewpoint. Hopefully by the end of this chapter you will have a clearer understanding of the issues surrounding childcare and will be able to determine, in an objective and unbiased fashion, what forms of childcare are, and are not, desirable.

Phases of attachment development

Attachments develop in several distinct phases. These are given below (based on the work of Schaffer, 1996):

1 **Pre-attachment phase** (birth to 3 months) – from six weeks, babies become attracted to other humans, preferring them to objects and events. This preference is demonstrated by smiling at people's faces.

2 **Indiscriminate attachment phase** (3 to 7/8 months) – babies begin to discriminate between familiar and unfamiliar people, smiling more at known people, though they will still allow strangers to handle and look after them.

3 **Discriminate attachment phase** (7/8 months onwards) – babies begin to develop specific attachments, staying close to particular people and becoming distressed when separated from them. They avoid unfamiliar people and protest if strangers try to handle them.

4 Multiple attachments **stage** (9 months onwards) – babies form strong emotional ties with other major care-givers, like grandparents, and non-care-givers, like other children. The fear of strangers weakens, but attachment to the mother figure remains strongest.

Key terms

Multiple attachments – forming emotional ties with many carers

Cupboard love theory – attachments formed with people who feed infants

Explanations of attachments

There are two main explanations of attachment behaviour:

- **learning theory**, which sees attachments as developing through conditioning processes
- **Bowlby's theory**, which sees attachment as a biological device to aid survival.

Learning theory

Learning theory explains all behaviour as acquired through experience via the process of association. **Classical conditioning** occurs where a stimulus becomes associated with a response, while **operant conditioning** involves learning behaviour due to its consequences via the use of reinforcements: stimuli presented after a response that increase the likelihood of the response reoccurring.

Figure 2.2 The learning theory of attachment is also known as the cupboard love theory, as care-givers are seen as satisfying babies' basic physiological needs

Attachments are seen as occurring through classical conditioning, where babies learn to associate care-givers with food, an **unconditioned** or **primary reinforcer**, due to the pleasure food gives. Care-givers are a **conditioned** or **secondary reinforcer**. As care-givers satisfy babies' physiological needs, learning theory is also known as cupboard love theory.

Care-givers come to be rewarding in their own right, with babies feeling secure in their presence without the need for food.

Attachments may also occur through operant conditioning, where care-givers become associated with reducing the unpleasant feeling of hunger and thus become a source of reinforcement (reward).

Research studies of learning theory

- Schaffer and Emerson (1964) studied 60 babies every four weeks throughout their first year, then again at 18 months. Mothers were asked about the babies' protests in various separation situations, including being left alone in a room, being left with a babysitter and being put to bed. The babies were clearly attached to people who were not involved in their physical care (notably fathers). Also, in 39 per cent of cases, the mother (usually the main carer) was *not* the baby's main attachment figure, suggesting that feeding is not the primary explanation of attachment.
- Dollard and Miller (1950) calculated that in their first year, babies are fed 2,000 times, generally by their main carer, which creates ample opportunity for the mother to become associated with the removal of the unpleasant feeling of hunger, a form of negative reinforcement. This implies support for the idea that attachments are learned through operant conditioning.
- Fox (1977) studied the attachment relationships between mothers, babies and metapelets on Israeli kibbutzim (a kibbutz is a communal farm). Metapelets provide full-time care for newborn children, allowing mothers to work, though some time is spent with parents. In general, children were more attached to their mothers, some appearing to have little or no attachment with metapelets. As metapelets did the majority of the feeding, this suggests learning theory to be flawed.

A fuller account of Fox's (1977) study of kibbutz children taken from the journal *Child Development* can be found at http://www.richardatkins.co.uk/atws/document/93.html

Classic research

'Even baby monkeys need comfort more than food' – Harry Harlow, 1959

Figure 2.3

Harlow studied learning theory using rhesus monkeys. He separated newborns from their mothers, raising them in isolation in cages. Each cage contained a 'baby blanket'. The baby monkeys were found to become distressed whenever the blanket was removed, a reaction similar to that observed when a baby monkey is separated from its mother. This suggested that attachment was not based on association with food.

Aim: To test learning theory by comparing attachment behaviour in baby monkeys given a wire surrogate mother producing milk with those given a soft towelling mother producing no milk.

Procedure: Two types of surrogate mother were constructed – a harsh 'wire mother' and a soft 'towelling mother'. Sixteen baby monkeys were used, four in each of four conditions.

1. A cage containing a wire mother producing milk and a towelling mother producing no milk.
2. A cage containing a wire mother producing no milk and a towelling mother producing milk.
3. A cage containing a wire mother producing milk.
4. A cage containing a towelling mother producing milk.

The amount of time spent with each mother, as well as feeding time, was recorded.

A loud noise was used to test for mother preference during stress.

A larger cage was also used to test the monkeys' degree of exploration.

Findings: Monkeys preferred to cling to the towelling mother when given a choice of surrogate mothers, regardless of whether she *continued ...*

A good video about Harlow, containing original footage of the study, can be found at http://www.youtube.com/watch?v=MmbbfisRiwA&feature=related

with links to other relevant videos.

...continued

produced milk; they even stretched across to the wire mother to feed while still clinging to the towelling mother.

Monkeys with only a wire surrogate had diarrhoea, a sign of stress.

When frightened by a loud noise, monkeys clung to the towelling mother in conditions where she was available.

In the larger cage conditions, monkeys with towelling mothers explored more and visited their surrogate more often.

Conclusions: Monkeys have an innate, unlearned need for contact comfort, suggesting that attachment concerns emotional security more than food.

Contact comfort is associated with lower levels of stress and a willingness to explore, indicating emotional security.

Evaluation:

- This study involved animals and therefore we cannot necessarily extrapolate (generalise) the results to humans.
- There are ethical issues involving the separation of baby monkeys and the stress caused to them.

Research in focus

Harlow used monkeys to study attachments. Animal studies have several strengths and weaknesses. For instance, monkeys are close to humans in evolutionary terms, so what is true for monkeys may be true for humans. However, Harlow's study was unethical. Babies were separated from mothers at birth, undergoing prolonged periods of stress. Harlow himself said he would not repeat the study.

Compose a list of the strengths and weaknesses of animal experimentation and see whether you can reach some conclusions about whether they should be permitted and, if so, under what conditions and for what purposes.

Evaluation

Evaluation of learning theory

- Conditioning best explains the acquisition of simple behaviours, but attachments are generally complex behaviours with an intense emotional component. This, coupled with the fact that attachments develop with people who do not feed babies, casts doubt on the learning theory.
- Schaffer (1971) commented that 'cupboard love' theories put things the wrong way round. Babies do not 'live to eat', but 'eat to live', thus they are active seekers of stimulation, not passive recipients of nutrition.
- Bowlby (1973) reported that babies only periodically need food, but continually need the protection of emotional security that proximity to attachment figures provides. This suggests that food is not the main reason for formation of attachments.
- Although conditioning and reinforcement via feeding play a part, research suggests that food is not the main explanation for the formation of attachments, casting doubt on the 'cupboard love' theory.
- Behaviourist explanations are **reductionist** because they take complex human behaviours and try to explain them in the simplest terms possible. Behaviourism does not consider internal processes or seek to explain the emotional nature of attachments, simply how they arise as behaviours.

Bowlby's theory (1951, 1969, 1973)

Bowlby rejected cupboard love theory, citing Harlow's research with monkeys (see Classic research section earlier in this chapter), as well as Lorenz's 1935 study of imprinting in goslings and other bird species. Imprinting is a form of attachment in which some young birds learn to follow the first large, moving object they see during a specific time (critical period) after hatching; this tendency is instinctive and requires no learning.

Applying these ideas to humans, Bowlby claimed that emotional bonds had evolutionary and biological functions. These bonds evolved because, in the distant past, when humans faced predators, a mechanism was needed to ensure that offspring stayed close to care-givers, thus obtaining protection and increasing their survival chances. Via evolution, human infants became genetically programmed to behave towards their mothers in ways that enhanced survival. These innate species-specific attachment behaviours are known as social releasers and include:

- crying – which attracts parents' attention
- looking, smiling and vocalising – which maintain parental attention and interest
- following or clinging – which gain or maintain physical closeness to parents.

These attachment behaviours are part of a baby's response repertoire from a very early stage. They function in an automatic, stereotyped way to begin with and may be triggered initially by lots of people. But, during the first year, these behaviours become focused on a few individuals and thus become organised into more flexible and sophisticated behaviour systems.

Key terms

Imprinting – a form of attachment where offspring follow the first large moving object encountered

Critical period – a specific time period within which an attachment must form

Social releasers – infant social behaviours stimulating adult interaction and care-giving

Monotropy – an innate tendency to become attached to one particular adult

So, the primary function of attachment is to gain security and increase survival chances. However, as well as protection, attachments help to teach children how to form later adult relationships which will be vital for reproduction. This only works if mothers respond to infant attachment behaviours, resulting in the evolution of a complementary maternal attachment system, ensuring mothers' responsiveness to infants' signals. This does not have to be with biological children: babies need an adequate mother figure, not necessarily their natural mother.

Figure 2.4 Lorenz being followed by goslings, which had imprinted on him after hatching

Bowlby sees attachment functioning like a control system which is geared to maintain a steady state, namely, to stay close to the mother. When that state is attained, attachment behaviour is 'quiet' – babies have no need to cry or cling and can thus get on with playing and exploring. When the state is threatened – if the mother disappears from view or a stranger approaches – attachment behaviours are activated to restore it. Generally, attachment behaviours are evident when children are distressed, unwell, frightened or in unfamiliar surroundings, but which particular responses are produced change as children age and become more competent, cognitively and behaviourally.

Bowlby believes that there is a critical period for the formation of attachments: mothering must take place within a certain time period if children are to form attachments. He saw mothering as useless for *most* children if delayed until after 12 months and useless for *all* children if delayed until after 2½–3 years.

According to Bowlby, babies display monotropy, an innate tendency to become attached to one particular adult, who interacts with them the most sensitively,

A compre-hensive web-based account of the life and work of John Bowlby, including his collaborations with Mary Ainsworth and the Robertsons taken from the journal *Developmental Psychology*, can be found at http://www.psychology.sunysb.edu/attachment/online/inge_origins.pdf

usually the biological mother. This attachment is unique: it is the first to develop and the strongest of all, forming a model for relationships that the infant will expect from others. This is known as the **internal working model** – it creates a consistency between early emotional experiences and later relationships. For Bowlby, 'Mother love in infancy is as important for mental health as vitamins and proteins for physical health.'

Research studies into Bowlby's theory

- By imprinting newly-hatched goslings onto himself, Lorenz (1935) found that certain animals have an innate tendency to respond immediately and consistently to specific forms of stimuli, like visual markings or sounds, usually displayed by a parent. They are drawn to the stimuli and will thus follow instinctively anyone exhibiting such stimuli and seem content when near them and distressed when not. This suggests that such innate 'pre-programming' provides an evolutionary advantage, as by staying close to parents and siblings, newborn animals are less likely to fall victim to predators and other environmental dangers.
- Rutter (1981) found that mothers are not special in the way Bowlby claimed. Infants display a whole range of attachment behaviours towards various attachment figures other than their mothers and there is no particular attachment behaviour used specifically and exclusively towards mothers.
- Schaffer and Emerson (1964) (see section on Research studies of learning theory on page 39) found that multiple attachments are the norm, going against Bowlby's idea of monotropy. Another contradiction to his theory was that 39 per cent of children had a main attachment with someone other than the mother (or main carer).
- Lamb (1982) studied the relationships and attachments infants had with many people like fathers, grandparents and siblings. He found that different attachments served different purposes rather than being a hierarchy. For example, infants go to fathers for play, but mothers for comfort, going against the idea of monotropy.

Figure 2.5 Children have attachments to different people for different purposes

Evaluation

Evaluation of Bowlby's theory

- Imprinting applies mainly to **precocial** animals – those that are mobile soon after birth – therefore attachment may not simply be a human form of imprinting.
- Bowlby's conceptualisation of attachment as essentially human imprinting implies that it is not important what form of interaction occurs between care-givers and infants, and that mere exposure is sufficient. Schaffer and Emerson (1964) noted that attachments were most likely to those displaying **sensitive responsiveness** (being sensitive to an infants' needs and responding to them).
- Schaffer and Emerson's (1964) study can be interpreted as evidence for monotropy. Although one-year-old children tended to have multiple attachments, they retained one primary attachment despite multiple care-givers.
- Fathers can be 'mothers' too. Bowlby considers that fathers are not of direct emotional importance to infants, with their main role being to provide emotional and financial support to mothers. In contrast, the findings of Schaffer and Emerson suggest that fathers can be attachment figures in their own right.

continued ...

...continued

- There is much evidence to support aspects of Bowlby's theory, for instance the **continuity hypothesis**, where there is a consistency between early emotional experiences and later relationships.
- Bowlby's theory suffers from bias and it has been championed by those who believe women should not work, but should stay at home to look after children.

Strengthen your learning

1. What is an attachment?
2. Outline the phases of attachment development.
3. At what age does a baby form its first attachment?
4. How does learning theory explain attachments occurring through a) classical conditioning and b) operant conditioning?
5. Why does Fox's (1977) study of Israeli children (see page 39) cast doubt on learning theory as an explanation of attachment?
6. a) Give details of Harlow's (1959) study on baby monkeys.
   b) Do the findings support learning theory?
   c) Explain your answer.
7. Give one strength and one weakness of using monkeys to study attachments.
8. Give a brief evaluation of learning theory.
9. Why did Bowlby become interested in attachment theory?
10. How does Bowlby's theory explain the occurrence of attachments?
11. What is imprinting?
12. Explain Bowlby's idea of a critical period.
13. Explain a) multiple attachments and b) monotropy.
14. Give a brief evaluation of Bowlby's theory.

Assessment Check

1 Outline and evaluate explanations of attachment. [12 marks]

2 a) What is meant by the term attachment? [2 marks]
  b) The following statements relate to explanations of attachment:

  A Attachments develop as a result of reinforcement.
  B Attachments develop during the oral stage.
  C Attachment behaviours have a survival value.

Copy and complete the table below by writing which statement, **A**, **B** or **C**, describes each explanation of attachment. [2 marks]

Description	Explanation
	Learning theory
	Evolutionary perspective

3 a) Outline the learning theory explanation of attachment. [4 marks]
  b) Give one weakness of the learning theory explanation of attachment. [2 marks]

4 Explain what Bowlby meant by a) monotropy and b) the critical period. [2 + 2 marks]

5 Outline and evaluate Bowlby's theory explanation of attachment. [12 marks]

Examination guidance:

1 This is a long-answer question, requiring an outline of at least two explanations for six marks and an evaluation of these for a further six marks.

2 a) This requires an explanation of the term attachment, with partial or muddled answers receiving one mark and accurate and clear answers two marks.
  b) The answers are provided, but must be inserted into the correct parts of the table. One description will be left over.

3 a) This requires an outline of learning theory, so describing other explanations or including evaluative material is not creditworthy.
  b) Requires a weakness, with one mark for a correct answer and an additional mark for valid elaboration.

4 Monotropy and critical periods are key elements of Bowlby's explanation, so candidates should be able to explain these.

5 This is a long-answer question focusing on Bowlby's theory, so any material on learning theory, etc. is irrelevant unless used as an evaluation.

Key terms

'Strange Situation' – an observational testing procedure measuring the quality of attachments

Stranger anxiety – distress shown by infants when in the presence of unfamiliar persons

Types of attachment and the uses of the 'Strange Situation' in attachment research

Several attachment styles have been identified, with research carried out in different countries and cultures. Initial research was conducted by Mary Ainsworth and her 'Strange Situation' testing procedure. This testing method has become the accepted way to identify and measure attachment styles.

Ainsworth worked with Bowlby in the 1950s and then studied mother–child relationships in the Ganda tribe of Uganda. Over nine months she observed 26 mothers, with infants ranging in age from 15 weeks to 2 years, for hours at a time. In addition to her observations, Ainsworth carried out interviews with the mothers. From these data she identified three types of attachments:

1 **Securely-attached** (Type B). These children were willing to explore, had high stranger anxiety, were easy to soothe and were enthusiastic at the return of their carer. Care-givers were sensitive to their charges.

2 **Insecure-avoidant** (Type A). These children were willing to explore, had low stranger anxiety, were indifferent to separation and avoided contact at the return of their care-giver. Care-givers tended to ignore their charges.

3 **Insecure-resistant** (Type C). These children were unwilling to explore, had high stranger anxiety, were distressed at separation and sought and rejected contact at the return of their care-giver. Care-givers were ambivalent to their charges, demonstrating simultaneous opposite feelings and behaviours.

In 1971 she conducted a similar study in Baltimore, USA, visiting 26 mother–child pairs every 3–4 weeks for the babies' first year of life. Each visit lasted 3–4 hours. Interviews and naturalistic observations were used, with the latter playing a greater role.

Ainsworth concluded that there were two distinct features of attachment, both with an adaptive survival value. Firstly, infants seek proximity to their mothers, especially when feeling threatened. Secondly, secure attachments allow infants to explore – vital for cognitive and social development – using their attached figure as a safe base to explore from and return to.

Classic research

'The Strange Situation' – Mary Ainsworth *et al.*, 1978

Figure 2.6 Mary Ainsworth (left) pioneered the 'Strange Situation' testing method

The 'Strange Situation' testing method was devised to make sense of the data Ainsworth had collected. It was hoped that it would prove a valid measure of attachments.

Aim: To see how young infants between 9 and 18 months behave under conditions of mild stress and novelty, in order to test **stranger anxiety**, separation anxiety and the **secure base concept**. Ainsworth wanted to examine the individual differences between mother–child pairs in terms of the quality of their attachments.

continued ...

...continued

Procedure: The Strange Situation comprised eight episodes. Each of these lasted for about three minutes, except episode one which lasted for 30 seconds.

Every aspect of participants' behaviour was observed and videotaped, with most attention given to **reunion behaviours** – the babies' responses to the mothers' return. Data were combined from several studies. In total 106 infants were observed.

The Strange Situation was a novel environment – an 81 square foot area divided into 16 squares to help record movements.

Five categories were recorded: (i) proximity- and contact-seeking behaviours, (ii) contact-maintaining behaviours, (iii) proximity- and interaction-avoiding behaviours, (iv) contact- and interaction-resisting behaviours and (v) search behaviours.

Every 15 seconds, the category of behaviour displayed was recorded and scored on an intensity scale of 1 to 7.

Table 2.1 details the eight episodes of the Strange Situation:

Findings: In general, the babies explored the playroom and toys more enthusiastically when just the mother was present than either a) after the stranger entered or b) when the mother was absent. The researchers classified the unexpected variety of reunion behaviours in terms of three attachment types:

- Fifteen per cent were insecure-avoidant (Type A), ignoring their mother and showing indifference towards her. Play was hardly affected whether she was present or absent. They showed little stress when she left and actively ignored or avoided her on returning. They responded to the mother and stranger in similar ways, being most distressed when left on their own.
- Seventy per cent were securely-attached (Type B), playing happily while their mother was present, whether or not a stranger was present, but becoming upset when she left, with play being seriously disrupted. When their mother returned, they wanted immediate comfort, then quickly calmed down and started playing again. Overall, they treated the mother and stranger very differently.

Table 2.1

Episode	Persons present	Brief description
1	Mother, baby, observer	Observer introduces mother and baby to experimental room, then leaves.
2	Mother, baby	Mother is passive while the baby explores.
3	Stranger, mother, baby	Stranger enters. First minute: stranger silent. Second minute: stranger converses with mother. Third minute: stranger approaches baby. After three minutes, mother leaves unobtrusively.
4	Stranger, baby	First separation episode. Stranger's behaviour is geared towards that of the baby.
5	Mother, baby	First reunion episode. Stranger leaves. Mother greets and/or comforts baby, then tries to settle baby again in play. Mother then leaves, saying 'bye-bye'.
6	Baby	Second separation episode.
7	Stranger, baby	Continuation of second separation. Stranger enters and gears her behaviour to that of the baby.
8	Mother, baby	Second reunion episode. Mother enters, greets baby, then picks up baby. Meanwhile, stranger leaves unobtrusively.

continued ...

...continued

- Fifteen per cent were insecure-resistant (Type C), being fussy and wary, even when their mother was present and crying more than Types A and B. When the mother left, they became distressed. On her return, they wanted contact but simultaneously showed anger and resisted contact, like putting their arms out to be picked up, but immediately struggling to get down, demonstrating ambivalence towards her.

Conclusions: Sensitive responsiveness is the crucial factor determining the quality of attachments. Sensitive mothers see things from the baby's perspective, correctly interpreting signals and responding appropriately to the baby's needs. Such mothers are also accepting, cooperative and accessible. Sensitive mothers tend to have securely-attached babies, whereas insensitive mothers tend to have insecurely-attached babies.

Evaluation: see Evaluation box below.

Key terms

Sensitive responsiveness – perceiving and responding appropriately to infants' needs

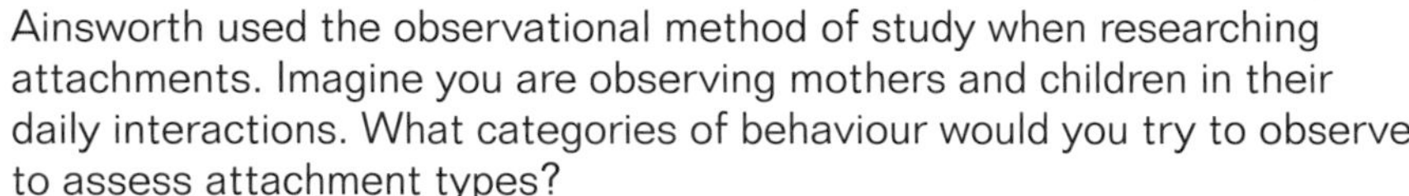

You are the researcher

Ainsworth used the observational method of study when researching attachments. Imagine you are observing mothers and children in their daily interactions. What categories of behaviour would you try to observe to assess attachment types?

It is important to establish **inter-observer reliability**. Explain what this is and how you would ensure it was established in your study.

To view an informative video about the Strange Situation go to http://www.youtube.com/watch?v=QTsewNrHUHU

Further footage with some film of Ainsworth herself can be found at http://www.youtube.com/watch?v=SHP_NikTkao'

Evaluation

Evaluation of the Strange Situation

- Van Ijzendoorn and Schuengel (1999) report that Ainsworth's Uganda and Baltimore studies are the most important in the history of attachment research, because their findings that parental sensitivity causes attachment security are supported by subsequent studies using larger samples.
- The Strange Situation has attained an **established methodology**, becoming the **paradigm** or accepted method of assessing attachments.
- The Strange Situation assumes that attachment types are fixed characteristics of children, but classification can change if family circumstances, like mothers' stress levels, alter. Therefore attachment style is not a permanent characteristic.
- The Strange Situation is an artificial way of assessing attachment, as it is laboratory based with mother and stranger acting to a 'script'. This is far removed from everyday situations and thus lacks ecological validity. Brofenbrenner (1979) found that infants' attachment behaviour is much stronger in a laboratory than when at home.
- The Strange Situation focuses too much upon the behaviour of infants, and not enough on that of mothers, which could affect results.
- Although mothers do leave children for brief periods with strangers, like unfamiliar babysitters and childminders, the ethics of a research method that deliberately exposes children to stress are questionable.

continued ...

...continued

- Is the Strange Situation a valid measure of attachment types? Main and Weston (1981) found that children acted differently depending on which parent they were with. Children might be insecurely attached to their mothers, but securely attached to their fathers; demonstrating that attachment patterns reflect qualities of distinct relationships rather than the characteristics of children. This suggests that it is not attachment types that are being measured, but relationships between individuals, such as between care-givers and infants.
- Main *et al.* (1985) found that 100 per cent of infants securely attached before 18 months were still securely attached at 6 years, and that 75 per cent of those who had been anxious-avoidant remained so. This suggests that the Strange Situation is reliable, as children tested at different times generally demonstrate identical attachment types.
- Main and Solomon (1986) found an additional attachment type, **insecure-disorganised** (Type D), displayed by a small number of children, whose behaviour is a confusing mixture of approach and avoidance behaviours.

To further your understanding of the measurement of attachment styles, go to

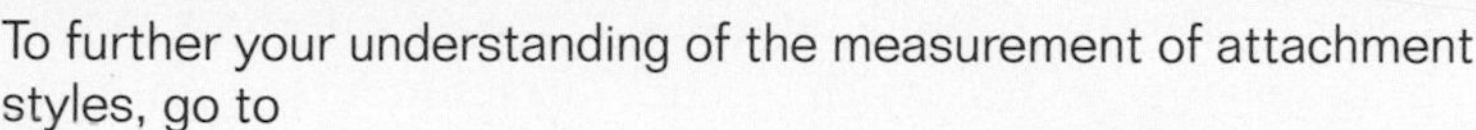

http://www.richardatkins.co.uk/atws/page/55.html

where you will find details of self-report and clinical measures.

Key terms

Continuity hypothesis – the idea that there is consistency between early emotional experiences and later relationships

Supplementary learning

Figure 2.7 The continuity hypothesis believes that securely attached children go on to develop emotionally stable adult relationships

The continuity hypothesis

The internal working model sees attachments as reflected in later relationships. Therefore securely attached children will be emotionally and socially stable as adults and able to have secure, trusting, loving relationships. In contrast, insecure attachments will result in troubled relationships in later life. Thus there is continuity between earlier and later relationship types. The continuity hypothesis also believes that attachment types of children are reflected in their own parenting styles when they have children of their own. If true, this could have dire consequences, as failing to achieve secure attachments could condemn individuals to a life of fractured relationships, divorce and a cycle of poor parenting.

Hazan and Shavers (1987) developed the 'love quiz', a questionnaire assessing infants' early attachment types and their later adult romantic relationships, finding continuity between early and later relationships. For example, insecure-avoidant children had cold, rejecting mothers and as adults, harboured a fear of intimacy, had emotional highs and lows and suffered from jealousy that often sabotaged relationships.

Zimmerman *et al.* (2000) measured attachment types of infants aged between 12 and 18 months

...continued

and then again at 16 years, finding that early attachment type was not a good predictor of later relationships. They concluded that other life events, like parental divorce, had more impact, weakening the continuity hypothesis.

Weinfield *et al.* (2003) studied the stability of attachment from infancy to adulthood in a sample of 57 participants selected for poverty and high risk of poor developmental outcomes, like high incidences of child maltreatment. No significant continuity between adult and infant attachment was found, suggesting that attachment types are vulnerable to difficult life experiences and do not necessarily remain constant.

Overall it seems that although early attachments can affect later adult relationships, other life events have a strong impact too.

Key terms

Culture – identifiable groups of people bound together by attitudes, values, goals and customs

Cross-cultural study – comparison of findings from people of different cultures

If you would like to assess your own attachment style, go to http://psychology.about.com/library/quiz/bl-attachment-quiz.htm where you will find a questionnaire based on the work of several researchers, including Hazan and Shaver's love quiz.

Cultural variations in attachment

Bowlby believed that attachments evolved and had a survival value. If this is true then attachment patterns should be similar across different cultures, regardless of child-rearing styles, with secure attachments dominating. However, if different patterns of attachment were found cross-culturally, it would suggest that attachments are determined environmentally through different child-rearing practices. Belsky (1999) proposes an evolutionary reason for different cross-cultural attachment types. He suggests that insecure attachment types are associated with weak adult relationships and early sexual activity, which could be useful in environments with a high death rate, as people would need to reproduce at a young age and not get too emotionally involved with people who may die young.

Child-rearing styles vary considerably cross-culturally; in some cultures one person does the majority of care-giving, while in others many carers are involved. There are also variations across cultures as to how different attachment types are perceived. For instance, what in our culture is perceived negatively as an insecure-avoidant attachment type is seen as an independent attachment type in Germany, a culture where independence is valued positively. Not surprisingly, a higher proportion of this attachment type is found in Germany.

Figure 2.8 Are attachment patterns similar or different across cultures?

Cross-cultural studies using the Strange Situation have shown differences both *within* and *between* cultures. However, such studies tend to use the Strange Situation testing procedure and this may not be suitable for use in all cultures and thus produce misleading results.

Contemporary research

Figure 2.9 A Dogon mother with her child

'Infant–mother attachment among the Dogon people of Mali' – McMahan True, Pisani, Oumar, 2001

Constant physical proximity, breastfeeding on demand and instant response to distress are the norm within the Dogon culture. This study therefore provides a rare insight into the attachment styles of children brought up according to natural parenting practices, thus providing a contrast to the more usual studies performed on western cultural samples.

Aim: To examine whether infant attachment security is linked to the quality of mother–infant communication and to see whether mothers of secure infants respond more sensitively to their infants than mothers of insecure infants.

Procedure: Forty-two mother and infant pairs from rural villages were used as participants, with infants ranging in age from 10 months to 12½ months at first assessment. The Strange Situation testing method was used to assess attachment styles. The results were compared to those from four North American samples, with a total of 306 mother–infant pairs tested.

Table 2.2 compares the attachment styles from the Dogon and western samples.

In the Dogon sample, many children had their grandmother as principal carer during the day. Attachment classifications were, however, unaffected by the type of primary care-giver, because mothers remained closely involved with children through regular breastfeeding and co-sleeping during the night.

Positive correlations were found between maternal sensitivity and infant security ratings and the quality of mother–infant communications and infant security ratings.

Conclusions: Children raised through natural child-rearing principles have significantly higher rates of secure attachment and a total absence of insecure-avoidant attachments, a fact explained by the incompatibility of Dogon child-rearing practices with practices associated with avoidant styles in western cultures. In Dogon culture there is no maternal rejection of attachment bids, intrusion or lack of physical contact.

The data suggest that naturally parented children show a trend towards greater attachment security and an absence of avoidant attachment, when compared to western cultures.

Evaluation:

- The distribution of attachment styles among the Dogon, with a high proportion of secure attachments and no avoidant attachments,

Type of culture	Percentage of secure attachments	Percentage of disorganised attachments	Percentage of resistant attachments	Percentage of avoidant attachments
Dogon	67	25	8	0
Western	55	15	8	23

Table 2.2 Comparison table of attachment styles in Dogon and western cultural samples

continued ...

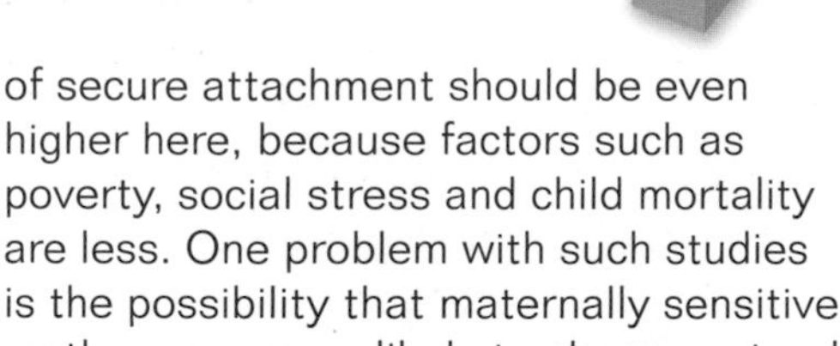

...continued

is even more remarkable considering the mortality rate of up to 45 per cent of infants before the age of 5 and the high rates of social and economic stress (a high proportion of mothers with HIV and high levels of poverty).

- The findings are backed up by two similar studies. Tomlinson *et al.* (2005), using a South African sample, and Zevalkink *et al.* (1999), using an Indonesian sample, both found high levels of secure attachment and low levels of avoidant attachment.
- Comparable studies are needed of infants naturally parented in western cultures. Rates of secure attachment should be even higher here, because factors such as poverty, social stress and child mortality are less. One problem with such studies is the possibility that maternally sensitive mothers are more likely to choose natural parenting procedures and this could affect findings.
- The Strange Situation procedure contains elements unfamiliar to Dogon infants, like being left with strangers, therefore this creates the risk that infants are being wrongly classified as insecurely attached.

Key terms

Imposed etic – using techniques relevant to one culture to study another

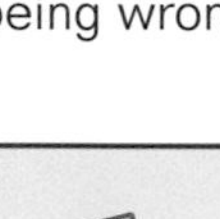

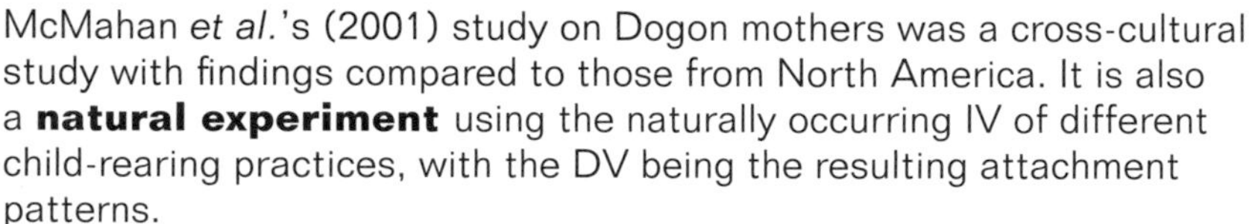

Research in focus

McMahan *et al.*'s (2001) study on Dogon mothers was a cross-cultural study with findings compared to those from North America. It is also a **natural experiment** using the naturally occurring IV of different child-rearing practices, with the DV being the resulting attachment patterns.

If behaviours are identical in different cultures, what does this tell us about the origins of those behaviours? If behaviours are different, what does this tell us?

The use of the Strange Situation in non-western cultures is an example of an imposed etic. Explain what this means.

Why do some psychologists not consider natural experiments to be true experiments?

In what situations would a natural experiment be used?

Compile a list of the advantages and disadvantages of natural experiments.

Research studies into cross-cultural variations in attachment

- Van Ijzendoorn and Kroonenberg (1988) reviewed 32 Strange Situation studies from eight countries, involving over 2,000 children. They found a similar pattern to Ainsworth, with secure attachment the most common type, followed by insecure-avoidant and insecure-resistant. Insecure-avoidant was not common in Japan or Israel, but insecure-resistant was. Marked differences were found in the results of the two Japanese studies reviewed. In one there were no insecure-avoidant children, while in the other, the pattern was like that found by Ainsworth, suggesting that there may also be differences within cultures.

- Kyoung (2005) used the Strange Situation to compare 87 Korean families with 113 American families. There were notable differences: the Korean infants did not stay close to their mothers and when Korean mothers returned, they were more likely to play with their infants. There were, however, a similar proportion of securely-attached children in both cultures, suggesting that different child-rearing practices can lead to secure attachments.
- Grossmann and Grossmann (1991) found that German infants tended to be classified as insecurely attached. This may be due to different child-rearing practices, as German culture requires 'distance' between parents and children. This indicates that there are cross-cultural variations in attachment.
- Malin (1997) found that young Aboriginal children in Australia are actively discouraged from exploring by threats and distractions of food. This inhibits children from using their mothers as a safe base from which to explore and can lead to children being incorrectly labelled as insecurely attached, backing up the later findings of Yeo (2003) (see Psychology in action section on page 52).

Evaluation

Evaluation of cross-cultural variations in attachment

- The different patterns of reaction to the Strange Situation reflect cultural values and practices. For example, the greater frequency of insecure-avoidant children in Germany reflects a cultural emphasis on early independence training.
- The greater frequency of insecure-resistant attachment type in Japan may result from stress during the Strange Situation due to infants' unfamiliarity at being left with strangers. Japanese children are rarely separated from their mothers, so separation episodes are upsetting for these children. In contrast, Rogoff (2003) found that black American children have many care-givers and are encouraged to be friendly to strangers and thus the Strange Situation activates their interest to explore. This shows that the Strange Situation has different meanings in different cultures and child-rearing practices need to be inspected in order to interpret findings based on the Strange Situation.
- Cross-cultural studies in psychology can suffer from an imposed etic, where researchers analyse findings in a biased manner in terms of their own cultural beliefs, wrongly imposing cultural-specific beliefs onto other cultures.
- In collectivist cultures, secure attachments are less likely to lead to sociability with strangers and sociability is not perceived as a form of social competence. Okonogi (1992) found that behaviours desirable in the West were perceived as inappropriate in Japan, where children are taught to fear and avoid strangers. Again implying that the Strange Situation may not be an appropriate testing procedure for use with non-western cultures.
- The fact that attachment patterns vary cross-culturally and that the Strange Situation may not be applicable in all cultures, suggests that attachment theory is **culture-bound** and applicable only to western cultures.

Key terms

Culture-bound – behaviours applicable to specific cultures

Psychology in action

Flawed assessment of Aboriginal children

In Australia, a practical use of attachment theory and the Strange Situation has been the emphasis in the children's court on bonding and attachment assessments to determine whether a child remains with its carers. This seems an excellent use of psychology and one with positive implications for society. However, Yeo (2003) raised concerns about how this is applied to Aboriginal children who are nine times more likely to be in out-of-home care. Indeed, Aboriginal children comprised 25 per cent of children in care in 2000. It is feared that assessments of Aboriginal children are being made on what the dominant Australian culture constitutes as competent parenting, with a disregard for Aboriginal cultural practices. Therefore life-changing decisions are being made based on evidence that is culturally inappropriate for Aboriginals and the continuation of this policy will undoubtedly have a negative impact on Aboriginal communities.

Aboriginal children are often cared for and breastfed by many women within their community. Children are cared for by women interchangeably and are often brought up by women who are not their natural mothers. Aboriginal children are rarely left in the presence of strangers. Therefore the assessment of Aboriginal children in line with Australian cultural values may lead to Aboriginal children being incorrectly assessed as having insecure attachments, taken away from their communities and placed in care.

Practical applications based on psychological research can have positive implications for society, but only if based on appropriate methodology.

Strengthen your learning

1 Describe the characteristics of a) secure attachment, b) insecure-avoidant attachment, c) insecure-resistant attachment and d) insecure-disorganised attachment.

2 a) Outline the procedures of the Strange Situation.
  b) What is the most common form of attachment?
  c) Ainsworth deemed sensitive responsiveness to be crucial. What is sensitive responsiveness?
  d) Give a brief evaluation of the Strange Situation.

3 Outline a) the continuity hypothesis and b) the temperament hypothesis.

4 Explain why having different attachment types may have an evolutionary benefit.

5 a) What conclusions did McMahan *et al.* (2001) reach after researching the child-care practices of the Dogon people?
  b) Were McMahan's findings backed up by similar research studies?

6 What have other studies of cross-cultural variations of attachment revealed?

7 Why might the Strange Situation testing procedure not be suitable for all cultures?

8 Give a brief evaluation of studies into cross-cultural variations in attachment.

9 What concerns does Yeo (2003) have about the placement of Aboriginal children into institutional care?

Assessment Check

1 Outline features of infants' behaviour recorded with the Strange Situation. [3 marks]

2 The following statements relate to types of attachment:

- **A** Strong and contented attachment, developing through sensitive responsiveness.
- **B** An attachment type where infants seek and reject intimacy.
- **C** An attachment type characterised by a lack of a consistent pattern of social behaviour.
- **D** An attachment type where infants shun intimacy and social interaction.
- **E** An attachment type that develops through classical conditioning.

Copy and complete the following table to match the statement, A, B, C, D or E, to the type of attachment. [4 marks]

continued ...

...continued

Description	Type of attachment
	Insecure-avoidant attachment
	Insecure-disorganised attachment
	Secure attachment
	Insecure-resistant attachment

3 Outline and evaluate what psychologists have discovered about cultural variations in attachment. [12 marks]
4 Outline two behaviours characteristic of an insecure-resistant attachment type. [4 marks]
5 The Strange Situation is a method used for the observation of children's attachment behaviours.
   a) Explain one ethical issue relevant to such observational studies of young children. [2 marks]
   b) Explain how a researcher could deal with this ethical issue. [2 marks]

Examination guidance:

1 Relevant answers to this question could contain material on exploration, separation behaviour, stranger anxiety and reunion behaviour.
2 Answers are provided, but must be inserted into the correct parts of the table. One description will be left over.
3 This is a long-answer question. Six marks are available for an outline and six additional marks for an evaluation, possibly based on the degree of research support, relevant methodological points and practical applications, like recommendations for child-rearing practices.
4 One mark is available for each relevant behaviour, with an additional mark for elaboration.
5 This question requires knowledge of research methods, namely ethical issues and how to deal with them.

The effects of the disruption of attachment

The maternal deprivation hypothesis (Bowlby, 1951)

If Bowlby is correct and attachments are vital for healthy psychological development, the disruption of the mother–child bond should result in negative outcomes, with serious and permanent damage to a child's emotional and intellectual development. The **maternal deprivation hypothesis** (MDH) was based on studies conducted in the 1930s and 1940s of children raised in orphanages and residential nurseries. Bowlby saw the lack of maternal care as the common factor leading to negative outcomes, like poor IQ scores and even, in some instances, death. There were, however, several methodological faults with these studies which Bowlby did not consider.

Research studies of the MDH

- Goldfarb (1943) compared 15 children raised in social isolation in institutions from 6 months of age until 3½ years of age with 15 children who had gone straight from their natural mothers to foster homes. At age three, the socially isolated children lagged behind the fostered children on measures of abstract thinking, social maturity, rule following and sociability. Between the ages of 10 and 14 years, they continued to perform poorly, with an average IQ of 72 compared to the fostered children's IQ of 95.
- Spitz (1945, 1946) studied children raised in poor-quality South American orphanages. Members of staff were overworked, untrained and rarely talked to the children or picked them up, even for feeding. Children received no affection and had no toys. The children displayed **anaclitic depression**, a reaction to the loss of a loved object, including fear, sadness, weepiness, withdrawal, loss of appetite, weight loss, inability to sleep and developmental retardation.

Key terms

Affectionless psychopathy – lacking a social conscience

Separation – temporary or permanent absence of an attachment figure

Deprivation – separation from an attachment figure

Privation – never having formed an attachment

For a fuller account of the work of John Bowlby and Mary Ainsworth, whom he greatly influenced, go to http://www.psychology.sunysb.edu/attachment/online/inge_origins.pdf

- Bowlby (1944) compared 44 juvenile thieves with a control group of non-thieves who had suffered emotional problems. Thirty-two per cent of the thieves were affectionless psychopaths, possessing no social conscience. None of the control group was classed in this way. Eighty-six per cent of the affectionless psychopaths had experienced maternal separation, compared to 17 per cent of the thieves who were not affectionless psychopaths. This suggests that maternal deprivation can have serious and long-lasting negative effects.

Evaluation

Evaluation of the MDH

- The Goldfarb study did not use random samples, so it is possible that the fostered children were naturally brighter, more sociable and healthier than the socially isolated children and that is why they were fostered rather than placed in institutional care.
- The institutions provided an unstimulating environment and it may have been the lack of stimulation rather than the absence of maternal care that led to retarded development.
- Bowlby failed to distinguish between **privation** and **deprivation**. Privation refers to never having formed an attachment, while deprivation refers to the loss through separation of the attachment figure. The institutional studies demonstrate the effects of privation, yet Bowlby's theory concerned deprivation.

Research in focus

In his study of juvenile thieves, Bowlby carried out interviews with children and mothers. Why is an interview a form of self-report? What other forms of self-report are there?

Interviews can be structured, semi-structured or unstructured. Explain the differences between these types, giving advantages and disadvantages of each.

Although interviews are relatively easy to conduct and generate lots of data, they do have faults. Explain the following weaknesses: a) leading questions, b) social desirability bias and c) interviewer reliability. (See the section on interviews in Chapter 3, Research methods, page 82.)

You are the researcher

Bowlby's (1944) study compared juvenile thieves and non-thieves by interviewing mothers and children. A higher proportion of the thieves had experienced maternal separation than the non-thieves.

Imagine you are conducting this study using a structured interview technique. Create a set of questions you would ask. These should be relevant to the factors being investigated. Explain how these questions could generate both **quantitative** and **qualitative** data, giving examples of each to show understanding. How would you analyse these different forms of data? (For guidance see pages 102–112 in Chapter 3, Research methods.)

Deprivation and privation

Attachments can be damaged in several ways, firstly by privation, where attachments do not form in the first place, or from deprivation, either by short-term separation, like being in daycare, or long-term separation, like family break-ups. Studies of privation and deprivation show that they have different types of developmental effects.

The effects of deprivation

Short-term deprivation

Short-term deprivation consists of brief, temporary separations from attachment figures, like being in daycare or a short period of hospitalisation. Bowlby (1969) described the components of distress caused by short-term separation as protest, despair and detachment. These are outlined in greater detail below:

- **Protest** – the immediate reaction to separation involves crying, screaming, kicking and struggling to escape, or clinging to the mother to prevent her leaving. This is an outward, direct expression of the child's anger, fear, bitterness and confusion.
- **Despair** – protest is replaced by calmer, more apathetic behaviour. Anger and fear are still felt inwardly. There is little response to offers of comfort, instead the child comforts itself, for example by thumb-sucking.
- **Detachment** – the child responds to people again, but treats everyone warily. Rejection of the care-giver on their return is common, as are signs of anger.

Figure 2.10 The Robertsons made a series of groundbreaking films of children's separations

Research studies of short-term deprivation

- In the 1960s, Robertson and Robertson made a series of films called 'Young children in brief separation', which documented how young children's brief separation from their mothers affected their mental state and psychological development. One film (1969) featured John, a sensitive child aged 17 months, who had enjoyed a close and stable relationship with his mother. He experienced extreme distress while spending nine days in a residential nursery while his mother was in hospital having a baby. According to Bowlby, he was grieving for his absent mother.
- Robertson and Robertson (1969) believed that John's extreme distress was caused by a combination of factors: loss of his mother, strange environment and routines, multiple care-takers and lack of a mother substitute. On his mother's return, John threw a tantrum and struggled to get free of her, escaping into his father's arms.
- Douglas (1975) found that separations of less than a week for children below 4 years of age were correlated with behavioural difficulties.
- Quinton and Rutter (1976) found that behavioural problems were more widespread in samples of adolescents separated from attachment figures during their first five years through hospitalisation, than among adolescents without this feature in their backgrounds.

Figure 2.11 Nurses' shifts are now designed so they have regular contact with the same children

Evaluation

Evaluation of short-term deprivation

- Much evidence linking short-term separation to negative outcomes is correlational and cannot show causality. Kagan *et al.* (1978, 1980) found no direct causal link between separation and later emotional and behavioural difficulties.
- Robertson and Robertson (1971) found that the negative effects of short-term separation are avoided by taking separated children into their own home and providing them with an alternative attachment and a normal home routine. This suggests that negative outcomes are not inevitable and that the provision of alternative care provides a stimulus to the formation of new relationships.
- Barrett (1997) argued that individual differences in reactions to short-term separation have not been considered. For instance, securely attached children and more mature children cope well with separations, implying that it is only some children that experience distress.
- The Robertsons' work led to radical changes in hospital practices. Nurses' shifts were designed so they had regular contact with the same children, enabling them to form alternative bonds during their hospitalisation. Visiting hours were changed to allow regular contact with attachment figures and children were encouraged to bring familiar items with them.

Key terms

Institutional care – child-care provided by orphanages and children's homes

Long-term deprivation

Long-term deprivation consists of prolonged or permanent separations from attachment figures, including death of a parent, imprisonment, adoption, placement in institutional care and divorce.

Research studies of long-term deprivation

- Schaffer (1996) found that almost all children are affected adversely by divorce, at least in the short term.
- Hetherington and Stanley-Hagan (1999) found that about 25 per cent of children experience long-term adjustment problems when their parents divorce, but that most children are resilient enough to adapt. This suggests that negative outcomes to children's development are more short term than long term.
- Furstenberg and Kiernan (2001) found that children experiencing parental divorce score lower than children in first-marriage families on measures of

Evaluation

Evaluation of long-term deprivation

- It seems logical that long-term separation has a greater negative effect upon children's development than short-term separation and research backs this up.
- Richards (1987) found that attachment disruption through divorce leads to resentment and stress, while death of an attachment figure is more likely to result in depression than delinquency. This implies that separation through different causes produces different outcomes.
- Demo and Acock (1996) found that children vary widely in reactions to divorce and noticed that some children develop better attachments to parents after divorcing. This may be due to the removal of the negative environment of marital conflict and also to parents being more attentive and supportive to children after divorcing. This implies that divorce does not necessarily incur negative effects.
- Research into divorce allows psychologists to formulate strategies to help children cope with divorce. Indeed some American states have a legal requirement for parents planning to divorce to attend an education programme. This teaches them to understand and avoid the difficulties concerning disrupted attachments their children may face, like providing emotional warmth and support and keeping to consistent rules.

social development, emotional well-being, self-concept, academic performance, educational attainment and physical health, suggesting that divorce has wide-ranging negative effects on children's development.

- Rodgers and Prior (1998) found that children experiencing two or more parental divorces have the lowest adjustment rates and the most behavioural problems, suggesting that changes in attachment relationships increase the likelihood of children reacting negatively.

Supplementary learning

The effects of divorce

The nature, severity and duration of the effects divorce has upon attachment are influenced by several factors, including:

- continuity of contact with the non-custodial parent
- the financial status/lifestyle of the custodial parent
- whether the custodial parent remarries and the nature of the resulting stepfamily.

The effects can include:

- Lower levels of academic achievement and self-esteem.
- A two to three times higher incidence of anti-social and delinquent behaviour and other problems of psychological adjustment during childhood and adolescence.
- Earlier social maturity, with certain transitions to adulthood – like leaving home, beginning sexual relationships, cohabiting or getting married and getting pregnant – occurring earlier.
- Increased tendency in young adulthood to more job changes, lower socio-economic status and depression, plus a greater likelihood to be divorced themselves.
- More distant relationships in adulthood with parents and other relatives.

Psychology in action

Mothers in prison

Figure 2.12

What should be done with the children of mothers and pregnant women sent to prison? There were 14 women's prisons in England in 2006, containing 4,463 prisoners, of which 55 per cent had a child under 16 and 33 per cent a child under five. Twenty per cent were single parents. Between 2003 and 2004 there were 126 births in custody.

Is it better for a child to be separated from its mother and looked after elsewhere or stay in prison with its mother? Should a newborn baby be taken from its mother and not allowed to form an attachment with her?

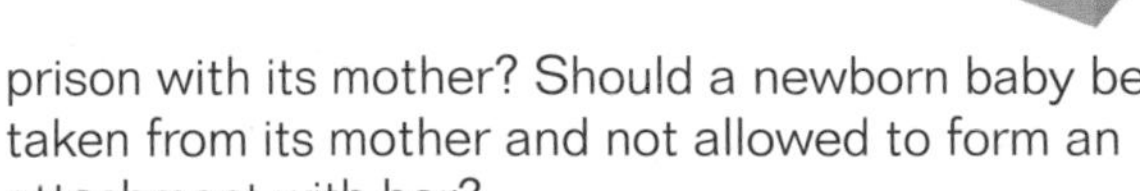

Psychological knowledge has helped form the working practices of the seven Mother and Baby Units (MBUs) currently existing in the prison service, two of which allow babies to stay with their mothers up to 9 months of age and five up to the age of 18 months. Women with a poor past history of parenting are less likely to be given places, but each application is assessed on an individual basis by a multi-disciplinary team, focusing on the best interests of the child. For example, if a mother has an 18-month-old child in an MBU, but is due for release shortly, the child may stay with her.

If a mother is serving a long sentence and is given a place on an MBU then in due course she will be separated from her child, though this is planned well in advance with social services and other family members involved.

This type of practice is an excellent example of how psychology is applied in the real world, in what is obviously a sensitive area.

If you would like to read more about prison practices for mothers and their children and the role of the MBUs, go to http://www.hmprisonservice.gov.uk/prisoninformation/prisonservicemagazine/index.asp?id=5730,18,3,18,0,0

and

http://www.hmprisonservice.gov.uk/adviceandsupport/prison_life/femaleprisoners/

The effects of failure to form attachment (privation) and institutional care

A number of case studies have been undertaken to see whether children who have endured extreme privation can recover and if so, to what extent. Privation is more likely than deprivation to lead to lasting damage and affectionless psychopathy, where individuals develop permanent emotional damage. Results can be contradictory; some individuals show signs of full recovery while others make little if any improvement.

Studies of institutional care, where children are raised in orphanages and children's homes are regarded as examples of privation as they generally have no opportunities to form attachments.

Classic research

Longitudinal study of institutional care – Barbara Tizard and Jill Hodges, 1978

Figure 2.13

Tizard and Hodges studied children born to single mothers who were transferred into institutional care within the first 4 months of their life and who therefore had not formed attachments with their mothers. High staff turnover and the policy of the institution not to let their carers form relationships with children prevented substitute attachments forming.

Aim: To perform a longitudinal study that followed a group of children from early life to adolescence, investigating the permanence of the effects of privation.

Procedure: 65 children placed into an institution before 4 months of age formed the sample. By 4 years of age, 24 children had been adopted and 15 had been restored to their natural homes. There was also a control group of children raised in their natural homes.

The children were assessed at ages 4 and 8, with the sample reduced to 51 children, and then again at age 16, though only 11 of the restored children, five of those remaining in institutional care and 23 of the adopted children were traced (more children had been adopted after age 4).

Assessment took the form of interviewing the children, their parents/adoptive parents and their teachers and getting them to complete questionnaires on attitudes and behaviour.

Findings: At age 4 those children who were still in the institutions were attention seeking and clingy towards adults in an indiscriminate fashion. They exhibited problems in relating to peers, showing argumentative styles of interaction. They did not appear to care deeply about specific carers, and showed no preference towards individual carers. The adopted children were indiscriminately and excessively friendly towards strangers.

At age 8 most adopted children had formed close attachments to their adoptive parents, but only some of those who had returned to their biological families had done so. The ex-institution group as a whole had no more problems than the control group, according to their parents, but their teachers thought they were attention seeking, restless and disobedient with poor peer relationships. The restored children exhibited the worst behavioural problems at school.

At age 16 most adopted children were similar to the control group in having mutually satisfying family relationships. But the restored children often had poor family relationships with the children and their parents having difficulty in showing affection towards each other. The parents reported feeling

continued ...

...continued

closer to their other children. Outside the family, the adopted and restored children were more likely to seek adult affection and approval and have difficulties with peer relationships. They were less likely to have a special friend or see peers as a source of emotional support and more likely to be friendly towards any peer, rather than choosing friends.

Conclusions: The finding that all ex-institution children had difficulties with peer relationships suggests early privation does have negative effects. However, children who do not enjoy close, lasting relationships early in life can still form attachments later on, as the adopted children developed close relationships with their adoptive parents. These attachments are, however, dependent on the adults concerned being nurturing and child-centred.

Evaluation:

- Children who were more socially responsive may have been chosen for adoption and thus found it easier to form attachments to their adoptive parents (though this does not explain why they had relationship problems outside their families).
- The sample suffers from **atypical sample attrition**, where, over time, a certain type of participant (e.g. the more troubled children) drops out, thus affecting the reliability of the results.
- There was no independent check of the accuracy of answers given in the interviews and questionnaires and parents/adoptive parents and their children may have found it difficult to be objective about each other. In addition, it is unlikely that the teachers were completely objective, as they knew which children were ex-institutional. This suggests the reliability and validity of the data may be questionable.

Research studies of privation

- Koluchova (1972, 1991) reported on identical Czech twins Andrei and Vanya whose mother died soon after she gave birth. When their father remarried, the stepmother locked them in a cellar for 5½ years, giving them regular beatings. The father was mainly absent from the home due to his job. Discovered at age 7, the twins were undeveloped physically, lacked speech and did not understand the meaning of pictures. The doctors who examined them were confident in predicting permanent physical and mental damage. Initially the boys were given physical therapy and put into a school for children with severe learning difficulties. They were then adopted by two nurturing, child-centred sisters. By age 14 their intellectual, social, emotional and behavioural functioning was near normal. As adults, both married and had children, one of them working as an instructor and the other as a computer technician. Both lack abnormalities, are stable and enjoy secure relationships.
- Freud and Dann (1951) reported on six children placed in the Nazi concentration camp at Tereszin, who were orphaned at a few months of age having formed no maternal attachments. They were taken at age 3–4 to the Bulldog Bank Centre in West Sussex. They had little language, did not know what to do with toys and were hostile to adults. They were, however, devoted to each other and refused to be separated. Very gradually they became attached to their carers and made rapid developments in physical and intellectual capabilities. It was not possible to trace the children fully as adults, so it is not known how full their recovery was.
- Curtiss (1977) and Rymer (1993) reported on Genie, a girl denied human interaction, beaten and strapped into a potty seat until her discovery at age 13. She could not stand erect or speak, spending most of her time spitting. She received years of rehabilitation and was tested constantly, developing some language abilities and improving her intellectual capacities. In 1971 her IQ was

38, while in 1977 it had risen to 74. At 18 she returned to the care of her mother, staying for only a few months before moving to a succession of six different foster homes and receiving further abuse. She then deteriorated physically and mentally and went to live in a home for people with learning difficulties.

A fuller account of the story of Genie, complete with updates can be accessed at http://www.feralchildren.com/en/showchild.php?ch=genie

while a more complete account of the Bulldog Bank children case study can be found at http://www.childrenwebmag.com/articles/key-child-care-texts/an-experiment-in-group-upbringing-by-anna-freud-and-sophie-dann

Evaluation

Evaluation of privation

- Case studies of children who have endured extreme privation tend to be used as a study method, as it would not be ethically possible to set up experiments into this area.
- It may be that the close attachments the Czech twins and the Bulldog Bank children had to each other can explain why they made lasting recoveries, while Genie, who had no attachments, made little progress.
- Case studies are dependent upon retrospective memories that may be selective and even incorrect. There is no way of knowing fully what happened to these individuals before discovery. Genie's mother, for example, often gave conflicting stories of what happened to her daughter.
- Bowlby's viewpoint that the negative effects of maternal deprivation are irreversible seems, given the more recent evidence, to be overstated. Individuals who endure negative experiences often subsequently endure further negative experiences, as was the case with Genie who suffered more abuse when fostered. Those whose abuse was followed by positive experiences, like the Czech twins, did, however, recover.
- The findings of privation research suggest that recovery is possible if individuals encounter a subsequent loving and nurturing relationship.

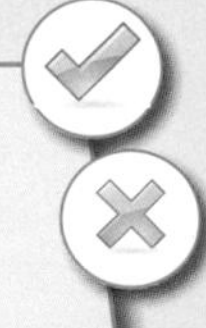

You are the researcher

Tizard and Hodges used questionnaires to assess children's attitudes and behaviours in their longitudinal study of institutional care.

Try to compose some questions relevant to this study. These should be easily understandable, unambiguous and not leading in any way. They should be written in such a way that the answers are easy to analyse. Ensure that some questions are open questions producing qualitative data and some are closed questions producing quantitative data. (See Chapter 3, Research methods page 81 for guidance.)

Research in focus

Tizard and Hodges' (1978) study of institutional care is an example of a longitudinal study: one carried out over a long period of time at regular intervals.

Longitudinal studies show **trends**. Explain what this means.

A disadvantage of longitudinal studies is they are prone to atypical sample attrition. With reference to the study of Tizard and Hodges, explain what is meant by this and the negative effect it can have.

IN THE NEWS

Abandoned boy said to have been raised by a dog

Figure 2.14 Feral children Romulus and Remus: fact or fiction?

A Mowgli-like wild boy who appears to have been raised by a dog since he was 3 months old has been discovered living in a remote part of Siberia seven years after he was abandoned by his parents.

Andrei Tolstyk was discovered by social workers who wondered why the 7-year-old had not enrolled at school. Deprived of human contact for so long, Andrei could not talk and had adopted many dog-like traits, including walking on all fours, biting people, sniffing his food before he ate it and general feral behaviour.

His mother left home when he was 3 months old, entrusting Andrei's care to his alcoholic invalid father who appears to have abandoned the boy soon afterwards and drifted away.

Andrei reportedly forged a close bond with the only other living thing around, the family guard dog, which somehow helped the young baby survive and grow up.

Source: adapted from Andrew Osborn's article in the *Independent*, Wednesday 4 August 2004. Copyright of the *Independent*.

Historical records document many instances of feral children raised by animals. Romulus and Remus, the founders of Rome, were said to have been suckled by a she-wolf. However, discoveries of children like Andrei show us that such stories are not mere fables. Abandoned by his parents before the age at which attachments could form, Andrei appears to be an example of acute privation. However, it seems he forged a bond with the dog that raised him. Andrei was placed in an orphanage, made friends there and began to communicate in sign language.

Strengthen your learning

1 a) Outline Bowlby's maternal deprivation hypothesis (MDH).
   b) The MDH was based on research conducted in the 1930s and 1940s of children raised in orphanages and residential nurseries. In what ways did such research support the MDH?
   c) What criticisms can be made of these studies?

2 Explain the difference between a) privation and deprivation and b) short-term and long-term separation.

3 Describe the components of distress caused by short-term separation.

4 What has research told us about the effects of short-term separation?

5 Give a brief evaluation of studies into the effects of short-term separation.

6 What has research told us about the effects of long-term separation?

7 Give a brief evaluation of research into the effects of long-term separation.

8 a) What factors influence the severity and duration of the effects of divorce upon attachment?
   b) What can these effects consist of?

9 a) How has privation generally been studied?
   b) What have psychologists learned from studies of privation?
   c) Why might some children appear to recover from the effects of privation while others do not?
   d) Why are studies of institutional care generally regarded as examples of privation?

10 Give a brief evaluation of privation studies.

Assessment Check

1 Outline the effects of disrupting attachment bonds. [6 marks]
2 Two-year-old Laura had a loving, secure attachment to her mother. While her mother was in hospital, psychologists decided to observe Laura's reaction to having her attachment disrupted.
   a) Outline two behavioural categories the psychologists could observe. [4 marks]
   b) Outline one strategy that could be employed while Laura's mother is in hospital to minimise any potential negative effects. [3 marks]
3 Research has demonstrated some negative effects of institutional care. Betty grew up in a children's home from birth, but at the age of three was adopted and went to live with her adoptive parents. Outline some possible negative effects of institutional care on Betty. [6 marks]
4 Discuss the effects of failing to form attachments. [12 marks]

Examination guidance:

1 The requirement in this question is to outline, therefore any evaluation would not gain credit.
2 In part a) behavioural categories, such as playing independently, need to be outlined and in part b), knowledge of the subject area must be applied to the scenario given, like the provision of opportunities for alternative attachments.
3 This is a scenario question on the negative effects of institutional care. Such effects should be focused directly upon the scenario given to gain the maximum credit.
4 This question refers to privation effects and would be best answered by reference to relevant case studies, with evaluation of these in terms of their methodology and practical applications.

Key terms

Day care – temporary care provided by non-family members or people not well known to a child outside of the home

Social development – acquiring relationships with others and the social skills needed to fit into a cultural group

Day care

The care of children outside of the family home raises passionate arguments. From a psychological viewpoint this is problematic as it is difficult to get an unbiased, objective outlook. Political and religious opinions motivate people instinctively to find day care either beneficial or harmful. For instance, many on the political right see a woman's place as in the home looking after children. However, there is also the issue of economic necessity – for many families it is essential that both parents work and so children need some form of day care. In 2004, women with children under the age of five comprised 52 per cent of the British workforce.

Day care refers to temporary care (i.e. not 24-hour care) of children outside the home. It is provided by people who are not family members and are not well known to the child, taking place in nurseries, crèches and kindergartens. Day care does not include institutional forms of child-rearing, like fostering and community homes, or health-related forms of care like hospitalisation.

Some see day care as harmful to children, while others see it as beneficial. The main points for debate are:

1. Whether day care is harmful for certain age groups.
2. Whether there are individual differences between children in terms of how day care affects them.
3. What constitutes good quality day care?

The effects of day care on social development

Bowlby's work on maternal deprivation influenced many women with young children to avoid working, as the use of nurseries and crèches was condemned as likely to lead to long-term emotional damage. Subsequently, however, psychologists have studied the possible benefits of day care upon a child's social development, like the heightened opportunities for interaction. They have also examined the negative aspects of day care, with a view to formulating practices that will ensure that day care is a positive and beneficial experience for both children and parents. Two main areas of interest have been the effects of day care upon children's aggression levels and upon the development of peer relationships.

Arguments against day care

- That separation from the primary care-giver results in deprivation leading to short- and long-term damage to social development.
- That day care is inferior to home care, as home care offers a more loving and stimulating environment.
- That day care brings negative outcomes, research evidence showing that children raised at home have superior social development.

Arguments for day care

- That good-quality day care is run by motivated, well-trained practitioners who provide a stimulating environment. Activities not available at home are offered and there are opportunities for interaction with other children.
- That high-quality day care has positive effects on social development and that any negative effects of day care are due to poor quality of provision. Good-quality day care is associated with the sensitivity of the carers to the children in their care.
- That day care makes better mothers, as mothers who are free to work experience lower levels of stress, frustration and depression and interact and respond to their children in a more positive and healthy manner.

Key terms

Peer relationships – relationships with people of equal standing

Home care – parental care given to children in their home environment

Research in focus

The study of day care is affected heavily by political/philosophical views about the raising of children and the position of women within society. Research into day care often produces conflicting results. There is a good chance that this occurs due to **experimenter bias**, a form of **investigator effect**.

Explain what is meant by experimenter bias and why this may occur with studies of day care.

What are investigator effects in terms of a) **direct effects** and b) **indirect effects**? How do they differ from **participant effects**? (See Chapter 3, Research methods page 100 for more details.)

Research studies of the negative effects of day care upon aggression

- Durkin (1995) reported that pre-schoolers who had been in day care since infancy were more prone to aggressiveness, negative social adjustment, hyperactivity and anxiety than those who started day care later. This suggests that the age children enter day care is important.
- Egeland and Heister (1995) found that insecurely attached children progressed well with day care, while securely attached children became aggressive. They suggested that insecurely attached children required compensatory care, while securely attached ones reacted aggressively to the extra attention of day care. This implies that certain types of children are negatively affected by day care.
- In 2003, the National Institute of Child Health and Human Development (NICHD) found from mothers' reports that children who averaged 30 hours or more of childcare per week were more likely to demonstrate problem behaviours, including heightened levels of aggression. This suggests that the amount of time spent in day care is related to aggression levels.

- Dmietrieva *et al.* (2007) found that the more children in kindergarten classes who had extensive histories of childcare, the more aggressive and disobedient were all the children in the class. This suggests that heightened levels of aggression can be transmitted between children.

Research studies of the positive effects of day care on aggression

- Hagekull and Bohlin (1995) found that Swedish children from disadvantaged families who experienced high-quality group day care had lower aggression levels than other children. Boys were found to benefit the most. This suggests that the quality of day care is important in determining aggression levels and that for some children, day care has a compensatory effect on aggression levels.
- A 2004 study carried out by NICHD found that children who spent the longest number of hours in day care had the lowest levels of aggression. This suggests that day care can have a positive effect on aggression levels. An earlier NICHD study found the opposite results, but used observations made by mothers rather than the more objective observations of teachers and carers used in this study.
- Doherty (1996) found that there is less likelihood of aggression if a child attends regular day care, though the importance of high-quality care – like low staff–child ratios, trained staff and stimulating activities – was acknowledged.

You are the researcher

An important factor when researching the effects of day care is the quality of the care provided.

Design a study comparing two nurseries identified as providing high- and low-quality day care. What type of study would this be? What design would you use? What would be your IV?

From what you have learned about day care, what would be the important factors you would compare the nurseries on? Explain how you would measure each of these factors.

Contemporary research

Early child care and physical aggression – Anne Borge *et al.*, 2004

Figure 2.15 Does early child care lead to increased levels of aggression?

Some studies indicate aggression levels to be heightened in children receiving day care. Anne Borge and her team compared aggression levels in children receiving day care with those raised at home. Family features, like level of maternal education, were considered, enabling the researchers to form clear conclusions.

Aim: To test claims that group day care is associated with increased risks of physical aggression in children.

Procedure: Data from a maternal questionnaire on 3,431 Canadian 2–4 year olds were used to compare rates of physical aggression shown by children raised at home by their mothers and those attending group day care. Data collection was undertaken by a single home visit with the person most knowledgeable about the child, in 90 per cent of cases this was the mother.

A family risk index, using occupational status, maternal education, number of siblings and degree of family functioning, was utilised to assess the contribution of family features to aggression levels.

continued ...

...continued

Findings: Aggression was more common in children raised by their mothers than those attending group day care. Analysis centred on whether higher rates of aggression occurred within certain sub-groups and after taking family features into consideration (which were found to be associated with levels of aggression), physical aggression was found to be more common in children from high-risk families raised at home. Such families had low levels of maternal education, three or more siblings, low socio-economic status and poor family functioning.

Conclusions: Home care is associated with higher levels of aggression in pre-school children, especially those from high-risk families.

Evaluation:

- As a large, representative sample was used and the effects of family features were taken into account, the findings seem valid.
- Group day care seems to protect against aggression for children from high-risk families, possibly as day care lessens the child's exposure to family risk or because it provides positive learning opportunities not available at home.

Evaluation

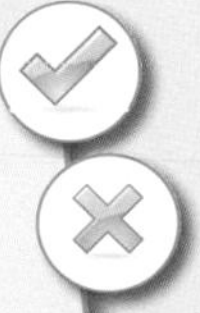

Evaluation of the effects of day care on aggression

- Family features, like the quality of the home environment, parental attitudes and maternal sensitivity, were a stronger indicator of children's aggression levels and social development than quantity of day care received. This suggests that quantity of day care is not the most important factor in determining aggression levels.
- The rating of some pre-schoolers as aggressive may reflect the fact that their day care experiences encourage them to get their own way. This may not be as 'nice' as the behaviour of other children, but it does not necessarily indicate lasting maladjustment.
- Hock *et al.* (1995) reported that aggressive and 'difficult' children are more likely to be placed in day care as their parents need a break and that some parents may choose to work, as they do not have positive interactions with their children. This suggests other factors, rather than day care alone, to be responsible for elevated aggression levels.
- Smith *et al.* (1998) believed that aggressive behaviour was confused with rough-and-tumble play and that evidence of heightened aggression in day care children is a misinterpretation of non-aggressive behaviour.
- Maccoby (1980) found that most aggressive behaviour in day care actually was not aggression, as it concerned conflicts over possessions. Children were not trying to hurt each other, but instead were removing an obstacle to something they wanted.
- Heightened levels of aggression may be apparent among children in day care simply because there is greater social interaction and more opportunity for aggression to arise.

Research in focus

Borge *et al.*'s (2004) study into child care and aggression used data from questionnaires. Questionnaires are a form of self-report. What does this mean?

Questionnaires use open and closed questions. Explain the difference between these types of questions and state the strengths and weaknesses of both.

Questionnaires produce quantitative and qualitative data. Explain each of these, giving examples to show understanding.

Borge mainly used questionnaire data from mothers. What criticisms can be made of this? (See Chapter 3, Research methods, for guidance.)

Research into the negative effects of day care on peer relations

- Gunnar *et al.* (1997) measured cortisol levels as an indicator of stress and found that day care was more challenging for less socially competent children who had negative interactions with peers. This indicates that day care may harm peer relationships in some children.
- Vlietstra (1981) used teacher ratings of New Zealand children aged 2½–4½ years and found that those attending half day care got on better with peers than those attending full day care. This suggests that the amount of day care received affects peer relationships.
- Vandell and Corasaniti (1990) used observations and ratings by teachers and parents, finding that Texan children with extensive day care developed poor peer relationships. The daytime carers of these children were untrained and staff–child ratios were high. This suggests that quality of day care is important in the development of positive peer relationships.
- Guralnick *et al.* (1996) found that children with disabilities, like limited communication, motor and social skills, interacted with peers less often and are less well accepted, suggesting that day care may not be beneficial for all children in developing peer relations.

Research into the positive effects of day care on peer relations

- Clarke-Stewart *et al.* (1994) found that children with the greatest ability to negotiate with peers were those who experienced group-based day care rather than home care, suggesting that day care is superior in fostering good peer relationships.
- Hartup and Moore (1990) found that from the age of two, day care permits children to interact more extensively with peers, learn the rules of social interaction and to resolve disputes with peers constructively. This implies that day care is a useful vehicle for achieving positive relationships with peers.
- Schenk and Grusek (1987) found that children attending day care were more likely to help a child in need, even though home-care and day-care children demonstrated equal knowledge of the appropriate response to someone in need. This suggests that day care gives children the confidence to react positively to peers.
- Rubenstein and Howes (1983) found that day care encourages interactions with familiar peers, leading to a reduction in anxiety when meeting unfamiliar peers. This implies that day care has psychologically healthy outcomes.

Evaluation

Evaluation of the effects of day care on peer relations

- The majority of research suggests that day care provides most children with enhanced opportunities for social contact and the development of social skills, helping to create positive peer relationships.
- Day care may actually harm the development of peer relationships in some children, especially those with poor social competence and motor skills. Indeed day care may provide ample opportunity for these types of children to be identified and bullied by other children.
- It is essential for the development of positive peer relations that high-quality day care is provided: carers should be well trained and staff–children ratios should be kept low. There is also evidence that too much day care has a negative impact on peer relationships.

Supplementary learning

Other studies of the effects of day care on social development

- Scarr (1998) found that children in day care were more likely to obtain lower language and cognitive scores and to be rated lower on social and emotional development, suggesting that poor-quality day care can put development at risk.
- Hegland and Rix (1990) found no differences in the aggression and assertiveness levels of children experiencing day care and those experiencing home care. This indicates that day care does not necessarily lead to increased levels of aggression. This was backed up by Melhuish *et al.* (1990) on a study of British 6-year-old children.
- DiLalla (1998) argued that day care inhibits social development, as children with little or no day care behave more pro-socially.

Evaluation

Evaluation of day care research

- Assessing the effects of day care on children is not easy, due to the huge variation in types and quality of day care. In addition, the subject area is contaminated by bias. Belsky (2009) suggests that policy makers should stop selectively embracing data consistent with their pre-existing viewpoints and dismissing data which is not in line with it.
- High-quality day care, like that provided in Sweden, leads to positive developmental outcomes. However, in many countries, only the wealthy can afford such care and the vast majority of children have lower quality care with negative consequences.
- Quantity versus quality. Good quality day care is not related to quantity; sensitive care-giving is more crucial than the quantity of time carers spend with children.
- Much research involves correlations, which show relationships between variables, but not cause-and-effect relationships. Other variables may be involved, like working mothers being more stressed and contributing to heightened aggression levels.
- Different methods of rating children's behaviour, like using teacher ratings rather than parental ratings, may lead to differences in findings. This suggests that differences in research findings are due to methodological reasons.

How research into attachment and day care has influenced child-care practices

It was originally believed that disrupting a child's maternal attachment through sending a child to day care led to serious, irreversible consequences. However, more recent research indicates that high-quality day care can be of benefit and factors creating opportunities to implement practical applications advantageous to children's development have been identified.

Research indicates that young children attending day care for considerable periods are at risk of having attachments adversely affected. Belsky and Rovine (1988) found that 43 per cent of babies who attended day care for at least 4 months before their first birthday and for more than 20 hours per week were likely to develop insecure attachments compared to 26 per cent of 'home-reared' babies. This was supported by Violata and Russell's (1994) meta-analysis of 88 studies, which found that children with over 20 hours of day care a week suffered negative effects on social development. This implies

Figure 2.16 Shy children do not develop well socially in day care

that young children should only attend day care for short periods and that policy makers and employers should consider this when formulating the workloads of mothers returning to work.

Research indicates that day care is not beneficial to all children. Pennebaker *et al.* (1981) found that certain children, particularly shy ones, did not incur positive social development with day care, while a 1997 NICHD study found that insecurely attached children in day care did not develop well socially. The research suggests that children should be assessed before entering day care, so those vulnerable to the negative consequences of day care can be catered for. This creates a problem, though, as such assessments would be intrusive into personal details, like parenting background.

Borge *et al.*'s (2004) research suggested that day care protects against aggression for children from high-risk families. This was supported by Hagekull and Bohlin's (1995) findings that Swedish children from disadvantaged families experiencing high-quality group day care had aggression levels in line with those of other children; boys benefited especially. The implication is that policy makers should ensure that such children are identified and provide sufficient funds to enable these children to receive high-quality day care, as the benefits to society are worthwhile.

Figure 2.17 A staff to children ratio of 1:3 is ideal

Smith *et al.* (1998) believe that child-minding could provide an economic form of day care with high adult-to-child ratios. This is considered best when provided by relatives like grandparents. Mayall and Petrie (1977, 1983) and Bryant *et al.* (1980) found that children seemed insecure in the homes of child-minders, scoring below average on tests of language and cognitive ability. However, no control groups were used, so outcomes may have been due to home circumstances. If child-minders are trained and given provision to offer a good standard of care, there is no reason why such care could not be at least equal to high-quality day care. More research is needed in this area.

Day care may not just be beneficial to children, but to mothers too. Day care permits a break from the stresses of child care and an opportunity to work, bringing financial rewards and other benefits, like enhanced self-esteem and lower levels of depression. Ultimately this allows mothers to interact with their children in a more meaningful and constructive manner. Mooney and Munton (1997) reviewing 40 years' research, concluded that there is no evidence that working mothers stunt children's emotional or social development, while Rout *et al.* (1997) found working mothers superior to non-working mothers on levels of mental health, reporting less depression and stress. This emphasises the benefits rather than the costs of having multiple roles.

The most striking implication of research into day care is that high-quality day care can be beneficial but that low-quality day care can be harmful. The characteristics of high-quality day care are detailed in Table 2.3.

Table 2.3 The characteristics of high-quality day care

Components of high-quality day care	Description of component
Verbal interaction	Encouraging regular two-way communications between carers and children is stimulating and helps cement relationships
Stimulation	Good provision of toys, books, interaction, etc.
Sensitive emotional care	Use of carers sensitive and responsive to children's needs
Low staff turnover	Achieved by providing a good working environment, training and financial reward
Consistency of care	Having the same carers tending a child allows secure attachments to form
Low staff–children ratio	A staff to children ratio of about 1:3 is ideal, though this varies with age. Smaller groups are easier for younger children to deal with
Mixed-age groups	Groups comprising younger and older children allow younger children the opportunities to learn social behaviours through observation and imitation
Structured time	Activities should be structured as part of a routine, creating a predictable, calming environment, with some free play time available too

Although the financial cost of providing high-quality day care for everyone, or to those who would benefit from it most, would be great, the benefits to society would cancel this out. High-quality day care has lasting benefits in helping to shape worthy, constructive individuals who function well and are of positive use to society. There would be huge savings in terms of mental health care and social welfare costs. It is, therefore, important that longitudinal studies are performed which evaluate the long-term benefits of day care.

Ultimately, as Clarke-Stewart (1989) says, 'maternal employment is a reality. The issue today, therefore, isn't whether infants should be in day care but how to make their experiences there and at home supportive of their development and of their parents' peace of mind.'

Strengthen your learning

1. What is day care?
2. Why is it difficult to get an objective, unbiased view of the effects of day care?
3. Summarise the arguments for and against day care.
4. What important factors has research identified concerning:
   a) the negative effects of day care upon aggression
   b) the positive effects of day care upon aggression
   c) the negative effects of day care upon peer relations
   d) the positive effects of day care upon peer relations?
5. Compile a brief evaluation of the effects of day care upon a) aggression and b) peer relations.
6. Outline the procedure and findings of Borge *et al.*'s (2004) study into aggression.
7. Compile a general evaluation of day care research. (Evaluation of the effects of day care on aggression and peer relations would be relevant, but what other points can be considered?)
8. Outline the ways in which research into attachment and day care can have implications for child-care practices.
9. Describe the components of high-quality day care, giving an example of each to demonstrate understanding.

Assessment Check

1 In order for Bryher to gain permission to open 'Brightways', a new day care facility for children below the age of five, she must demonstrate how Brightways would promote social development.

Outline how Bryher could promote the social development of children. [6 marks]

2 Outline and evaluate how research into attachment and day care has influenced child-care practices. [12 marks]

3 Outline two characteristics of high-quality day care on children's social development. [2 + 2 marks]

4 What have research studies demonstrated about the effects of day care on aggression OR peer relations? [4 marks]

Examination guidance:

1 To gain good marks for this question, knowledge of how to promote the social development of children in day care needs focus on the scenario given.

2 This is a long-answer question. Six marks are available for an outline and six additional marks for an evaluation. The focus of the answer must be on how research into attachment and day care has influenced child-care practices to gain credit.

3 With this question, one mark is earned by identifying a characteristic, with an additional mark for elaboration. If more than two characteristics are offered, all are marked, but only the best two are credited.

4 This requires candidates to offer material on the effects of day care on either aggression or peer relations. Be careful not to do both, as credit will only be given for the best one.

End of chapter review

- Attachments are enduring, two-way, emotional ties to specific other persons, developing in set stages within a fairly rigid time-scale.
- Learning theory sees attachments as developing through conditioned processes. With classical conditioning, babies associate care-givers with the primary reinforcer of food, while with operant conditioning, care-givers are reinforcing as they become associated with reducing the unpleasant feeling of hunger.
- Bowlby believed that there is a critical period, a time period in which attachments must form.
- Bowlby believed that babies display monotropy, an innate tendency to attach to a particular person, creating an internal working model of consistency between early emotional experiences and later relationships.
- The Strange Situation testing procedure has identified several attachment types and has become the standard measuring technique.
- Sensitive mothers interpret and respond to a baby's needs appropriately and tend to have securely attached infants. Insensitive mothers tend to have insecurely attached infants.
- The continuity hypothesis sees a link between earlier and later attachment types, while the temperament hypothesis sees children's innate personalities as a better indicator of attachment types.
- Child-rearing styles vary across cultures, with variations in how different attachment types are perceived in different cultures.
- Although the Strange Situation testing procedure reveals similar cross-cultural attachment patterns, differences within and between cultures have also been found.
- The Strange Situation is not applicable to all cultures, suggesting that attachment theory is culture-bound, applicable only to western cultures.
- Bowlby's maternal deprivation hypothesis was based on studies of institutionalised children and believes serious, permanent damage occurs if a baby is separated from its main attachment figure in the first five years of life.
- Short-term deprivation leads to protest, despair and detachment, though these are avoidable if separated children are provided with an alternative attachment and a home-based routine.
- Long-term separation consists of prolonged or permanent separations from attachment figures, including death of a parent, imprisonment, adoption, placing in institutional care and divorce.
- Research suggests that the effects of long-term separation are more severe than those of short-term separation and that long-term separation through different causes produces different outcomes.
- Privation is more likely than deprivation to lead to lasting damage and affectionless psychopathy.
- Due to political and philosophical bias it is difficult to gain objective views of the effects of day care, with many bodies motivated instinctively to find day care either of benefit or harm.
- Opponents of day care argue that separation results in damage to social development and that home care is of superior quality.
- Day care makes better mothers, as those free to work experience lower levels of stress, frustration and depression and interact and respond to children in a more positive and healthy manner.
- Family features are better indicators of children's aggression levels than the amount of day care received.
- Heightened levels of aggression are more apparent in children receiving day care as there is more opportunity for social interaction.
- Research suggests that day care gives enhanced opportunities for social interaction, leading to positive peer relations, though day care may harm the development of peer relationships in some children.
- Positive peer relations develop when day care is of high quality.
- Research suggests that young children should only attend day care for short periods and that some are vulnerable to incurring negative effects.
- High-quality day care is characterised by verbal interaction, stimulation, sensitive emotional care, low staff turnover, low staff–children ratio, consistency of care, mixed age groups and structured time.
- High-quality day care is costly in financial terms, but is beneficial to society.

3 Research methods

Introduction

Research methods are the means by which psychologists construct and test theories concerning the mind and behaviour. Without research methods there would be no theories or practical applications, indeed no scientific discipline called psychology. There are many different research methods, each with their own strengths and limitations and each applicable in different circumstances. Research methods are examined as a separate topic, but also within all other subject areas studied, which makes it perhaps the most important topic of all.

Understanding the specification

- With questions involving methods and techniques, candidates are expected to demonstrate knowledge and understanding of the research methods listed, including their advantages and weaknesses.
- With questions involving investigation design, candidates are expected to be familiar with the features of investigation design listed in the specification.
- With questions on data analysis and presentation, candidates are expected to be familiar with the features of data analysis, presentation and interpretation listed in the specification.
- The central guiding principle to answering questions on research methods is to be able to relate them to research based on the actual topics studied, as that is the format in which examination questions will occur. There is not a separate section of the AS examination where research methods are examined alone, they occur in conjunction with other topics you will have studied.

Key terms

Investigation design – the planning and construction of research methods

Methods and techniques

Figure 3.1 Carpenters choose the most appropriate tool for the job. Similarly, psychologists must choose the most appropriate research method

There are several research methods in psychology. Like a carpenter selecting the most appropriate tool, psychologists choose the most appropriate method for research. No single method is perfect. You need to know what these methods are including their advantages and weaknesses.

Quantitative research methods involve measurement of numerical quantity, like the number of stressful incidents experienced, while **qualitative** research methods involve measurement of quality, such as describing the emotional experience of each stressful incident.

Key terms

Research methods – the means by which explanations are tested

The experimental method – a research method using random assignment of participants and the manipulation of variables to determine cause and effect

IN THE NEWS

'The greatest moment in science. Almost.'

Twenty years ago today the world of science went crazy. As crazy as someone can go with a test tube in each hand. Which, as it turned out, is very crazy. At a press conference at the University of Utah on 23 March 1989, two chemists told a stunned world that its energy worries were over. Stanley Pons and Martin Fleischmann announced that, with little more than some special water and two metal electrodes, they could harness the power of the Sun in a laboratory flask. They had created a star in a jar.

The implications were extraordinary. Limitless energy. An end to the domination of the fossil-fuel industry. World peace. Cold fusion, as the effect became known, would save the day.

Stung into action, thousands of scientists tried it for themselves.

Source: adapted from David Adam, the *Guardian*, 23 March 2009. Copyright Guardian News & Media Ltd 2009.

Inevitably, not one of the scientists who tried to replicate the experiment found the same results and enthusiasm quickly waned. But what at first seems like a non-story is actually a very good illustration of the purpose of replication – where scientists follow exactly the procedures of research studies in order to check the results. In this particular case the research was found wanting. Either the researchers had witnessed a separate phenomenon or they had made methodological errors. The implications in this particular case were minor, but replication also serves as a check against scientists putting into action applications based upon flawed research, which could have serious negative consequences.

Research in focus

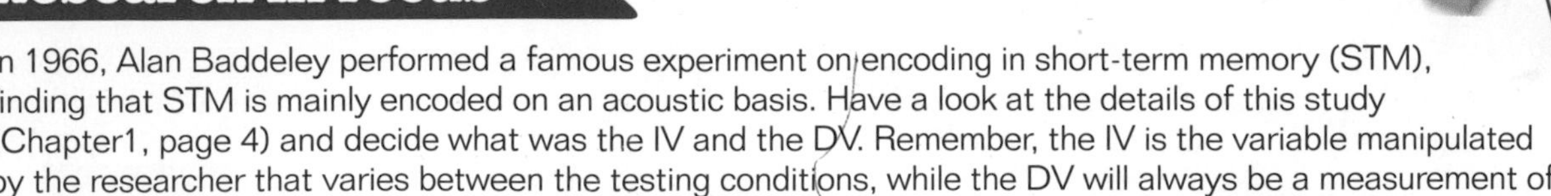

In 1966, Alan Baddeley performed a famous experiment on encoding in short-term memory (STM), finding that STM is mainly encoded on an acoustic basis. Have a look at the details of this study (Chapter1, page 4) and decide what was the IV and the DV. Remember, the IV is the variable manipulated by the researcher that varies between the testing conditions, while the DV will always be a measurement of some kind.

The experimental method

The experimental method is a research method using random assignment of participants (see the section on Sampling techniques, page 98) and the manipulation of **variables** in order to determine cause and effect; variables being anything that can change or vary.

The researcher carrying out the experiment manipulates an independent variable (IV) to see its effect on the dependent variable (DV). The IV is the variable that is altered by the researcher; the DV is the measured result of the experiment. Any change in the DV occurs as a result of the manipulation of the IV. For example, alcohol consumption (IV) could be manipulated to see its effect on reaction time (the DV).

Extraneous variables are any other variables that may affect the DV. **Controls** are used to prevent extraneous variables from becoming confounding variables that 'confuse' the results.

There are several types of experiment, as described below.

Key terms

Independent variable – the factor manipulated by researchers in an investigation

Dependent variable – the factor measured by researchers in an investigation

Laboratory experiment – experiment conducted in a controlled environment allowing the establishment of causality

Laboratory experiments

In laboratory experiments, the researcher controls as many variables as possible. In other words, there is control over 'who, what, when, where and how'. This is done in a controlled environment using standardised procedures. Participants should be randomly allocated to experimental groups.

Advantages of laboratory experiments

- **High degree of control** – experimenters can control all variables. For example, the IV and DV can be very precisely **operationalised** or defined (see page 93) and measured. This leads to greater accuracy and objectivity.
- **Replication** – other researchers can repeat the experiment to check results.
- **Cause and effect** – as long as all other variables are controlled, we can assume the effect (change in the value of the DV) was caused solely by the manipulation of the IV.
- **Accurate measurements** – the laboratory facilitates the use of sophisticated technological equipment, which permits accurate measurements to be made.
- **Isolation of variables** – in the laboratory, individual pieces of behaviour can be isolated and rigorously tested.

Figure 3.2 Laboratory experiments take place in a controlled environment

Weaknesses of laboratory experiments

- **Experimenter bias** – experimenters' expectations can affect results and participants may be influenced by these expectations (see page 100).
- **Problems operationalising the IV and DV** – in order to gain precise measurements, the measurements themselves can become too specific and not relate to wider behaviour; for example, defining 'getting fatter', as putting on a certain amount of weight in a certain time.
- **Low external (ecological) validity** – high degrees of control can make experimental situations artificial and unlike real life and therefore it can be difficult to generalise results to other settings. Laboratory settings can be intimidating and people may not act normally.
- **Demand characteristics** – sometimes participants try to guess the purpose of experiments and act accordingly. In contrast, the 'screw you' effect is where participants guess the purpose of an experiment and act in a deliberately contradictory way (see page 99).

Research in focus

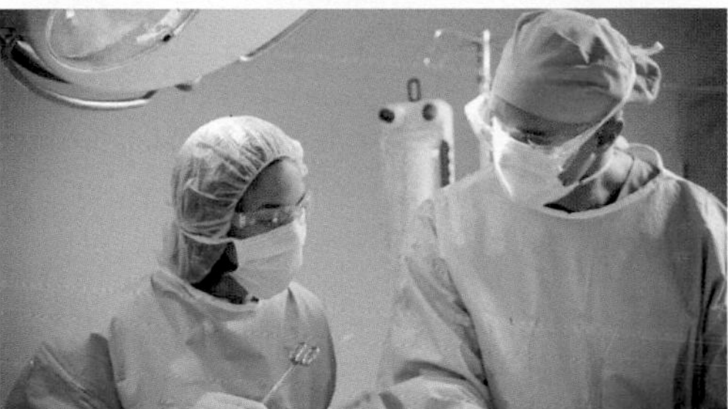

Figure 3.3 Nurses are more likely to obey doctors than follow hospital rules

Hofling (1966) performed an obedience experiment in the naturalistic setting of a hospital and found that the authority of doctors was a greater influence on nurses' behaviour than hospital rules.

Explain why initially it seems as if this study has high external validity, but why on closer inspection it seems that it actually has low external validity. (For further guidance see page 168.)

Field experiments

Field experiments are performed in the 'real world' rather than the laboratory. The IV is manipulated by the experimenter and as many other variables as possible are controlled.

Key terms

Field experiment – experiment conducted in a naturalistic environment where the researchers manipulate the independent variable

You are the researcher

Figure 3.4 Are people more willing to help males or females find change?

Construct a field experiment that looks at whether people are more willing to help females or males when asked to change a 20p piece for two 10p pieces.

Why would this be a field experiment rather than a laboratory or natural experiment?

What would be your IV and DV?

What type of sample would you be using?

Compose a suitable null hypothesis for your study. (See Chapter 3, Research methods, page 86 for more information about null hypotheses.)

Key terms

Natural experiment – experiment conducted in a naturalistic environment with a naturally occurring independent variable

Natural experiments

With natural experiments the IV occurs naturally; the experimenter does not manipulate it, but merely records the effect of the IV on the DV. This method can be used when it is unethical to manipulate the IV, such as studying the effect of stress on families. Strictly speaking, this is a **quasi-experiment**, as random allocation of participants is not possible. A good example of this would be McMahan *et al.*'s (2001) cross-cultural attachment study (see Chapter 2, page 49).

Advantages of field and natural experiments

- **High ecological validity** – due to the 'real world' environment, or naturally occurring environment, results relate to everyday behaviour and can be generalised to other settings.
- **No demand characteristics** – often participants are unaware of the experiment, and so there are no demand characteristics.

Weaknesses of field and natural experiments

- **Less control** – it is more difficult to control extraneous variables, either 'in the field' or in naturally occurring situations.
- **Replication** – it is difficult to replicate precisely field or natural experiments since the conditions are never exactly the same again.
- **Ethics** – there are ethical issues, like lack of informed consent, when participants are not aware that they are in an experiment. This applies more to field experiments, since in natural experiments the IV occurs naturally and is not manipulated by the experimenter.
- **Sample bias** – since participants are not randomly allocated to groups, there may be sample bias (see page 98).

Research in focus

McMahan *et al.* (2001) performed an experiment that looked at mother–infant attachments among the Dogon people of Mali and then compared them to western child-rearing practices. In the process, they highlighted some important differences.

Have a look at the study on page 49 and explain what features of the study make it a natural experiment.

Why are natural experiments referred to as quasi-experiments?

The study is also an example of a cross-cultural study and as such may suffer from an imposed etic. Explain what is meant by an imposed etic and why it may have occurred in this case.

You are the researcher

Design a natural experiment that would examine whether home-reared children are more aggressive than children who regularly attend day care.

Why would this be a natural experiment rather than a field or laboratory experiment?

What would your IV and DV be?

Previous research is rather contradictory, with some research suggesting that day care raises aggression levels, while other research says that day care reduces levels of aggression. Would a one-tailed (directional) or two-tailed (non-directional) hypothesis therefore be preferable? (See page 87 for more information about one-tailed and two-tailed hypotheses.)

Compose a suitable experimental hypothesis.

Strengthen your learning

1 Explain the role of independent and dependent variables in the experimental method.
2 a) What is the difference between laboratory, field and natural experiments?
 b) Give two strengths and two weaknesses of each of these types of experiment.

Assessment Check

A team of researchers showed a tray containing 30 unrelated items to an opportunity sample of young adult participants and elderly participants for 30 seconds, after which time the tray was removed from sight.
Participants were then instructed to recall as many items as possible.
The following results were found (figures represent the number of words correctly recalled):

	Young adults	Elderly
Mean score	9.1	9.2
Range	4.0	8.0

1 What were the IV and the DV in this study? [2 + 2 marks]
2 What experimental design was used in this study? [1 mark]
3 Explain one strength and one weakness of this experimental design in the context of this study. [2 + 2 marks]
4 Give one strength and one weakness of the sampling method used in this study. [2 + 2 marks]
5 What do the results tell us about age-related short-term memory capacity? [3 marks]

Examination guidance:

1 With this question it is important that you do not get the answers the wrong way round. The IV is the variable manipulated by the researchers, while the DV is a measurement of some kind.
2 This question is looking for the type of experimental design, not the type of experiment, such as laboratory, field or natural experiment.
3 One mark would be given for identifying a strength and a weakness, with a further mark available for elaboration of both. The full marks would only be awarded if the answers were in context.
4 Again, there is a mark each for a relevant strength and weakness, with a further mark for elaboration. As with Question 3, answers must be in context to gain the full marks.
5 This question requires reference to the results quoted to draw out valid conclusions.

Non-experimental (alternative) research methods

Studies using correlational analysis

Correlational analysis involves measuring the relationship between two or more co-variables to see if a trend or pattern exists. As an example, see Holmes and Rahe's (1967) study into life events and stress-related illness on page 123.

- A **positive correlation** occurs where one co-variable increases as another co-variable increases, for example ice cream sales increase as the temperature increases.
- A **negative correlation** is where one co-variable increases while another co-variable decreases, for example raincoat sales decrease as the temperature increases.
- A **correlation coefficient** is a numerical value expressing the degree to which two variables are related. Measurements range from +1 (perfect positive correlation) to –1 (perfect negative correlation). The closer the

Key terms

Correlational analysis – measuring the relationship between co-variables

correlation to a perfect correlation, the stronger the relationship between the two variables. If there is little correlation, the result will be near to zero (0.0) (see figure 3.25, page 109).

Figure 3.5 Ice cream sales increase as the temperature increases

Advantages of correlational analysis

- **Allows predictions to be made** – once a correlation is found, predictions can be made, such as predicting the number of ice creams that will be sold on hot days.
- **Allows quantification of relationships** – correlations show strength of relationship between co-variables. A correlation of +0.9 means a high positive correlation, while a correlation of –0.1 indicates a weak negative correlation.
- **No manipulation** – correlations don't require manipulation of behaviour and are used when experiments may be unethical.

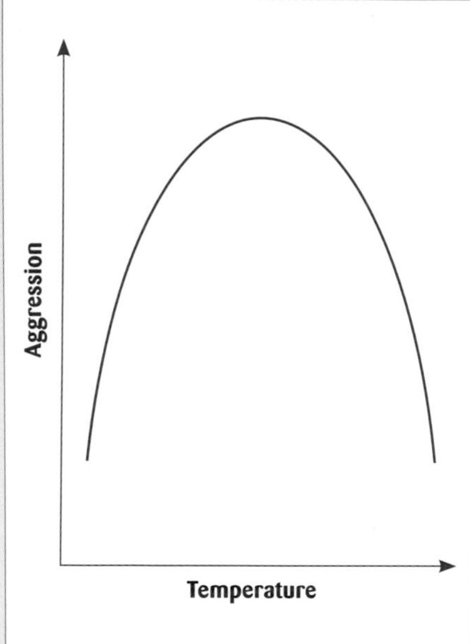

Figure 3.6 The curvilinear relationship between temperature and aggression

Weaknesses of correlational analysis

- **Quantification problem** – seemingly low correlations, for example +0.28, can be significant (meaningful) if the number of scores recorded is high. Conversely, with a small number of recorded scores, correlations that seem high, such as +0.76, are not always significant.
- **Cause and effect** – correlations aren't conducted under controlled conditions and therefore do not show causality, i.e. that one variable caused the other. This makes interpretation of results difficult.
- **Extraneous relationships** – other variables may influence the measured variables. For example, holidays occur in the summertime and people eat ice creams on holiday; therefore, the variable 'holiday' is related to both temperature and ice cream sales.
- **Only works for linear relationships** – correlations only measure **linear** (straight-line) relationships. The relationship between temperature and aggression is a **curvilinear** relationship. This appears to be a zero correlation, and yet there is an obvious relationship between the two variables – as temperature increases, aggression levels do too up to an optimum point. After this point, any further increase in temperature leads to a decline in aggression levels.

Research in focus

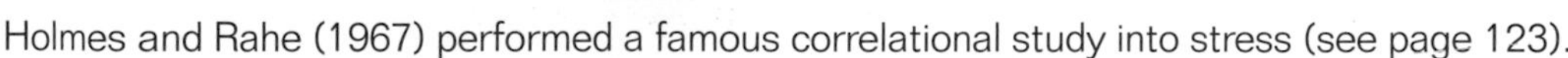

Holmes and Rahe (1967) performed a famous correlational study into stress (see page 123).

What were the two co-variables in this study?

Was a negative or positive correlation found? Explain what this means in terms of the study.

Correlations do not show causality. Explain what is meant by causality and outline what other factors may have contributed to the results.

What kind of graph would be used to plot the data from this study?

Observational studies

Most psychological studies involve the observation of behaviour, whether it is observing children in a school playground or observing reaction speeds in a laboratory. Observation can occur as part of a laboratory study, as in Milgram's (1963) study of obedience (see page 163), however most observations involve the measurement of naturally occurring behaviour in the real world, so-called naturalistic observations. Observations should only occur in circumstances where people expect to be observed.

> **Key terms**
>
> **Naturalistic observations** – surveillance and recording of naturally occurring events

There are two main types of observation:

1 **Participant observation** involves observers becoming actively involved in the behaviour of the people being studied. The researchers experience a more 'hands-on' perspective of those being observed. Participant observation can either be **overt**, where people are told they are being observed (for example Zimbardo *et al.*'s 1973 prison simulation study, where students volunteered to be observed playing the roles of guards and prisoners with the researcher having the position of prison commandant), or **covert**, where participants remain unaware of being observed (such as Festinger's 1957 study where he infiltrated a cult who were prophesising the end of the world).

2 **Non-participant observation** involves researchers observing behaviour from a distance; they do not become actively involved in the behaviour being studied, for example Ainsworth's 1971 Strange Situation study (page 44).

The distinction between participant and non-participant observations is not always clear, since it may be difficult for observers to participate fully in some behaviours, like gang warfare.

Advantages of observational techniques

- **High external validity** – since observed behaviour takes place in the natural environment, participants behave naturally and results can be generalised to other settings.
- **Practical method** – can be used in situations where deliberate manipulation of variables would be unethical or impractical, for example studying football hooliganism. It is useful where cooperation from those being observed is unlikely and where the full social context for behaviour is needed. It is particularly useful when studying animals or children.
- **Few demand characteristics** – participants are usually unaware of being observed and so there are few demand characteristics (see page 99).

Weaknesses of observational techniques

- **Cause and effect** – causality cannot be inferred, since the variables are only observed, not manipulated. There is also little control of extraneous variables.
- **Observer bias** – if observers know the purpose of the study, they may see what they want to see. Observers need to produce **reliable** (consistent) results. When there is more than one observer, the observations of one observer can be correlated (checked) against those of another observer to see if they are observing in the same, consistent way and thus have **inter-rater reliability** (also known as **inter-observer reliability**). Sometimes one observer changes their method of observation over time. For example, the behavioural categories they were using at the beginning of the study can alter by the end

of the study. A comparison from the start of the observation to the end of the observation would check this to ensure they have **intra-rater reliability**.

- **Replication** – although it is possible to check for both inter- and intra-rater reliability, it is often difficult to accurately check reliability and validity (see page 94) of observations, since the lack of control means conditions can never be repeated exactly.
- **Ethics** – if participants are unaware of being observed, issues of invasion of privacy and **informed consent** arise. If participants are informed of the study, then there is a possibility of demand characteristics.
- **Practical problems** – sometimes it is difficult to remain unobserved and there can be practical problems when making recordings, such as video/audio, of some behaviours. Furthermore, it is often difficult to categorise observed behaviours accurately (see Design of naturalistic observations, page 90).

Research in focus

A 2004 study by the National Institute of Child Health and Human Development (NICHD) found that children who spent the longest number of hours in day care had the lowest levels of aggression.

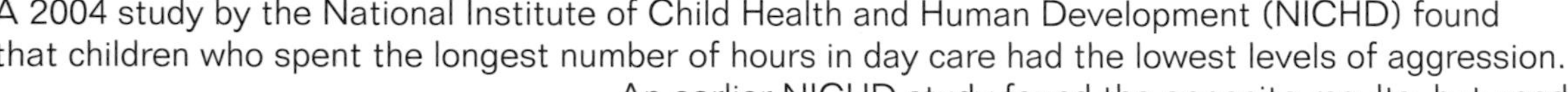

Figure 3.7 Research into day care can find conflicting results

An earlier NICHD study found the opposite results, but used observations made by mothers rather than those made by teachers and carers.

Can you think of an explanation why these similar studies into the effects of hours of day care on aggression levels, which both used observational techniques, should have found such different results?

The establishment of inter-rater reliability could have created clearer results.

Explain what inter-rater reliability is and how it would be established.

You are the researcher

Construct an observational study that examines whether females choose more healthy options than males from the school/college cafeteria.

Figure 3.8 Is there a gender difference in food choice?

You will need to decide what categories of food you are going to have, such as very healthy, healthy, unhealthy and very unhealthy.

You will need to examine the menu or the food on offer and decide which category each food item goes into. When these decisions have been made, you will need to construct a coding sheet into which you can incorporate your categories and record your data.

You will need to make a decision about what to do with people who buy several items that go into different categories.

Why will it be important to establish inter-observer reliability? How will you establish it?

Self-report techniques, including questionnaires and interviews

Questionnaires

Self-report techniques are research methods in which participants give information about themselves without researcher interference. One type of self-report technique is the questionnaire. Questionnaires are a written method of data collection where respondents record their own answers to a pre-set list of questions. They are usually concerned with people's behaviour, opinions and attitudes. Two main types of question are used.

1 **Closed (fixed) questions** – responses are fixed by the researcher. They usually involve tick boxes, for example, do you believe in UFOs, 'yes' or 'no', or a range of fixed responses such as, do you attend your local football team's home games 'always', 'usually', 'sometimes', 'never'. Such answers are easy to quantify, but restrict participants' answers.

2 **Open questions** – these allow participants to answer in their own words. They are more difficult to analyse, but allow freedom of expression and greater depth of answers. For example, what kinds of music do you like and why?

> **Key terms**
>
> **Self-report techniques** – participants giving information about themselves without researcher interference
>
> **Questionnaires** – self-report method where participants record their own answers to a pre-set list of questions

Advantages of questionnaires

- **Quick** – relative to other methods, large amounts of information can be gathered in a relatively short period.
- **Large samples** – questionnaires can be completed without researchers present. Postal questionnaires can gain very large samples for the cost of a stamp.
- **Quantitative and qualitative analysis** – closed questions provide quantitative data that is easy to analyse statistically. Answers can be pre-coded for computer input and instant analysis. Open-ended questions provide richer, fuller detail and the respondent does not feel as constrained in their answers.
- **Replication** – since questionnaires use standardised questions, it is fairly easy to replicate studies. This is particularly true of questionnaires using closed questions.

Weaknesses of questionnaires

- **Misunderstanding** – designing questionnaires is difficult. Participants may misunderstand or misinterpret questions. For example, what do you mean when you say you 'usually' do your homework? There can be problems with using technical terms, emotive language and leading questions.
- **Biased samples** – questionnaires are suitable for people who can read and are willing and able to spend time completing them. Certain types of people may be more willing to fill in questionnaires and not be representative of the whole population.
- **Low response rates** – questionnaires are an uneconomical research method as they can get very low return rates.

Figure 3.9 Social desirability: in the 1980s, voters were reluctant to admit that they supported the Conservative Party, but the Tories kept on winning

- **Superficial issues** – questionnaires, particularly those using closed questions, are not suitable for sensitive issues requiring detailed understanding.
- **Social desirability/idealised answers** – participants may lie to present themselves in a positive light or to answer questions on particularly sensitive issues, for example questions to do with sexual behaviour. Participants may also answer as they would like to be, rather than how they actually are.

Research in focus

Kiecolt-Glaser (1984) performed a study into immunosuppression in medical students (see page 120) in which, among other measures, she used a questionnaire to assess psychiatric symptoms, loneliness and life events. Questions on such sensitive areas could easily fall prey to socially desirable and idealised answers. Explain what these features are and how they could have created a source of bias.

You are the researcher

Compose three open and three closed questions for a questionnaire examining peoples' smoking habits and attitudes to smoking.

What type of data would:

a) the open questions generate?

b) the closed questions generate?

Explain how:

i) social desirability bias could affect the answers given.

ii) idealised answers could affect the answers given.

Interviews

Key terms

Interviews – self-report method where participants answer questions in face-to-face situations

Interviews involve researchers asking questions in face-to-face situations. There are three broad types.

1 **Structured** (formal) – a questionnaire is read to participants and the interviewer writes down responses. These interviews are identical for all participants and involve simple, quantitative questions. Interviewers do not need much training.

2 **Unstructured** (informal) – these are less controlled, involving an informal discussion on a particular topic. While topics are predetermined, the direction of the interview is not, allowing interviewers to explore areas of greatest interest. Friendly rapport between the interviewer and respondent is important in order to gain the required level of detail and understanding. Interviewers need considerable training and expertise to conduct such interviews.

3 **Semi-structured** – combines a mixture of structured and unstructured techniques, producing quantitative and qualitative data.

Advantages of interviews

- **Complex issues** – complicated or sensitive issues are best dealt with in face-to-face interviews. This is particularly true of unstructured interviews, where a natural flow of conversation can make respondents feel relaxed and enhances the quality of the answers.

- **Ease misunderstandings** – ambiguities or misunderstandings can be clarified within the interview. Interviewers can follow up interesting answers and explore them more fully. Questions can be adapted to the individual needs of respondents, making the interview more productive for all concerned.
- **Data analysis** – the variety and flexibility of interviews allows for the analysis of both quantitative and qualitative data. Structured interviews in particular produce data that can be analysed in quantitative form fairly easily.
- **Replication** – the more standardised or structured the interview, the easier it is to replicate. Unstructured interviews are less easy to replicate but other researchers can review data produced.

Weaknesses of interviews

- **Interviewer effects** – interviewers may inadvertently bias respondents' answers. This can even occur as a result of the interviewer's appearance. For example, would men be less willing to admit to being sexist to a woman? Interviews are subject to demand characteristics and social desirability bias.
- **Interview training** – with structured interviews there is less training required. However, a great deal of skill is required to carry out unstructured interviews, particularly those concerned with sensitive issues. It is not always easy to obtain highly trained interviewers.
- **Ethical issues** – these can arise when participants do not know the true purpose of the interview. There is also a danger that participants may reveal more than they wish to.
- **Respondent answers** – some respondents may be unable to put into words their feelings about a particular topic. This applies mainly to structured interviews.

Research in focus

Figure 3.10 How important is the gender of an interviewer?

In 1994, Linda Williams interviewed 129 women who had been sexually abused in childhood, finding that 38 per cent could not recall the abuse (see page 198).

In what way might the results have been different if a man had interviewed the women?

For what reasons would an unstructured interview technique be the best method of conducting such interviews?

Case studies

Case studies are in-depth, detailed investigations of one individual or a small group. They usually include biographical details, behavioural information and experiences of interest. Case studies allow researchers to examine particular individuals in great depth. Explanations of behaviour are outlined in descriptive ways and subjective reports are often used too, describing what an individual

Key terms

Case studies – in-depth, detailed investigations of one individual or a small group

feels or believes about particular issues. For example Koluchova's (1972) study of the 'Czech twins' (see page 59).

Bromley (1986) argues that case studies are 'the bedrock of scientific investigation' and that psychologists' preoccupation with experimental procedures has led to a neglect of this area.

Advantages of case studies

- **Rich detail** – case studies provide greater depth and understanding about individuals and acknowledge human diversity. Information relates to a real person, not an average gathered from many.
- **The only possible method to use** – case studies allow psychologists to study behaviours or experiences so unique they could not have been studied any other way. The method also allows 'difficult' areas to be explored, where other methods would be unethical, such as the effects of sexual abuse.
- **Useful for theory contradiction** – just one case study can contradict a theory. Curtiss (1977) reported on the case study of Genie (see page 59), which helped to question evidence regarding critical stages of language development.

Weaknesses of case studies

- **Unreliable** – case studies are criticised for being unreliable (lacking consistency), as no two case studies are alike and therefore results cannot be generalised to other people. But do we always have to find universal truths of behaviour?
- **Researcher bias** – sometimes researchers conducting case studies may be biased in their interpretations or method of reporting, making it difficult to determine factual information.
- **Reliance on memory** – case studies are often dependent upon participants having full and accurate memories. This can be a problem in certain cases, for example where participants suffer from **false memory syndrome** (see page 20).

Research in focus

Figure 3.11 How can psychologists study war orphans?

In 1951, Freud and Dann conducted a harrowing case study on a group of war orphans (see page 59).

Why was the case study method the only viable way of studying these children?

What weaknesses of the case study method may apply to this particular study?

Strengthen your learning

1 a) What are correlations?
b) What is the difference between a positive and a negative correlation?
c) Give two strengths and two weaknesses of correlations.

2 a) What do naturalistic observations involve?
b) What is the difference between participant and non-participant observations?
c) Give two strengths and two weaknesses of observations.

3 a) What are questionnaires?
b) What is the difference between open and closed questions?
c) Give two strengths and two weaknesses of questionnaires.

4 a) What are interviews?
b) What is the difference between structured, unstructured and semi-structured interviews?
c) Give two strengths and two weaknesses of interviews.

5 a) What are case studies?
b) Give two strengths and two weaknesses of case studies.

Supplementary learning

Other research methods

Aside from research methods covered already, several other types often feature within the topics covered by the AS specification. These include:

Longitudinal studies

As the name suggests, **longitudinal studies** occur over an extended period of time, usually at set intervals. Their chief strength is that they show **trends** (changes over time) and are in that sense superior to the more common **cross-sectional studies** which occur at a set moment in time and thus may display non-typical behaviour and therefore not be representative. Aside from the obvious weakness of taking a long time to perform with no guarantee of worthwhile results, longitudinal studies suffer from **atypical sample attrition** where, over time, certain types of participant drop out making the remaining sample non-representative.

An example would be Tizard and Hodges' (1978) study of institutionalised children (see page 58), where a group of children raised in various scenarios were studied from infancy to adolescence.

Cross-cultural studies

These are a type of natural experiment, where the naturally occurring IV is different cultural practices. **Cross-cultural studies** can often give an insight into the origin of behaviours. If behaviours are cross-cultural, in other words are found in all cultures, they they are assumed to be genetic in origin, such as speaking a language. If behaviours are not cross-cultural, and therefore not found in all cultures, then they are assumed to be learned, such as the ability to speak English. A common weakness is that of an **imposed etic**, where research procedures and tests applicable to one culture are not valid when applied to another culture. An example would be Yeo's (2003) study of the wrongful assessment of Aboriginal children by white Australian cultural values, leading to many children being placed in care (see page 52).

Meta-analysis

A **meta-analysis** combines the results of several studies into a common research area to give a more typical overview. This has the considerable advantage of avoiding the formation of incorrect conclusions by focusing on the results of an unrepresentative study. A weakness is that sources of bias are not controlled, meaning that badly designed and executed studies may be included, with a negative impact upon results. An example would be Geddes *et al.*'s (2008) study into the effectiveness of anti-psychotic drugs (see page 206).

Assessment Check

A team of researchers recorded the number of hours of day care that individual children received and the degree of sociability they displayed to their peers. The researchers found that as the number of hours in day care increased, the degree of sociability also increased.

1 What kind of correlation does this research show? [1 mark]
2 Outline one strength and one weakness of using correlational research to investigate the effects of day care on sociability. [2 + 2 marks]
3 What type of graph would be used to display the correlational data? [1 mark]
4 The scale used to record the degree of sociability was one that was proven to be reliable. What does this mean in the context of this study? [2 marks]

Examination guidance:

1 In this question, the type of correlation must be identified not described to gain credit.
2 One mark each is given for a valid strength and weakness, with a further mark for elaboration that applies to the amount of day care and sociability.
3 The type of graph must be correctly identified, not described, to gain credit.
4 One mark would be earned by explaining reliability, with a further mark for elaboration that is in context.

Key terms

Aim – a precise statement of why a study is taking place

Hypotheses – precise testable research predictions

Investigation design

Aims

An aim is a precise statement of why a study is taking place, for example to investigate the effect of alcohol on reaction times. It should include what is being studied and what the study is trying to achieve.

Hypotheses

A hypothesis is more precise than an aim and predicts what is expected to happen. As an example, your hypothesis might state that 'alcohol consumption will affect reaction times'. Hypotheses are testable statements. There are two types:

1 The **experimental (alternative) hypothesis** – a prediction that differences in the DV, the variable being measured, will be beyond the boundaries of chance, as a result of manipulation of the IV, the variable being manipulated.

Differences in the DV resulting from manipulation of the IV are known as **significant differences**. For example, you might state that 'alcohol consumption will significantly affect reaction times'.

The term 'experimental hypothesis' is only used with the experimental method. Other research methods use the term 'alternative hypothesis'.

2 The **null hypothesis** – this is 'the hypothesis of no differences'. It predicts that the IV will not affect the DV. Any differences in results will be due to chance factors, not the manipulation of the IV and will therefore be not significant. This wording can be incorporated into a null hypothesis. For example 'there will be no significant difference in reaction times as a result of alcohol consumption'.

One of the two hypotheses will be supported by the findings and thus be accepted, with the other one being rejected.

There are two types of experimental/alternative hypotheses:

- **Directional ('one-tailed') hypothesis** – this predicts the direction of the results. For example, you might predict that there will be a significant reduction in the speed of reaction times as a result of alcohol consumption. It is called directional because it predicts the particular direction in which the results can go.
- **Non-directional ('two-tailed')** – this predicts that there will be a difference, but not the direction of the results. For example, 'there will be a significant difference in the speed of reaction times as a result of alcohol consumption'. Reaction times could either get quicker or slower, and so these are referred to as 'non-directional' hypotheses.

Directional hypotheses are used when previous research evidence suggests that results will go in one particular direction, or when replicating a previous study that has also used a directional hypothesis.

Research in focus

Have a look at Geddes *et al.*'s (2008) study of the effectiveness of anti-psychotic drugs on page 206.

For this study write a suitable:

a) one-tailed (directional) experimental hypothesis

b) two-tailed (non-directional) hypothesis

c) null hypothesis.

Experimental design

There are three main types of experimental design: the repeated measures design, the independent groups design and the matched pairs design.

Repeated measures design

In the repeated measures design (RMD), each participant is tested in both (or indeed more) conditions of the experiment.

Advantages of the repeated measures design

- **Group differences** – as the same people are measured in both conditions, there are no participant variables (differences between individuals) between the conditions.
- **More data/fewer participants** – as each participant produces two scores, twice as much data is produced compared with an independent measures design (IMD). Therefore half as many participants are needed to get the same amount of data. As it is not always that easy to get participants for psychology experiments, this can be a blessing.

Weaknesses of the repeated measures design

- **Order effects** – with an RMD participants are doing both conditions and the order in which they do these conditions can affect the results. Participants may perform **worse** in the second condition due to fatigue or boredom (**negative order effect**) or perform **better** due to practice or learning

Key terms

Repeated measures design – experimental design where each participant performs all conditions of an experiment

(**positive order effect**). **Counterbalancing** can control this, where half the participants do Condition A followed by Condition B, and the other half do Condition B and then Condition A. This counterbalancing procedure is known as 'ABBA', for obvious reasons.

- **Lost participants** – if a participant drops out of the study, data are 'lost' from both conditions.
- **Guessing aim of study** – by participating in both conditions, it is more likely that participants may guess the purpose of the study. This makes demand characteristics more common.
- **Takes more time** – a gap may be needed between conditions to counter the effects of fatigue or boredom. In addition, each condition might require different materials. In a memory test, for example, you could not use the same list of words for both conditions. These issues involve more time and effort.

Research in focus

Explain why Jenness's (1932) study into informational social influence (see page 154) is an example of a repeated measures design.

Why may order effects have occurred in this study?

In what ways was the design superior to having used an independent groups design?

Figure 3.12 Jenness's jelly bean experiment used a repeated measures design

You are the researcher

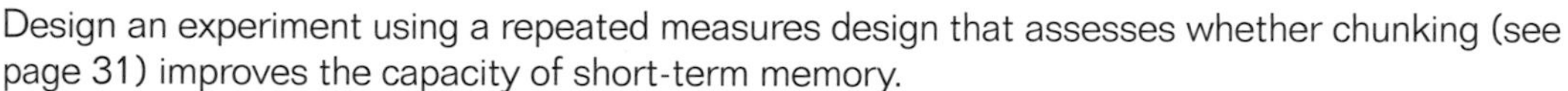

Design an experiment using a repeated measures design that assesses whether chunking (see page 31) improves the capacity of short-term memory.

How might order effects have a negative impact on your results?

Part of your design must incorporate a means of controlling for such order effects.

Key terms

Independent groups design – experimental design in which each participant performs one condition of an experiment

Independent groups design

In the independent groups design (IGD), different participants are used in each of the conditions, therefore each group of participants is independent of the other. Participants are usually randomly allocated to each condition to balance out differences (see Sampling page 98).

Advantages of the independent groups design

- **Order effects** – as different participants do both conditions there are no order effects.
- **Demand characteristics** – participants do one condition each, therefore there is less chance that they can guess the purpose of the study.
- **Time saved** – both sets of participants can be tested simultaneously, saving time and effort.

Weaknesses of the independent groups design

- **More participants** – with participants each doing only one condition, twice as many participants as needed as for an RMD.
- **Group differences** – differences in results between the two conditions may be due to participant variables (individual differences) rather than manipulations of the IV. This is minimised by random allocation of participants to each condition.

Research in focus

Have a look at Coxon and Valentine's (1997) study into the effects of age on eyewitness testimony (page 25).

Why was the independent groups design the only experimental design that could be used?

How might participant variables have had a negative effect upon the findings?

Why were more participants needed in this study than if a repeated measures design been used?

You are the researcher

Design an experiment using an independent groups design that examines whether females have a better memory for faces than males.

Why would an independent groups design be the only possible design to use?

Due to a lack of previous research evidence in this area, you will need to compose a suitable two-tailed (non-directional) hypothesis.

Matched pairs design

The matched pairs design (MPD) is a special kind of RMD. Different, but similar, participants are used in each of the conditions. Participants are matched on characteristics important for a particular study, such as age. Identical (monozygotic) twins are often used as they form perfect matched pairs, sharing identical genetic characteristics.

Key terms

Matched pairs design – experimental design where participants are in similar pairs, with one of each pair performing each condition

Advantages of the matched pairs design

- **Order effects** – as different participants do both conditions there are no order effects.
- **Demand characteristics** – participants do one condition each, therefore there is less chance of them guessing the purpose of the study.
- **Time saved** – both sets of participants can be tested at the same time, saving time and effort.
- **Group differences** – participant variables are more closely matched between conditions than in an IGD.

Weaknesses of the matched pairs design

- **More participants** – with participants each doing only one condition, twice as many participants are needed as for an RMD.
- **Matching is difficult** – it is impossible to match all variables between participants. The one variable missed might be vitally important. Also,

even two closely-matched individuals will have different levels of motivation or fatigue at any given moment in time.

- **Time consuming** – it is a lengthy process to match participants. This can become almost a research study in itself.

You are the researcher

Design an experiment using a matched pairs design that examines whether people's running ability is improved after a 6-week period of weight training or a 6-week period of circuit training. You will need to decide which important variable to match your participants on.

Previous research indicates that circuit training would be more beneficial, therefore compose a suitable one-tailed (directional) hypothesis.

Psychology in action

Practical applications

Figure 3.13 A beneficial aspect of the working memory model is its application to children with learning difficulties

Psychological research is performed to test out hypotheses in a rigorous scientific manner, in order that knowledge can be gained and plausible explanations for behaviour can be created. However, just as important are the practical uses to which such knowledge can be put that will benefit humanity. As long as such practical applications are based on solid, unbiased, properly analysed and replicated research, then there is every chance that psychology can indeed be of positive use to society and help create a better world.

Baddeley and Hitch's (1974) working memory model (see page 12), which has had a multitude of research performed upon it, has suggested many beneficial applications, especially for children with learning difficulties relating to impairments of working memory. For instance, Alloway (2006) has recommended several methods to assist such children (see page 17), while Klingberg *et al.* (2002) devised a computerised method to help sufferers of Attention Deficit Hyperactivity Disorder (ADHD) who tend also to have a poor working memory (see page 17).

Strengthen your learning

1. What is the purpose of an aim in a psychological investigation?
2. a) What is meant by a hypothesis?
   b) What is the difference between a directional (one-tailed) and a non-directional (two-tailed) hypothesis?
3. Explain what is meant by each of the following: independent groups design, repeated measures design and matched pairs design. Give two strengths and two weaknesses of each.

Design of naturalistic observations

One weakness of naturalistic observations involves the development and use of appropriate behavioural categories. There are several ways in which data can be gathered in naturalistic observations, including visual recordings like videos and photographs, audio recordings or 'on-the-spot' note-taking using agreed rating scales or coding categories. The use of video or audio recordings tends to result in later analysis back in the 'lab' using such coding categories.

Behavioural categories

Observers agree on a grid or coding sheet on which to record the behaviour being studied. The behavioural categories chosen depend upon the subject matter under study. For example, in a study about the effect of age and sex on the speed of car driving, they might want to develop behavioural categories like those given in Table 3.1.

Key terms

Behavioural categories – dividing target behaviours into subsets of behaviours through use of coding systems

Table 3.1

Driver	Sex (M/F)	Age (estimate)	Number of passengers	Observed behaviour	Type of car	Speed (estimate in km per hour)	Safe driving rating 1 = very unsafe 5 = very safe
A	M	55	0	M-P	Saloon	40	2
B	F	21	2	T	Hatch	30	5
C							
D etc.							

Observed behaviour code

D = Distracted

T = Talking

M-P = Using mobile phone

… and so on

Rather than writing detailed descriptions of the behaviour observed, it is easier to code or rate behaviour according to previously agreed scales. Coding might involve numbers (such as age of driver) or letters to describe participant characteristics (such as M = male) or observed behaviours (such as T = talking, M-P = using mobile phone). Observed behaviour can also be rated on structured scales, such as 1–5 on a scale of 'safe driving'.

In practice, it is difficult to achieve standardisation between different observers, and considerable training is required before the actual observational sessions occur. **Inter-observer reliability**, where observers are coding behaviour in the same way (in other words are agreed as to which behavioural categories each piece of behaviour fits into), can be checked before the actual observation begins. One way to assess inter-observer reliability is to conduct a correlation of all the observers' scores. If there is a high degree of agreement between observers, then it is clear that they are observing and categorising behaviours identically. There is no certainty that behaviour is being observed correctly (validity), but it can be shown that behaviour is being observed consistently (reliability).

Design of questionnaires

As questionnaires can suffer from low response rates, it is essential that they are well designed. There are a number of important factors in questionnaire design.

- **Aims** – having an exact aim helps the questionnaire design. Determining how information gained will be used ensures that only those questions that address the aims are asked.
- **Length** – the longer the questionnaire, the more likely that people will not complete it. Questionnaires should be concise with unnecessary questions deleted.
- **Advice** – when designing questionnaires, seek advice from experts. Use examples of questionnaires that have proved successful as a blueprint.
- **Statistical analysis** – even at the design stage, statistical analysis of questionnaire responses should be considered. If a question is not going to be analysed, omit it.
- **Presentation** – questionnaires should look professional, should include clear, concise instructions and, if sent through the post, should be in an envelope that does not signify 'junk mail'. Leave spaces in the design of each page for respondents to include comments to questions as they see fit.
- **Question order** – start with simple, factual, biographical questions before moving on to more probing questions. However, initial questions also need to be interesting to motivate the respondents to complete the rest of the questionnaire. It is best to put essential questions in the first half of the questionnaire, since respondents often pay more attention to these questions or send them back half completed.
- **Question formation** – questions should be concise, unambiguous and easily understood. Ambiguity is avoided by not using complicated terms. Questions should probe only one dimension. For example, 'Do you like the content and design of this book?' is a poorly phrased question. If a respondent answers 'yes', we cannot be sure if they like the content, the design or both.
- **Incentives** – offering incentives for questionnaire completion helps provide additional motivation. Make it convenient for respondents to return questionnaires; pre-paid envelopes often achieve this.
- **Pilot study** – questionnaires should be tested on people who can provide detailed and honest feedback on all aspects of the design.
- **Measurement scales** – some questionnaires use measurement scales involving statements on which respondents rate levels of agreement or disagreement. For example:

  Rate your level of agreement with the following statement:

  'The Prime Minister is doing a good job.'

1	2	3	4	5
Strongly agree	Agree	Undecided	Disagree	Strongly disagree

There are usually a number of statements on a particular topic and the answers to these statements are combined to determine a single score of attitude strength. There are some problems with this approach. Firstly, it is not easy for respondents to judge answers and many respondents choose the middle score. When this happens it is impossible to know whether they have no opinion or cannot decide between their attitudes in both directions. The best known of these attitude scales is the **Likert scale**.

Design of interviews

The first decision when designing interviews is whether to choose a structured interview, where every participant answers the same questions, or an unstructured interview, where different questions are asked, or indeed a combination of the two (see page 82). There is also a decision regarding open and closed questions.

Decisions as to the most appropriate type of interviewer depend on what type of person is being interviewed, but there are some general interpersonal variables that can be considered, including the following:

- **Gender and age** – studies have demonstrated that the sex and age of interviewers affect respondents' answers when topics are of a sensitive sexual nature.
- **Ethnicity** – due to cultural upbringing, interviewers may have difficulty interviewing people from a different ethnic group to themselves. Word *et al.* (1974) found that white participants spent 25 per cent less time interviewing black job applicants than white applicants.
- **Personal characteristics and adopted role** – some people are just easier to get on with than others. Interviewers can adopt different roles within the interview setting and use of formal language, accent and appearance can also affect how someone comes across to the interviewee.

Interviewer training is an essential factor in successful interviewing. Interviewers need to listen appropriately and learn when to speak and when not to speak. Non-verbal communication is important in helping to relax the interviewee so that they will give natural answers. Difficult and probing questions about emotions are best left to the end of the interview, whereas initial questions are better for ascertaining factual information.

Operationalisation of variables

The term operationalisation means being able to define variables simply and easily in order to manipulate them (IV) and measure them (DV). Sometimes, this can be done easily. For example, if investigating the effect of alcohol consumption on reaction times, the IV could be 'operationalised' as the number of alcohol units consumed and the DV could be the speed of response to a flashing light. However, on other occasions it is more difficult. For example, how do you operationalise anger or stress levels? There is not always a 'best way' of operationalising variables. Researchers have to make judgements about whether they are actually measuring the variables they want to measure and present arguments to support this. A problem with the operationalisation of variables is that they often only measure *one* aspect of the variable.

> **Key terms**
>
> **Operationalisation** – the process of defining variables into measurable factors
>
> **Pilot studies** – small-scale practice investigations

IVs and DVs need to be operationalised accurately and objectively to maintain the integrity of research studies. Without accurate operationalisation, results are not reliable or valid, and cannot be replicated and checked.

Pilot studies

Pilot studies are small-scale 'practice' investigations where researchers check all aspects of their research, enabling any changes to the design, method or analysis to be made. Participants may also be able to suggest appropriate changes. For example, if participants admit that they guessed the purpose of the study and acted accordingly (demand characteristics), changes can be made to avoid this. Pilot studies improve the quality of research, help avoid unnecessary work and save time and effort.

The control of extraneous variables

In experiments, the IV is manipulated and the DV is measured and it is assumed that the IV causes any change or effect in the DV. Any other variables causing a change in the level of a DV are known as **extraneous variables**.

Extraneous variables must be controlled carefully and systematically so that they do not vary across any of the experimental conditions or, indeed, between participants. When designing an experiment, researchers should consider three main areas where extraneous variables may arise:

1 **Participant variables** – factors such as participants' age and intelligence, for example, should be controlled across the different experimental conditions.

2 **Situational variables** – the experimental setting and surrounding environment must be controlled. This may include the temperature and noise levels.

3 **Experimenter variables** – any change in personality, appearance and conduct of the researcher can affect the results. For example, female researchers may gain different results from male ones.

If extraneous variables are not controlled carefully, they can **confound** (confuse) results. When extraneous variables do vary from one condition to another, changes in the level of the DV may result not from the manipulation of the IV but from the presence of the extraneous variables. When this happens, they are called **confounding variables**. The presence of confounding variables can minimise the value of results.

For example, if researchers wished to investigate the effect of background music (Condition 1) or silence (Condition 2) on homework performance using two classes, they would have to control a number of extraneous variables, including age, homework difficulty, etc. If these were all successfully controlled, then the results would be trustworthy. However, if the researchers discovered that the participants in Condition 1 were considerably brighter than those in Condition 2, then intelligence would be a confounding variable. The researchers could not then be sure whether differences in homework performance were due to the presence of the music or due to intelligence levels. Results would be confounded and worthless.

Key terms

Reliability – the extent to which a test or measure of measurement produces consistent results

Validity – the extent to which results accurately measure what they are supposed to measure

Reliability and validity

Reliability and validity are essential in any type of psychological research. If results are reliable, they are consistent. If a study is repeated using the same method, design and measurements, the same results should be obtained and the results are said to be reliable.

If results are unreliable, they cannot be trusted. However, results can be reliable, but not be accurate. For example, if you add up 1+1 several times and each time calculate the answer as 3, then your result is reliable (consistent), but not valid (accurate). Sometimes measuring instruments may be reliably (consistently) producing inaccurate results.

To be valid, results must measure accurately what they are supposed to measure.

Research in focus

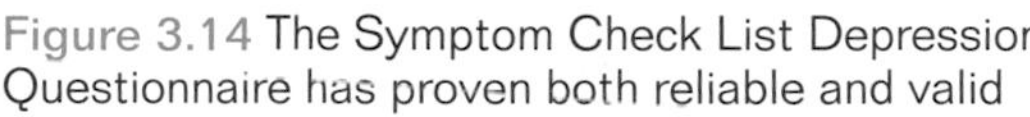

Figure 3.14 The Symptom Check List Depression Questionnaire has proven both reliable and valid

Garnefski *et al.* (2004) performed research on coping strategies by using the Cognitive Emotion Regulation Questionnaire (see page 137), which assesses what individuals think after experiencing threatening or stressful life events. They also used the Symptom Check List Questionnaire, which measures depression. Both of these questionnaires have proven to be reliable and valid.

Explain what it means in terms of Garnefski's research that these questionnaires are reliable and valid.

Why would it be possible for the questionnaires to be reliable, but not valid?

It is possible to test both reliability and validity, as described below.

- **Internal reliability** – whether a test is consistent within itself. For example, a set of scales should measure the same weight between 50 and 100 grammes as between 150 and 200 grammes.
- **External reliability** – whether a test measures consistently over time. An IQ test should produce the same measure for the same participant at different time intervals if intelligence has remained the same. This is called the **test–retest method.**
- **Internal validity** – whether the results are due to the manipulation of the IV. Results are said to be internally valid if they have not been affected by confounding variables. Various characteristics are required in order for an experiment to be internally valid. These are:
  - no investigator effects (see page 100)
  - no demand characteristics (see page 99)
  - use of standardised instructions
  - use of random samples (see page 98).
- **External (ecological) validity** – whether results are valid beyond the experimental setting and can be generalised to the wider population or to different settings or different time eras. For example, Milgram's obedience study (see page 163) has low external validity, as the sample was male and so cannot be generalised to females; it involved the artificial setting of Yale University laboratory and took place in the 1960s. It is often difficult to test whether a study has external validity, as it may only become clear when

research findings are found to either apply or not apply to different situations. Field and natural experiments, and naturalistic observations, are regarded as being high in external validity, because results can be generalised to other real-life settings.

Research in focus

Ainsworth's (1978) study of attachment (see page 44) is regarded as a paradigm study, or 'gold standard', for assessing attachment types.

However, Main and Weston (1981) claimed that the study lacked validity. Why would this be? (See Evaluation of the Strange Situation, page 46.)

Similarly why did Main *et al.* (1985) believe the Strange Situation to be reliable?

See if you can work out from McMahan *et al.*'s (2001) study why the Strange Situation may not be a valid measure of attachment in all cultures.

Key terms

Ethical issues – the rules governing the conduct of researchers in investigations

Ethical issues

High-quality research involves good ethical practice and ethical issues must be fully considered before research is conducted. In addition to formal ethical guidelines, most research institutions, such as universities, have ethical committees which meet to consider research projects before they commence. The British Psychological Society (BPS) publishes a Code of Ethics which includes the following.

- **Informed consent** – whenever possible, investigators should inform participants of the objectives of investigations. Parental consent should be obtained in the case of children under 16 years of age. Additionally, consent should be obtained from children old enough to understand a study.
- **Avoidance of deception** – the withholding of information or the misleading of participants is unacceptable if participants are likely to object or show unease once debriefed. Intentional deception of the participants over the purpose and general nature of investigations should be avoided wherever possible. Participants should not deliberately be misled without scientific or medical justification, though sometimes deception is unavoidable. There are a number of possible ways to deal with the problem of deception:
  a) **Presumptive consent** – this is gained from people of a similar background to participants in a study. If they state that they would have been willing to participate, then it is deemed that the actual participants would too.
  b) **Prior general consent** – this involves participants agreeing to be deceived without knowing how this will occur. As participants know they will be deceived, this can affect their behaviour.
  c) **Retrospective consent** – this involves asking participants for consent after they have participated in a study. However, they may not consent and yet have already taken part.

If deception is used, participants must be told immediately afterwards and given the chance to withhold their data from the study. Before conducting such a study, the investigator has a special responsibility to:

  - determine that alternatives which avoid deception are not available
  - ensure that participants are provided with sufficient information at the earliest stage
  - consult appropriately upon the possible effects of withholding information or deliberate deception.

- **Adequate briefing/debriefing** – all relevant details of a study should be explained to participants before and afterwards. A debrief is important if deception has been used. Participants should leave the study in the same state they started it. Debriefing does not provide justification for any unethical aspects of the procedure.
- **Protection of participants** – investigators have a responsibility to protect participants from physical and mental harm during the investigation. Risk of harm must be no greater than in ordinary life.
- **Right to withdraw** – participants are made aware that they can leave a study at any time, regardless of whether payment or inducement has been offered. This is difficult to implement during observations. Participants should also be aware that they can withdraw their data at any point in the future.
- **Confidentiality** – participants' data are confidential and should not be disclosed to anyone unless agreed in advance. Numbers should be used instead of names in any subsequent published articles. Confidentiality is easily confused with anonymity. Confidentiality means that data can be traced back to names, whereas anonymous data cannot, as the researchers collect no names. Confidential data collection is preferable in cases where participants might be followed up later.
- **Observational research** – observations are only made in public places where people might expect to be observed by strangers.
- **Giving advice** – during research, investigators may obtain evidence of psychological or physical problems of which a participant is, apparently, unaware. The investigators have a responsibility to inform the participant if they believe that by not doing so the participant's future well-being may be endangered.
- **Colleagues** – investigators share responsibility for the ethical treatment of participants with collaborators, assistants, students and employees. A psychologist who believes another investigator may be conducting research that is not in accordance with ethical principles should encourage that investigator to re-think what they are doing.

Before research is conducted, investigators must seek peer guidance, consult likely participants for their views, follow the BPS Code of Ethics, consider alternative research methodologies, establish a cost–benefit analysis of short-term and long-term consequences, assume responsibility for the research, and gain approval from ethical committees monitoring their research. If, during the research process, it becomes clear there are negative consequences resulting from the research, it should be stopped and every effort made to correct for the negative consequences. Any researcher having ethical concerns about a colleague should contact them in the first instance, and if their concerns are not allayed, contact the BPS.

Research in focus

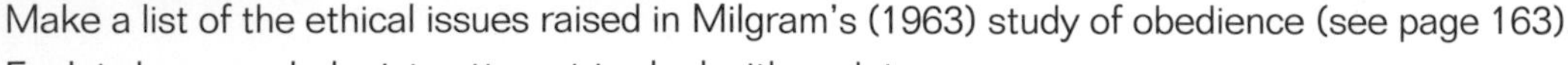

Make a list of the ethical issues raised in Milgram's (1963) study of obedience (see page 163).

Explain how psychologists attempt to deal with such issues.

In what ways can Jenness's (1932) study of informational social influence (see page 154) be regarded as ethically acceptable?

Assessment Check

Psychologists have carried out research into attachment behaviour. One possible ethical issue which might arise during this research is protection of participants from harm.

1 Explain ways in which psychologists could deal with this ethical issue. [4 marks]

2 a) Outline two further ethical issues psychologists have to consider when conducting research. [2 + 2 marks]

b) Explain one strategy psychologists might use to deal with the two ethical issues outlined in part a). A different strategy must be used in each part of your answer. [2 + 2 marks]

Examination guidance:

1 An answer is required that focuses on relevant strategies for dealing with this issue, such as incurring no harm in the study greater than everyday life. Describing the issue would not earn credit.

2 This question allows you to select issues of your own, but be sure you select issues and not ways of dealing with issues. Then move on in part b) to how you would deal with them, remembering that the question specifically forbids you from using the same answer twice. Choose your issues with care.

Key terms

Sampling – the selection of participants to represent a wider population

The selection of participants and sampling techniques

Psychological studies usually involve using **samples** drawn from larger **populations**. Sampling is essential to avoid studying entire populations. A sample should be representative of the population from which it is drawn and should therefore possess the same characteristics as the population. The term **target population** is used, as this is the group of people whom researchers target or generalise their results to. In general, the larger the sample, the better it is, but the more time consuming it is too. Psychologists use several sampling techniques to try to obtain unbiased samples.

Random sampling

Random sampling is where every member of a population has an equal chance of being selected. The easiest way to do this is to place all names from the target population in a hat and draw out the required sample number. Computer programs can also be used to generate random lists. This results in a sample selected in an unbiased fashion, although it can still result in a biased sample. For example, if ten boys' and ten girls' names were placed in a hat, there is a possibility that the first ten names drawn from the hat could all be boys' names. The selection was unbiased, but the resulting sample is biased.

Evaluation of random sampling

- The sample is likely to be representative and therefore results can be generalised to the target population.

- It is sometimes difficult to get full details of a target population from which to select a sample. In addition, not all members may be available or wish to take part, making any sample unrepresentative.

Opportunity sampling

Opportunity sampling involves selecting participants who are available and willing to take part. Sears (1986) found that 75 per cent of university research studies use undergraduates as participants simply for the sake of convenience.

Self-selected sampling

Self-selected sampling involves people volunteering to participate. They select themselves as participants, often by replying to adverts.

Evaluation of opportunity and volunteer sampling

- They are the easiest and most practical methods of ensuring large samples.
- Samples are likely to be biased and thus the findings cannot be generalised to the target population. Volunteers are generally more motivated and thus perform differently than randomly selected participants. Bauman (1973) found different results on reported sexual knowledge, attitudes and behaviour of undergraduate students dependent on whether they were willing or non-willing volunteers.

Research in focus

Both Kiecolt-Glaser's (1984) and Garnefski *et al.*'s (2003) studies into stress (see pages 120 and 137) used volunteer samples.

How did Garnefski gain her volunteers? How else can volunteers be found?

Explain why such samples may be unrepresentative and how this could have affected the results in both these studies.

A random sample may have been more preferable. What is a random sample and how would it be selected?

A random sample is not, however, guaranteed to be representative. Why not?

Figure 3.15 Many studies use volunteer samples

Demand characteristics

Social interactions affect peoples' behaviour and conducting research is no different. Research does not take place in a 'social vacuum', it involves interaction between researchers and participants and such interactions can affect research findings.

There are many features of research studies that enable participants to guess a study's purpose and what is expected of them. Such demand characteristics can involve participants:

- guessing the purpose of research and trying to please the researcher by giving the 'right' results

Key terms

Demand characteristics – a research effect where participants form impressions of the research purpose and unconsciously alter their behaviour accordingly

- guessing the purpose of the research and trying to annoy the researcher by giving the wrong results; this is called the **screw you effect**
- acting unnaturally out of nervousness or fear of evaluation
- acting unnaturally due to social desirability bias.

A technique that reduces demand characteristics is the **single blind procedure**. This is where participants have no idea which condition of a study they are in. In drug trials, for example, they would not know whether they were being given a real drug or a placebo drug (ineffective sugar pill).

You are the researcher

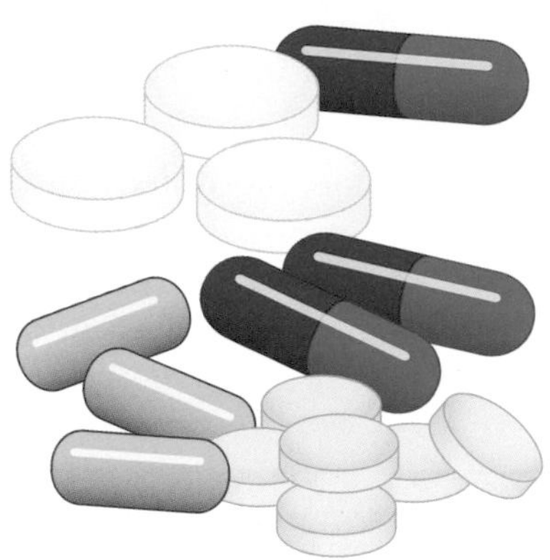

Figure 3.16 Drugs are often tested against placebos, but who gets which?

Researchers often assess the effectiveness of new drugs by comparing them with a placebo treatment (see page 216). Devise a study to assess the effectiveness of a new anti-depressant drug 'Aspiritor' using the single blind method to try to reduce the effects of demand characteristics. You are going to have to concentrate especially on how you would assign your participants to the test conditions.

What would be your IV and DV?

Which experimental design would you have to use?

Key terms

Investigator effects – researcher features influence participants' responses

Investigator effects

Investigators may inadvertently influence the results of their research. These investigator effects can occur in several ways:

- Certain physical characteristics of investigators may influence results, such as age or ethnicity. For example, male participants may be unwilling to admit sexist views to female researchers.
- Less obvious personal characteristics of investigators, like accent or tone of voice, can influence results. Participants may pick up on this and not act normally.
- Investigators may be accidentally biased in their interpretation of data.

A technique that reduces investigator effects is the **double blind procedure**. This is where neither participants nor investigators know which condition participants are in. They are both 'blind' to this knowledge. This prevents investigators from inadvertently giving participants clues as to which condition they are in and therefore reduces demand characteristics. There is, however, an investigator in overall charge who is aware of the allocation of participants to conditions.

Research in focus

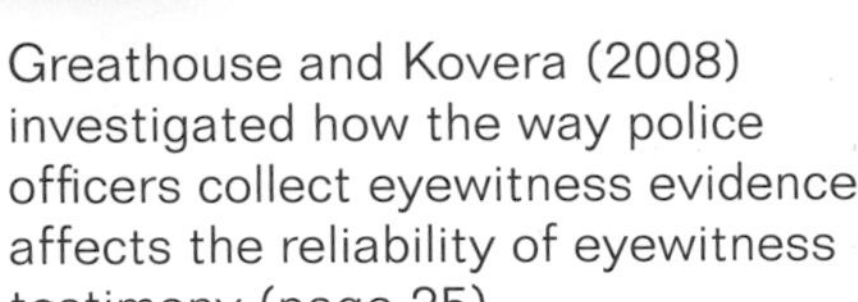

Greathouse and Kovera (2008) investigated how the way police officers collect eyewitness evidence affects the reliability of eyewitness testimony (page 25).

Explain how bias may have been occurring and how their recommendation of using a double blind procedure would actually have been administered.

Figure 3.17 Police interview procedures can affect the reliability of EWT

Psychology in action

The implications of research

Psychology, like all scientific disciplines, is underpinned by research studies which help to explain psychological phenomena by testing out hypotheses in a rigorous fashion. These can lead to the formation of many useful practical applications of benefit to people in all aspects of life.

For example, research into day care for children has identified several factors that have important implications about what high-quality day care should consist of, such as consistency of care, sensitivity of day care staff, low staff to child ratios and well-trained staff (see page 68). In this way it can be seen that psychology has transformed the way day care operates, as policy makers incorporate what research has taught us about desirable practice, into the actual ways in which day care must be provided. The implication is that our children are receiving a better standard of care that will, hopefully, turn out better-equipped individuals.

Strengthen your learning

1. When is inter-rater reliability established?
2. Outline two important factors when designing questionnaires.
3. Give two important interpersonal variables when selecting an interviewer.
4. a) What are pilot studies?
   b) What is their purpose?
5. Which three types of variables should researchers consider when trying to reduce the impact of extraneous variables?
6. a) What is meant by reliability?
   b) What is the difference between internal and external reliability?
   c) What is meant by validity?
   d) What is the difference between internal and external validity?
7. Explain how researchers can:
   a) obtain informed consent
   b) avoid deception
   c) debrief participants
   d) protect participants from harm
   e) ensure the right to withdraw
   f) establish confidentiality
   g) conduct observations in an ethical manner.
8. Explain what the following terms mean:
   a) random sampling
   b) opportunity sampling
   c) self-selected sampling.
9. Outline one technique for reducing the risk of demand characteristics.
10. In what ways may investigator effects occur?

Assessment Check

A situation in which disruption of attachment can occur is when a mother of a young child has to be away from home for a week due to work commitments. Researchers studied the behaviour of a young girl who experienced such disruption to attachment. Naturalistic observation of the girl before and after the separation was conducted, with each period of observation lasting for two hours.

a) Suggest two behavioural categories the researchers could use to record the girl's behaviour. [2 marks]

b) How might the researchers record the girl's behaviour? [2 marks]

c) Explain why a pilot study might be carried out before the main observation. [2 marks]

d) Explain:

i) Why the researchers would need to establish inter-rater reliability. [2 marks]

ii) How inter-rater reliability could be established. [2 marks]

Examination guidance:

Part a) merely calls for relevant identification of the categories, therefore any further description or explanation would not attract credit.

In part b) one mark would be earned by explanation of a relevant method with a further mark for elaboration. An alternative way of gaining both marks would be to supply two valid ways of recording the behaviour.

In part c) two relevant reasons could be given or one relevant reason with suitable elaboration.

With d) it is important to explain in i) what the purpose of inter-rater reliability is and in ii) a method of establishing it, in order to gain the marks on offer.

Data analysis and presentation

IN THE NEWS

'A GLASS OF WINE A DAY DOUBLES THE RISK OF CANCER'

Figure 3.18

The newspaper headline above seems to suggest a strong link between drinking alcohol and developing life-threatening illness. The story reported in the British press was taken from US research, which indicated middle-aged women drinking just a single glass of wine per day, half the recommended safe level, doubled their risk of contracting lobular cancer, a common type of breast cancer, when compared with people who didn't drink at all. It was reported further that scientists had concluded that excessive consumption of alcohol was causing a worldwide rise in breast cancer, pointing to the fact that in Britain the number of cases has risen by 80 per cent in the past thirty years. Over the same period, alcohol consumption had almost doubled.

This type of article is not uncommon in the popular press. Although highlighting issues that have a serious side to them, like the undesirability of excessive drinking, such articles show a basic misunderstanding of what scientific data display. The data talked about in this article, that cancer cases have increased at the same time that alcohol consumption has increased, are correlational evidence, which shows a relationship between two co-variables. But what the data do not show are that excessive drinking causes a rise in the incidence of cancer.

Correlational data do not display cause and effect relationships, only experiments are capable of doing that. It is important that scientific data are properly understood, in order that people comprehend fully the impact of scientific knowledge upon their daily lives.

Research involves the collection of data. Data can be analysed both quantitatively and qualitatively. In general, qualitative studies produce subjective, detailed, less reliable data of a *descriptive* nature, whereas quantitative studies produce objective, less detailed, more reliable data of a *numerical* nature.

Qualitative data	Quantitative data
Subjective	Objective
Imprecise non-numerical measures used	Precise numerical measures used
Rich and detailed	Lacks detail
Low in reliability	High in reliability
Used for attitudes, opinions, beliefs	Used for behaviour
Collected in 'real-life' setting	Collected in 'artificial' setting

Table 3.2 General summary of quantitative data and qualitative data

Analysis and interpretation of quantitative data

Psychological data can be presented in a number of ways. Although psychology as a science places emphasis on statistical analysis, data should also be presented in a visually meaningful way. Graphs and charts enable readers to 'eyeball' and help illustrate patterns in data. Correlations involve scattergrams and were previously discussed (see page 77). Other types of graphs exist for different types of research data. These will be discussed in detail below.

Key terms

Quantitative data – data occurring in numerical form

Graphs – easily understandable, pictorial representations of data

Bar charts

Bar charts show data in the form of categories that the researcher wishes to compare, such as males and females. Categories are placed on the x-axis (horizontal). The columns of bar charts should be the same width and separated by spaces. The use of spaces illustrates that the variable on the x-axis is not continuous. Data are 'discrete', such as the mean score of several groups. It can also involve percentages, totals or ratios. A bar chart can display two values together. For example, Figure 3.19 shows male and female groups divided into two further groups: those under and over 20 years of age.

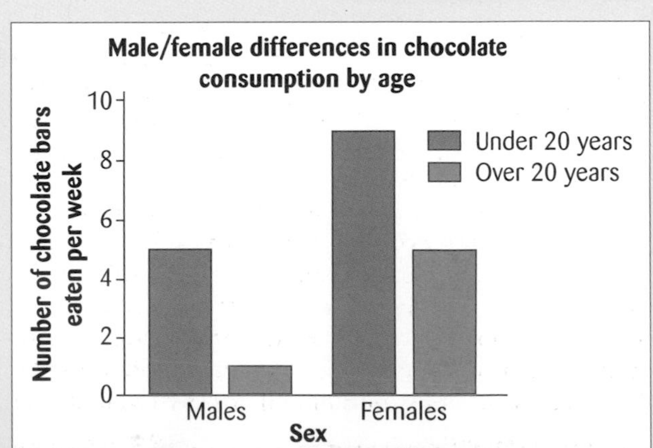

Figure 3.19 An example of a bar chart displaying two values together

You are the researcher

In an experiment into the effects of age on the accuracy of eyewitness testimonies, participants had to watch a video of a kidnapping and were then asked a mixture of non-misleading (truthful) and misleading questions. Researchers found that both young children and elderly participants got fewer non-misleading questions right than did young adult participants. However, elderly participants were less suggestible to misleading questions than were the children and young adults.

A summary of the results is found in Table 3.3.

Participants	Average number of non-misleading questions answered correctly (out of 20)	Average number of misleading questions answered correctly (out of 10)
Children	9	2
Young adults	17	4
Elderly	8	1

Table 3.3 Average number of non-misleading and misleading questions answered correctly by different age groups

Construct a bar chart to plot the data from this study. Your graph will need to be properly titled and labelled.

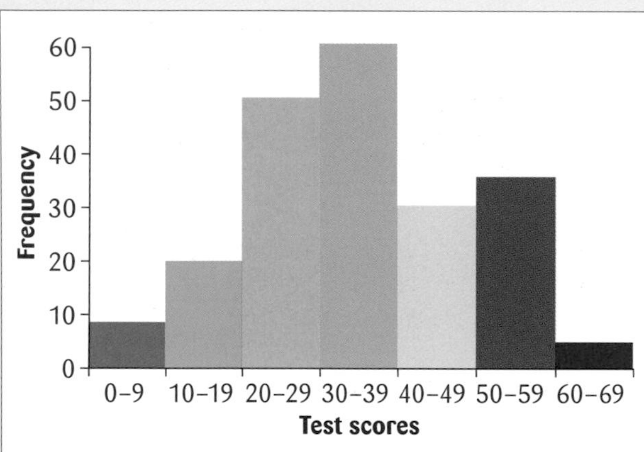

Figure 3.20 Example of a histogram

Histograms

Students often confuse **histograms** and bar charts. The main difference is that histograms are used for continuous data, such as test scores, like the example shown in Figure 3.20. These continuous scores or values should increase along the x-axis. The frequency of these values is shown on the y-axis (vertical). There are no spaces between the bars since the data are continuous. The column width for each value on the x-axis should be the same width per equal category interval. Thus the area of each column is proportional to the number of cases it represents throughout the histogram.

You are the researcher

A study was carried out to investigate the effect of the number of hours of day care children receive upon their levels of aggressiveness. It was found that the number of aggressive acts was relatively low and remained fairly unchanged for children receiving below 30 hours of day care a week. However, for those receiving more than 30 hours a week, there was an elevated level of aggressiveness.

A summary of the results is found in Table 3.4.

Construct a histogram to plot the data from this study. Your graph will need to be properly titled and labelled.

Number of hours day care a week	Average number of aggressive acts per week
0–5	1
5–10	3
10–15	2
15–20	4
20–25	2
25–30	3
30–35	9

Table 3.4 The average number of aggressive acts a week in children attending different hours of day care

Frequency polygon (line graph)

This is similar to a histogram in that the data on the x-axes are continuous. A **frequency polygon** is produced by drawing a line from the mid-point top of each bar in a histogram. The advantage of a frequency polygon is that two or more frequency distributions can be displayed on the same graph for comparison (see Figure 3.21).

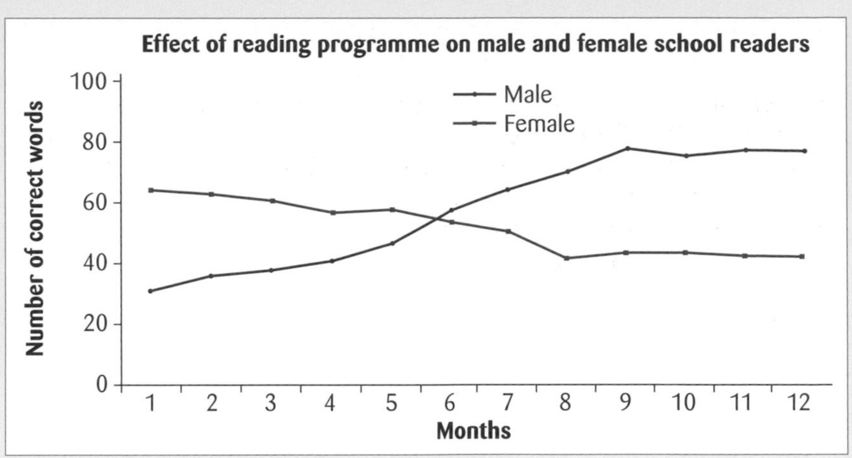

Figure 3.21 Example of a frequency polygon

You are the researcher

Figure 3.22 Some Scottish children learn Gaelic before they learn English

Many children in Scotland from the start of their school life have all their lessons in Gaelic. It has been found that although Gaelic-educated children initially lag behind their English-educated peers in scores of English language ability, they eventually catch up and then surpass their peers.

Using the data from Table 3.5, construct a frequency polygon to show the relative developmental progress of both Gaelic- and English-educated children in English language ability.

Your graph will need to be properly titled and labelled.

Age in years	Score on English language ability scale for Gaelic-educated children	Score on English language ability scale for English-educated children
3–4	3	10
4–5	4	11
5–6	7	12
6–7	9	12
7–8	10	14
8–9	15	17
9–10	20	18
10–11	21	19
11–12	24	20

Table 3.5 English language ability scores in Gaelic- and English-educated children

General points to consider with presentation of graphs and charts

- All graphs and charts must be fully labelled with appropriate titles. The x- and y-axes must be labelled accurately.
- Graphs and charts look best if the y-axis height is three-quarters the x-axis width.
- Only one graph or chart is used to illustrate a set of data.
- An appropriate scale should be used on the axes. Do not mislead by using inappropriate scales. Political parties often do this to present biased data.
- Raw data should not be presented. A chart or graph should be used instead to summarise the data. Each individual score is also not presented, as the raw data table will already show this.

Figures 3.23A and B show an example of how using inappropriate scales on graphs can mislead people. Both figures display data about the aggression rates of children attending different amounts of day care. However, if you wanted to suggest that day care is harmful in terms of increased aggressiveness in children, then you would be more tempted to use graph B, whose steeper curve seems to indicate stronger evidence for your belief. It does not. Both graphs display exactly the same data.

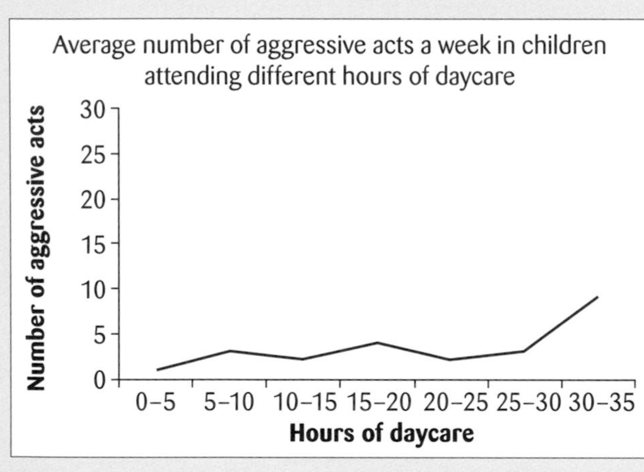

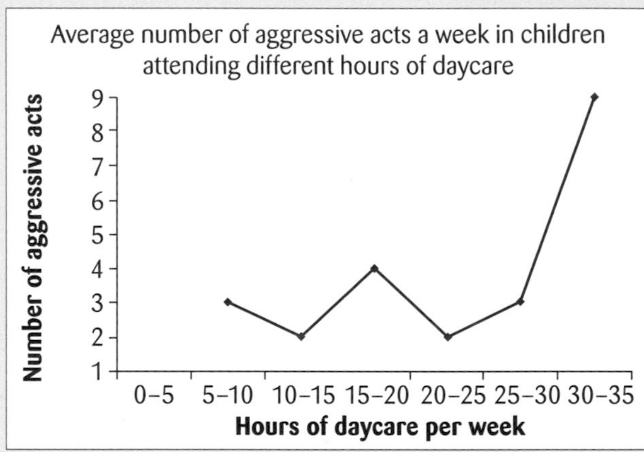

Figure 3.23 Using inappropriate scales to mislead

Measures of central tendency

> **Key terms**
>
> **Measures of central tendency** – methods of estimating mid-point scores in sets of data

Measures of central tendency are used to summarise large amounts of data into typical values or averages. These are ways of estimating mid-point scores. There are three averages: the **median**, the **mean** and the **mode**.

The median

The median is the central score in a list of rank-ordered scores. With an odd number of scores, the median is the middle number. With an even number of scores, the median is the mid-point between the two middle scores and therefore may not be one of the original scores.

The advantages of the median are:

- It is not affected by extreme 'freak' scores.
- It is usually easier to calculate than the mean.
- The median can be used with ordinal data (ranks), unlike the mean.

The weaknesses of the median are:

- It is not as sensitive as the mean, because not all the scores are used in the calculation.
- It can be unrepresentative in a small set of data. For example:

  1, 1, 2, 3, 4, 5, 6, 7, 8 – the median is 4

  2, 3, 4, 6, 8, 9, 12, 13 – the median is 7

The mean

This is where all the scores are added up and divided by the total number of scores. It is the mid-point of the combined values.

The advantages of the mean are:

- It is the most accurate measure of central tendency as it uses the interval level of measurement, where the units of measurement are of equal size (for example, seconds in time).
- It uses all the data in its calculation.

The weaknesses of the mean are:

- It is less useful if some scores are skewed, such as if there are some large or small scores.
- The mean score may not be one of the actual scores in the set of data.

The mode

This is the most common, or 'popular', number in a set of scores.

The advantages of the mode are:

- It is less prone to distortion by extreme values.
- It sometimes makes more sense than the other measures of central tendency. For example, the average number of children in a British family is better described as 2 children (mode) rather than 2.4 children (mean).

The weaknesses of the mode are:

- There can be more than one mode in a set of data. (For example, for the set of data 2, 3, 6, 7, 7, 7, 9, 15, 16, 16, 16, 20, the modes are 7 and 16.)
- It does not take into account exact distances between values.
- It does not use all the scores.

Measures of dispersion

Measures of dispersion are measures of the variability or spread of scores. They include the **range**, **interquartile range** and **standard deviation**.

Key terms

Measures of dispersion – measurements of the spread of scores within a set of data

The range

This is calculated by subtracting the lowest value from the highest value in a set of scores.

The advantages of the range are:

- It is fairly easy and quick to work out.
- It takes full account of extreme values.

The weaknesses of the range are:

- It can be distorted by extreme 'freak' values.
- It does not show whether data are clustered or spread evenly around the mean. For example, the range of the two sets of data below is the same, despite the data being very different.

  2, 3, 4, 5, 5, 6, 7, 8, 9, 21

  2, 5, 8, 9, 10, 12, 13, 15, 16, 18, 21

Interquartile range

This shows the spread of the middle 50 per cent of a set of scores. For example, the following set of data contains sixteen scores:

4, 5, 6, 6, 7, 8, 8, 9, 11, 11, 14, 15, 17, 18, 18, 19

Four scores are in the first 25 per cent, four scores are in the last 25 per cent and eight scores are in the middle 50 per cent. The middle eight scores begin with 7 and end with 15. The upper limit of the interquartile range lies between 15 and 17 and is calculated as the mean of these two values, i.e. 16. The lower limit of the interquartile range lies between 6 and 7, with the mean being 6.5. The interquartile range is the difference between the upper and lower limits (i.e. between 16 and 6.5) and in this instance is 9.5.

The advantages of the interquartile range are:

- It is fairly easy to calculate.
- It is not affected by extreme scores.

The weaknesses of the interquartile range are:

- It does not take into account extreme scores.
- It is inaccurate if there are large intervals between the scores.

Standard deviation

This is a measure of the spread or variability of a set of scores from the mean. The larger the standard deviation, the larger will be the spread of scores.

Standard deviation is calculated using the following steps:

i) Add all the scores together and divide by the number of scores to calculate the mean.

ii) Subtract the mean from each individual score.

iii) Square each of these scores.

iv) Add all the squared scores together.

v) Divide the sum of the squares by the number of scores minus 1. This is the variance.

vi) Use a calculator to work out the square root of the variance. This is standard deviation.

The advantages of standard deviation are:

- It is a more sensitive dispersion measure than the range since all scores are used in its calculation.
- It allows for the interpretation of individual scores. Thus in Figure 3.24 anybody with an IQ of 121 is in the top 5 per cent of the population, between +2 and +3 standard deviations of the mean.

The weaknesses of standard deviation are:

- It is more complicated to calculate.
- It is less meaningful if data are not normally distributed (see Figure 3.24).

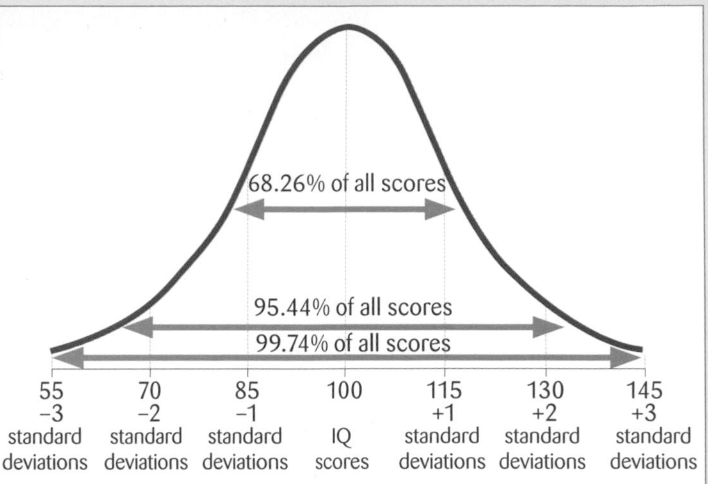

Figure 3.24 Standard deviation: IQ scores

You are the researcher

The following are individual participants' scores on a memory test:

14, 8, 12, 10, 8, 8, 7, 6, 13, 11, 6, 6, 6, 14, 15, 13, 8, 14, 8, 11

Calculate the following:

a) the median

b) the mean

c) the mode

d) the range

e) the interquartile range

f) the standard deviation

Analysis and interpretation of correlational data

Correlational methods have been discussed previously (see page 77). It is possible to have a positive correlation, negative correlation or no correlation at all. The stronger a correlation, the nearer it is to +1 or –1. Scattergrams (or scattergraphs) are a type of graph displaying to what extent two variables are correlated. However, a statistical test (**correlation coefficient**) has to be calculated to determine the exact nature of the correlation.

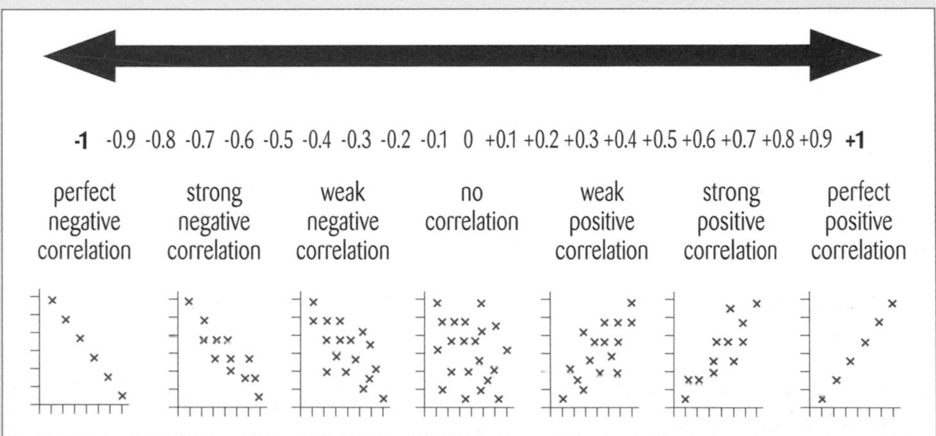

Figure 3.25 Scattergrams and correlation strength

You are the researcher

A correlational study into occupational stress levels and absenteeism among 12 police officers produced the following data.

Police officer number	Occupational stress level score	Days absent in a 6-month period
1	80	60
2	10	1
3	40	9
4	30	11
5	10	3
6	90	65
7	30	17
8	50	40
9	20	9
10	20	8
11	30	17
12	90	67

Table 3.6 The occupational stress scores and number of days absent of police officers over a 6-month period

Plot the data on a scattergram.

The graph should be properly titled and labelled.

What type of correlation does the scattergram display?

Key terms

Qualitative data – non-numerical data expressing meanings, feelings and descriptions

Content analysis – a method of quantifying qualitative data through the use of coding units

Analysis and presentation of qualitative data

Qualitative data involves meanings, experiences and descriptions. It is particularly useful when researching attitudes, opinions and beliefs. Data can consist of verbal, written or pictorial descriptions. The qualitative approach suggests that information about human experience loses much of its meaning and value when reduced to numerical form.

There is no single best way to analyse qualitative data and, as a fairly recent field, new methods are constantly emerging and developing.

Content analysis

Content analysis is commonly done with media research. It involves the quantification of qualitative material, in other words, the numerical analysis of written, verbal and visual communications. It can involve the analysis of speeches, graffiti, advertisements or newspapers. For example, Waynforth and Dunbar (1995) analysed the content of 'lonely hearts' columns to find out whether men and women were looking for different things in relationships.

Content analysis requires the development of **coding units** which can be used to categorise analysed material, such as the number of times women appear as housewives in TV adverts. Analysis can involve words, themes, characters or time and space.

Unit	Examples
Word	Count the number of slang words used
Theme	The amount of violence on TV
Character	The number of female bosses there are in TV programmes
Time and space	The amount of time (on TV) and space (in newspapers) dedicated to famine in Africa

Table 3.7 Coding units for content analysis

Categorising

This involves the grouping of common items together. For example, we could group students' perceptions of their Psychology course into: resources, peer/teacher relationships, teacher knowledge and so on. It is often difficult to decide on categories to use. Once categories have been selected, quantitative graphical techniques, like bar charts, can be used to present the data.

Quotations

Word-for-word quotations can be used to bring research findings to life. Quotes should 'tell it like it is' and typify what others have said during the research.

Qualitative data and naturalistic observations

Observers typically give running commentaries into a tape recorder, producing qualitative data. Such data can be coded or categorised and may help to add detail to quantitative data. The **diary method** is another technique where observers take notes on behaviour in a self-reported format. The diary method provides genuine information in the participants' own surroundings. However, participants often find it difficult to complete on a long-term basis.

Qualitative data and questionnaire surveys

Qualitative data are mainly collected from open-ended questions where participants give answers using their own words. Such data are less likely to be biased by interviewers' preconceived ideas. Analysis of such data can involve content analysis, categorisation or the use of quotations.

Qualitative data and interviews

Interviews are generally transcribed and may then be analysed using the qualitative techniques described earlier. Unstructured interviews are best for qualitative analysis. Interpretation of interview data is prone to subjective interpretation. However, this lack of objectivity is compensated by the detail generated.

Evaluation of qualitative data analysis

Qualitative data analysis tends to be subjective, although it is possible to check reliability and validity. Many qualitative researchers believe subjectivity and the personal opinions of participants strengthen research studies, though qualitative data analysis can be time consuming.

Strengthen your learning

1 What is the difference between quantitative and qualitative data?
2 What do the following display:
   a) bar charts
   b) histograms
   c) frequency polygons
   d) scattergrams?
3 Explain the following measures of central tendency and for each give one strength and one weakness.
   a) Mean
   b) Median
   c) Mode
4 What do the following measures of dispersion show and for each one give one strength and one weakness?
   a) The range
   b) The interquartile range
   c) The standard deviation
5 What is content analysis and how is it performed?

Assessment Check

One method of improving memory ability is to use chunking, where information is grouped into larger units by giving it a collective meaning. To investigate this, a team of researchers used two groups of participants. To the first group they gave a list of words and to the second group they gave the same list of words but with collective meanings by which they could group them together.

Both groups were asked to recall as many items as possible.

1 Suggest a one-tailed (directional) hypothesis for this investigation. [2 marks]
2 Why is it important that the same list of words is used by both groups of participants? [2 marks]
3 This investigation was conducted in a laboratory. Give one strength and one weakness of this method. [2 + 2 marks]
4 A random sample was used for this investigation.
   a) What is meant by a random sample? [2 marks]
   b) How might this be established? [1 mark]
   c) Give one strength and one weakness of a random sample. [2 + 2 marks]

Examination guidance:

1 For this question, one mark would be awarded for a partial or muddled answer, with two marks given for a full and clear answer.
2 One mark would be gained for a valid reason, with a further mark for elaboration that was in context.
3 One mark would be awarded each for a valid strength and weakness, with an additional mark for elaboration.
4 With this question it is important that you give the correct answers to the right parts of the question. For example in part a) do not explain how a random sample is established; this can only be done in part b) to gain credit.

End of chapter review

- Various psychological research methods exist, each with strengths and weaknesses. There's no single best method.
- The experimental method involves manipulation of an independent variable to determine effect on a dependent variable.
- Laboratory experiments occur in controlled environments.
- Laboratory experiments display causality, but have low external validity.
- Field experiments occur in naturalistic environments.
- Field experiments are high in ecological validity, but have low control over extraneous variables.
- Natural experiments occur in naturalistic environments with a naturally occurring IV and a measured DV.
- Natural experiments have no demand characteristics and weaknesses, but are difficult to replicate.
- Correlations measure the strength of relationship between two variables.
- Correlations are positive, where two co-variables systematically increase, or negative, where one co-variable systematically increases while another decreases.
- Correlations allow quantification of relationships, but lack causality.
- Observations measure naturally occurring behaviour and have high external validity, but are prone to observer bias.
- Questionnaires involve respondents recording written answers to pre-set open and/or closed questions.
- Questionnaires produce quantitative and qualitative data, but have low response rates.
- Interviews range from unstructured to fully structured and involve answering face-to-face questions.
- Interviews can deal with complex issues, but are subject to interviewer bias.
- Case studies involve detailed investigations of one individual or a small group and are richly detailed, but reliant on accurate memory.
- Aims indicate why studies take place, while hypotheses are testable statements.
- An experimental hypothesis predicts a significant difference in the DV due to manipulation of the IV. A null hypothesis predicts no significant difference.
- Experimental hypotheses are one-or two tailed, where the direction of difference is either predicted or not.
- There are three types of experimental design: independent groups design, repeated measures design and matched participants design.
- Operationalization of variables involves objectively defining variables in order to manipulate and measure them.
- Pilot studies are small scale pre-studies that identify potential problems.
- Results must be reliable and valid i.e. consistent and accurate.
- Reliability can be internal, where a test is consistent within itself, or external where a test is consistent over time.
- Validity can be internal where results are due to manipulation of the IV and not confounding variables, or external where results are generalizable beyond the laboratory environment.
- Research is conducted under ethical guidelines, involving informed consent, protection from harm, avoidance of deception and the right to withdraw.
- Samples are representative parts of populations, possessing their same characteristics.
- Demand characteristics occur when participants try to guess the purpose of a study and respond accordingly.
- Investigator effects involve some aspect of an investigator influencing participants' responses.
- Quantitative data involves numerical analysis of data.
- Graphs and charts visually illustrate data patterns.
- The mean, mode and median illustrate 'middle' values of data, each with strengths and weaknesses.
- The range, interquartile range and standard deviation illustrate 'the spread' of data, each with strengths and weaknesses.
- Qualitative data involves non-numerical analysis of data.
- Content analysis quantifying qualitative data by categorizing material into coding units.

Biological psychology

Introduction

Biological psychology concentrates upon the physiological aspects of the body that affect behavioural, thought and emotional processes, with particular emphasis upon brain mechanisms and the nervous system. The particular topic illustrated here is that of stress, with the focus on the body's reactions to threatening stimuli and methods of dealing with stressors.

Understanding the specification

- You should be able to outline how the body responds to stress in terms of the pituitary–adrenal system and the sympathomedullary pathway. As the specification says 'in outline', this means that the two systems do not need to be known in tremendous detail.
- You should know how the body is affected by stress in terms of illness and the effects of stress upon the immune system.
- You will look at stress in everyday life, concentrating firstly on how life changes and daily hassles affect stress levels.
- You need to study the stressors we are subjected to at work, before concentrating on the relationship between personality factors and stress.
- You must have knowledge of Type A behaviour, as it is mentioned in the specification, meaning you could be questioned specifically about it.
- Finally you must look at methods of stress management, with a requirement to have a working knowledge of two specific methods, namely the psychological method of cognitive behavioural therapy and the physiological method of drugs.

Stress

Stress as a bodily response

Stress is a general response to any demand made of the body. Stress occurs when there is a lack of balance between the perceived requirements of a situation and the perceived abilities to cope with those requirements, for example having a demanding job and feeling unable to meet those demands.

Many responses associated with stress are physiological ones. Although there are also behavioural and cognitive components, stress mainly manifests itself as a bodily response.

Stressors are simply sources of stress. In other words, anything causing stress is a stressor. If you are stressed due to a lack of money, then stress is what you feel, while the stressor is the lack of money.

Key terms

Stress – lack of balance between the perceived demands of a situation and perceived abilities to cope with such demands

Stressors – internal and external sources of stress

IN THE NEWS

Pet ownership reduces risk of developing cancer

In 2008 the press reported a novel way of protecting against Hodgkin's lymphoma, a deadly cancer of the immune system contracted by around 10,000 Britons each year. Research undertaken at Stanford University and the University of California, found pet owners were nearly 30% less likely to develop the condition than those who owned no pets. As the disease strikes those with weakened immune systems, it is believed the mere presence of pets safeguards against becoming ill by helping owners to relax, placing less pressure on the heart and they reap the benefits of lowered stress levels and stronger immune system functioning.

Figure 4.1

Psychological research has shown that stress can damage the immune system, leaving people vulnerable to stress-related illnesses, like cardiovascular disorders and cancer. This research seems to suggest that pet ownership helps to protect against reduced immune system functioning, by helping people to relax.

Key terms

Sympatho-medullary pathway – bodily system responding to acute, short-term stressors, comprised of the sympathetic nervous system and the sympathetic adrenal medullary system

Pituitary–adrenal system – bodily system responding to chronic, long-term stressors, comprised of the hypothalamus, the pituitary gland and the adrenal glands

The body's response to stress

There are two general ways in which the body responds to stressors: the sympathomedullary pathway, dealing with *acute* (short-term) stressors and the pituitary–adrenal system, dealing with *chronic* (long-term) stress.

The sympathomedullary pathway

The **sympathetic nervous system** (SNS) and the **sympathetic adrenal medullary** (SAM) **system** make up the sympathomedullary pathway.

Acute stressors activate the **autonomic nervous system** (ANS), which has two divisions.

1 The **sympathetic nervous system** (SNS), which is the 'troubleshooter'. It is highly responsive to stimuli and through activation is responsible for emotional states and heightened arousal.

2 The **parasympathetic nervous system** (PSNS), which is the 'housekeeper'. It is responsible for maintaining equilibrium and calming bodily processes.

These two divisions are essentially opposing forces, interacting to produce the bodily state at any given time. The sympathetic division is the component primarily activated by stressors.

When exposed to an acute stressor, the SNS is activated and, simultaneously, the SAM system stimulates the release of the hormone **adrenaline** into the bloodstream from the adrenal glands in the adrenal medulla. This hormone prepares the body for the 'fight-or-flight' response by boosting the supply of oxygen and glucose to the brain and muscles and suppressing non-emergency processes like digestion.

Research into the sympathomedullary pathway

- Taylor *et al.* (2000) found that acute stress produces the fight-or-flight response in men, but the 'tend and befriend' response in women. This different effect is believed to occur as women produce more oxytocin, a chemical promoting relaxation and nurturing, suggesting a gender difference in the activation of the sympathomedullary pathway.
- McCarty (1981) found that blood plasma levels of adrenaline and noradrenaline (another hormone) were equal in rats of varying ages before subjecting them to 1 minute of inescapable foot-shock, but that older rats had lower levels than younger rats after being shocked. This suggests that diminished responsiveness of the sympathomedullary pathway explains the reduced capacity of aged animals to adapt to stressful stimulation.
- Horwatt *et al.* (1988) found that if animals are exposed to the same stressful stimulus each day for several weeks, a number of adaptive changes occur in the sympathomedullary pathway. These include the increased production and storage of catecholamines, fight-or-flight hormones produced in response to stress. If such animals are then exposed to a novel stressful stimulus, they display an exaggerated response of the sympathomedullary pathway compared to animals exposed to the same stressful stimulus for the first time. This suggests that acute stress responses develop differently due to previous stress experiences.

You are the researcher

Design an experiment to test the hypothesis that acute stress produces the fight-or-flight response in males, but the tend and befriend response in females.

What experimental design would you use?

What would be the IV and DV? (You may wish to refer to Taylor *et al.*'s (2000) study for guidance.)

How would you gain a systematic sample?

Construct a suitable debriefing to read out after the study.

Explain how you would calculate from your data:

a) the mean b) the median c) the mode.

Research in focus

Research into stress is often based on animal experiments. Such research may suffer, however, from problems of extrapolation.

Explain what is meant by extrapolation and what this might mean in terms of stress-related research.

Evaluation

Evaluation of the sympathomedullary pathway

- A gender difference in the activation of the sympathomedullary pathway may occur due to women's evolutionary role in caring for offspring. If women fought or fled when faced with danger, offspring would be placed in danger, reducing reproductive success. A better policy is to bond with other group members, most probably females.
- Studies on human stress responses were mainly conducted on men, as researchers believed the monthly fluctuations in hormones experienced by women would create stress responses that varied too widely to be considered valid. Therefore, such results cannot be generalised to women.
- Much research into the sympathomedullary pathway involves animals and thus presents a problem of extrapolation, as the stress-related behaviour of animals might not represent that of humans, with humans more likely to have a cognitive element to their stress responses.

The pituitary–adrenal system

Prolonged, chronic stress activates the pituitary–adrenal system (alternatively known as the **hypothalamic–pituitary–adrenal axis** (HPA). This system is harder to initiate than the sympathomedullary system, being activated by stressors continuous over a period of time. Such stressors alert the **hypothalamus** within the brain to stimulate the release of the chemical messenger **corticotrophin-releasing hormone** (CRH) into the bloodstream. This in turn stimulates the pituitary gland to release **adrenocorticotropic hormone** (ACTH), which travels in the bloodstream to the adrenal glands just above the kidneys, triggering the release of stress-related hormones, the most important being **cortisol**. The production of cortisol permits a steady supply of blood sugar, which provides an individual with a constant source of energy, allowing the body to deal with the stressor. Additionally, cortisol release results in

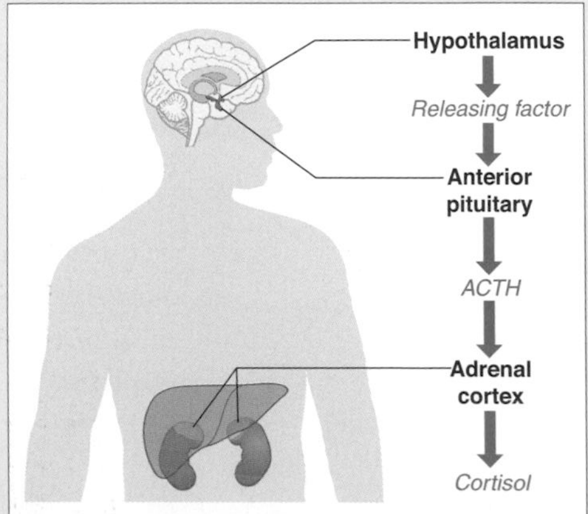

Figure 4.2 The hypothalamic–pituitary–adrenal axis

the capability to tolerate more pain than usual, but also leads to impaired cognitive ability and reduced immune system performance.

Research into the pituitary–adrenal system

- Heim *et al.* (2000) found that women who were sexually abused as children exhibited increased pituitary–adrenal and autonomic responses to stress, measured by levels of ACTH and cortisol, compared to women who were not sexually abused in childhood. This suggests that pituitary–adrenal system hyper-reactivity due to corticotrophin-releasing factor (CRF) hypersecretion is a consequence of childhood abuse. It is also suggested that CRF-receptor antagonists could be used to prevent and treat abnormal conditions related to early-life stress.
- Newcomer *et al.* (1999) found that participants given levels of cortisol high enough to produce blood sugar levels similar to those of people experiencing major stress events, like abdominal surgery, were significantly poorer at recalling prose passages than participants given levels of cortisol only high enough to produce a stress reaction similar to minor surgery, like having stitches out. This suggests that stressful stimulation of the pituitary–adrenal system has adverse effects on memory.
- Watson *et al.* (2004) compared the pituitary–adrenal system functioning of 26 people with bipolar disorder (manic depression), 27 people with bipolar disorder in remission and 28 healthy controls. They found heightened cortisol levels in bipolar sufferers, including those currently in remission. This suggests that pituitary–adrenal system dysfunction may be involved in the disease process underlying bipolar disorder.

Listen to an audio lecture given by Dr Robert Sapolsky, Professor of Neuroscience at Stanford University, on the disruptive effects of stress on memory and ageing, by going to http://www.exploratorium.edu/memory/robertsapolsky.html

Evaluation

Evaluation of the pituitary–adrenal system

- There are individual differences with response levels. Mason (1975) found that different individuals produce different levels of stress hormones when exposed to the same stressors.
- People respond in more active ways to stressors involving cognitive and emotional factors. Symington *et al.* (1955) found that conscious terminal cancer patients experienced more stress than those in a coma, as they indulged in a more stressful appraisal of their condition.
- The biological explanation of stress allows accurate, objective measures to be made.

Key terms

Immune system – bodily system that defends against disease

Stress-related illness and the immune system

The immune system consists of billions of cells travelling through the bloodstream. These cells are produced mainly in the spleen, lymph nodes, thymus and bone marrow. They move in and out of tissues and organs, defending the body against foreign bodies (**antigens**), such as bacteria, viruses and cancerous cells. The major type of cells are white blood cells (**leucocytes**), of which there are various types. Some immune cells produce and secrete **antibodies**, which bind to antigens and destroy them.

When stressed, the immune system's ability to fight off antigens is reduced and the risk of infection is more likely. Stress does not actually *cause* infections, but increases the body's susceptibility to infectious agents by temporarily suppressing immune function (**immunosuppression**).

Occasional production of cortisol and other corticosteroids does not harm the immune system, but if produced *continuously*, as with chronic, prolonged stress, they can interfere with leucocyte activity and the production of antibodies. Stressful events are linked to certain infectious illnesses, including influenza, herpes and chronic-fatigue disorder. It seems, therefore, that although cortisol helps protect against viruses and to heal injured tissues, too much cortisol suppresses the immune system, harming the very thing that protects us from infection.

Research into stress and the immune system

- Kiecolt-Glaser *et al.* (1995) gave small wounds to participants and measured how long they took to heal. They found the healing process took longer in women who cared for senile relatives. This was supported by other measurements of immune system functioning, indicating that prolonged chronic stress lessens immune system functioning.
- Vaernes and Torjussen (1991) reported a study of Norwegian air force personnel that showed a strong relationship between perceived work stress and complaints related to immune system activity. This demonstrated a link between work stress and immunosuppression, though the direction of this relationship is not clear as the data is only correlational.
- Cohen *et al.* (1993) performed a research study centring on the cold virus. Of those given the virus, it was found that people were more likely to catch a cold if they displayed high stress scores, suggesting that stress depresses the efficiency of the immune system.
- Evans *et al.* (1994) found short-term stress beneficial. Students who gave mildly stressful public presentations had increased levels of sigA, an antibody that improves the ability of the immune system to resist infection.

Evaluation

Evaluation of stress and the immune system

- Health practitioners can use findings gained from research into stress and the immune system to anticipate problems occurring as a response to stressful incidents and use appropriate therapies.
- A simple cause-and-effect relationship between stress and damage to the immune system is difficult to identify as other factors, like the unhealthy lifestyles of stressed individuals (such as smoking and drinking), may also be contributory factors.
- Changes in the functioning of the immune system may take some time to establish and may not be identifiable immediately by research. Longitudinal studies involving measurement of immune system functioning over an extended period would be required.
- Although most evidence suggests that stress damages the immune system, leading to greater vulnerability to infection and illness, there is a difference in the effects that acute and chronic stressors have. Acute stress is short-term and can be enjoyable, like the thrill of a horror film. Indeed acute stress can even result in improved immune system functioning (see Evans *et al.* above).

Classic research

Effect of immunosuppression in medical students – Janet Kiecolt-Glaser, 1984

Figure 4.3 Janet Kiecolt-Glaser

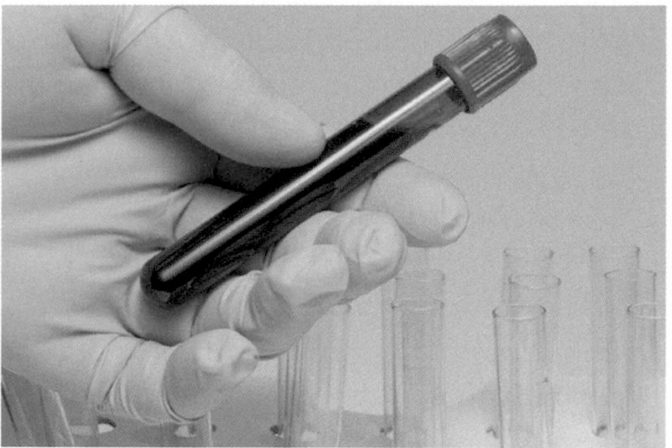

Figure 4.4 Blood samples can show immunosuppression

Aim/Hypothesis: To study the capability of the immune system in people facing stressful situations. The prediction was that immunosuppression, measured by the amount of natural killer cell activity, would be greatly reduced when stress levels were at their highest.

Procedure: Blood samples were taken from 49 male and 26 female volunteer first-year medical students one month before final exams and then again on the first day of the exams after two papers were sat. The blood samples were analysed for leucocyte activity, specifically how much natural killer cell activity, involved in fighting off viruses and tumours, was present.

Questionnaires were also given, assessing psychiatric symptoms, loneliness and life events.

Findings: As predicted, natural killer cell activity was greatly reduced in the second sample compared to the first. Immune responses were weakest in those scoring highly for loneliness, stressful life events and psychiatric symptoms, like depression and anxiety.

Conclusions: Stress is associated with reduced immune function, especially in individuals exposed to particular kinds of stressor.

Evaluation:

- The stressors used were naturally occurring, as opposed to other studies which used artificially induced stressors. In other words, the IV and DV were not artificially created.
- As the students were compared to themselves on the two occasions blood samples were taken, this controls for **participant variables**, like personality.
- We cannot be sure that it is the stressors causing changes in immune function; other non-controlled situational variables might also play a part.
- The sample of volunteer medical students was potentially not representative of the general population.

Strengthen your learning

1 a) What type of stress does the sympathomedullary pathway deal with?
  b) Outline how the sympathomedullary pathway operates in response to stress.

2 Explain why there might be a difference in the way males and females react to acute stress.

3 a) What type of stress does the pituitary–adrenal system deal with?
  b) Outline how the pituitary–adrenal system operates in response to stress.

4 a) Outline the role of the immune system.
  b) Why might prolonged stress damage the immune system?
  c) Outline two pieces of research which suggest that stress lessens immune system functioning (immunosuppression).

5 Explain how stress can result in cardiovascular disorders.

Supplementary learning

Stress and cardiovascular disorders

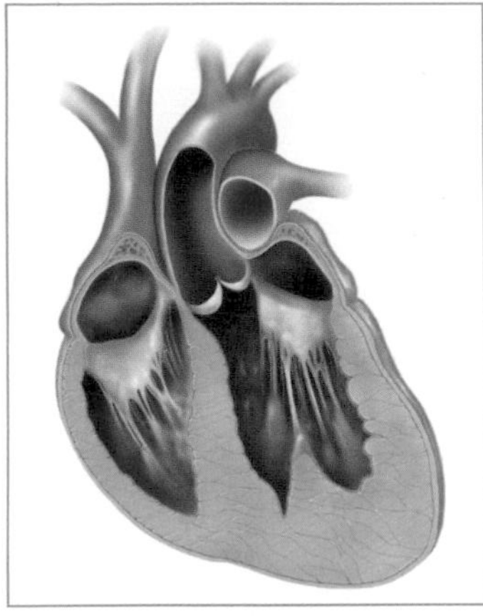

Figure 4.5 Chronic stress enhances the chances of developing cardiovascular disorders

Individuals exposed to prolonged, chronic stress have an enhanced risk of developing cardiovascular disorders (CVDs). These are disorders of the heart and blood vessels, like coronary heart disease and high blood pressure (**hypertension**), caused by the physical havoc that continual stress causes to the body.

Stress can lead to CVDs *directly* via activation of bodily stress systems or *indirectly* via stressed people's unhealthy lifestyles.

Research on stress and CVDs

Krantz *et al.* (1991) looked at 39 people with **myocardial ischaemia** (a condition where the heart receives a reduced blood flow) and their reactions to low-level stress. Those with the highest myocardial ischaemia readings, when stressed, had the highest increases in blood pressure, suggesting a direct link between low-level cognitive stress and physiological reactions leading to cardiovascular damage.

Evaluation

It may be unethical to cause distress to patients with CVD, but the justification is that the cognitive stressors were no more than those found in everyday life.

Maybe the patients with CVDs would show heightened myocardial ischaemia and blood pressure when relaxed, as well as when moderately stressed. As no control was used to compare their behaviour when stressed and not stressed, it is not possible to know.

Other research studies into stress and CVDs

Cobb and Rose (1973) compared the medical records of air traffic controllers (a highly stressful job) with those of other air traffic personnel and found that air traffic controllers had higher levels of hypertension, which increases the risk of heart disease.

Figure 4.6 Air traffic controllers have high levels of stress-related hypertension

Williams (2000) measured the anger levels of 13,000 healthy participants, as an indicator of acute stress. Those scoring highly for anger were more likely to suffer heart attacks.

Rozanski *et al.* (1999) found that some people are **hyper-responsive** to stressors. In other words, the sympathetic branch of their ANS reacts more than in other people, leading to more damage of the cardiovascular systems. This shows that there are individual differences in people's reactions to stress.

Key terms

Cardiovascular disorders – disorders of the heart and blood vessels

Assessment Check

1 Copy and complete the accompanying table, placing a letter P next to the two statemen that relate to the pituitary–adrenal system and a letter S next to the two statements that relate to the sympathomedullary pathway. [4 marks]
2 Outline the key features of a) the pituitary–adrenal system and b) the sympathomedullary pathway. [3 + 3 marks]
3 Outline the effect stress can have on the immune system. [6 marks]
4 In the last year Rhossili has endured an acrimonious separation from her boyfriend, been made redundant from her job and experienced the death of her mother. Increasingly she has been feeling physically and emotionally exhausted and is not getting enough sleep.
With reference to the statement above, outline the effects of stress-related illness on the immune system. [6 marks]
5 Discuss the relationship between the immune system and stress-related illness. [12 marks]

Statement	Letter
A system that responds to acute stressors	
Prepares the body for fight-or-flight response	
A system involving the hormone cortisol	
The system that defends against disease	
A system that responds to chronic stressors	

Examination guidance:

1 This is a selection question where you choose from the options available. This means that the correct answers are there, but must be identified and placed in the correct order. One description fitting none of the definitions is left over.
2 This question requires specific descriptions of bodily stress responses. Any irrelevant material or evaluation would not gain credit.
3 Sufficient description of how stress affects the immune system is needed to gain six marks. This could be achieved by making several brief points or fewer, more detailed points.
4 This is a scenario or stem question, requiring reference to information in the scenario to gain marks.
5 This is a long-answer question, with six marks available for outlining the relationship and six marks for evaluation. Suitable evaluation could make use of relevant research evidence.

Stress in everyday life

Much of the focus of stress-related research is upon the types of stressors encountered in everyday life, for instance life changes, like getting married, daily hassles, like travelling to work and workplace stressors, like job responsibility.

Psychologists have also looked at factors moderating the effects of everyday stressors, like personality factors, as well as performing research into the type of coping strategies individuals use when faced with such stressors.

Methods of stress management, both physiological and psychological, have been formulated, each method possessing its own strengths and weaknesses.

Life changes

Life changes are occasional events which result in major adjustments to lifestyle, such as the death of a loved one or moving house. There is a lot of variation in the impact life changes can have. For instance the ending of a relationship may be devastating for one person, but a blessing in disguise for another. In addition, when life changes do not occur, like not getting into university, they can be equally stressful in their impact.

Scales such as the **Social Readjustment Rating Scale** (SRRS) have been developed to try to measure the stressful effects of life events in order that possible links between life changes and stress-related disorders could be investigated.

Key terms

Life changes – occasional events incurring major adjustments to lifestyle

Classic research

The Social Readjustment Rating Scale – Thomas Holmes and Richard Rahe, 1967

Thomas Holmes noticed that he developed a cold every time his mother-in-law came to stay with him for a week or more. This observation was the starting point for his and Richard Rahe's attempt to develop a means of measuring the impact of various life-change stressors.

Aim/Hypothesis: To construct an instrument for measuring stress, with the prediction being that individuals are more likely to show symptoms of illness, both physical and psychological, following periods of stress and the greater the stress, the more serious the illness.

Procedure: The medical records of 5,000 patients were examined. A list of 43 life changes, which seemed to cluster in the months prior to the onset of patients' illnesses, was compiled. One hundred judges were told that 'marriage' had been assigned a value of 500 and they were to assign a number to each of the other life changes, indicating how much readjustment would be involved relative to marriage.

The average of the numbers assigned to each life change was divided by ten with the resulting scores becoming the value for each change.

The amount of life stress a person experiences in a given period is measured by the total number of life change units (LCUs). These units are calculated by adding the mean values associated with each life change that individuals have experienced during that time.

Findings: Most life changes were judged to be less stressful than getting married, with only six events, like death of spouse, being rated as more stressful. People with higher LCU scores for the preceding year were more likely to experience physical illness the following year. For example, someone scoring over 300 LCUs had an 80 per cent chance of becoming ill, with health problems including sudden cardiac death, non-fatal heart attacks, tuberculosis, diabetes, leukaemia, accidents and sports injuries.

Conclusions: Stress can be measured objectively as an LCU score. Stress can lead to illness. LCU scores can predict the chances of becoming ill, physically and/or mentally.

Evaluation:

- The 43 life changes listed are mainly negative, especially those with high LCU scores, so the SRRS may be confusing 'change' with 'negativity'.
- Some life events are ambiguous; for example, those referring to 'change in ...' could be positive or negative.
- Brown (1986) pointed out it might not be change, but rather unexpected, uncontrollable change that is stressful. When people were asked to classify undesirable life events on the SRRS, only those classified as 'uncontrollable' were correlated with later illness.
- A correlation does not indicate causality. Someone's general susceptibility to stress or their general level of health may also be important factors.
- Having a high LCU score suggests a health problem is imminent, but the nature of the health problem is not apparent. Different stress-related illnesses appear to be more or less associated with different forms of stressor.
- Holmes and Rahe did find a statistically significant correlation between LCU scores and subsequent measures of health, but the correlation was small. Therefore, the number and type of life changes experienced have some connection with subsequent health, but there is lots of variance and many individual differences in response to life change stressors not accounted for by the scale.
- A score for a particular life change indicates whether it is more or less stressful than other events, but does not say anything meaningful about the nature or extent of that particular event.

Other research studies into life changes as a source of stress

- Rahe *et al.* (1970) gave the SRRS to 2,700 sailors to assess the number of life changes undergone in the previous six months. Then, during a six-month tour of duty, individual health records were recorded for each sailor and from this illness scores were calculated. A significant positive correlation between LCUs and illness scores of +0.118 was found, suggesting a link between life changes and physical illness.
- Jacobs and Charles (1980) found that children with cancer were from families with higher life change scores than children with other illnesses, giving further support to the idea of an association between life events and illness.
- Li-Ping Tang and Hammontree (1992) measured the occupational stress levels and life changes of 60 police officers over a six-month period, finding a significant association with absenteeism levels, again implying a link between life stress and illness.

Figure 4.7 Rahe found a relationship between life changes and physical illness in sailors

Rank	Life change	Mean value
1	Death of spouse	100
2	Divorce	73
3	Marital separation	65
4	Jail term	63
5	Death of close family member	63
6	Personal injury or illness	53
7	Marriage	50
8	Fired from work	47
10	Retirement	45
11	Change in health of family member	44
12	Pregnancy	40
13	Sex difficulties	39
16	Change in financial state	38
17	Death of close friend	37
18	Change to different line of work	36
23	Son or daughter leaving home	29
27	Begin or end school	26
38	Change in sleeping habits	16
42	Christmas	12
43	Minor violations of the law	11

Table 4.1 A selection of life changes from the Social Readjustment Rating Scale (SRRS)

To read an illuminating interview with Richard Rahe about his and Thomas Holmes' work that appeared in *Health and Stress magazine* in 2007, go to http://www.stress.org/interview-Scope_Of_Stress.htm?AIS=5f9e687e7526fdafe89de9f7add05f72

Evaluation

Evaluation of life changes as a source of stress

- Many studies are retrospective and reliant on accurate and full memory, with participants being asked to recall illnesses and stressful life changes that occurred in the past. This may produce unreliable data.
- Most of the 43 life changes included in the SRRS are not everyday occurrences and daily hassles, due to their constant, repetitive nature, may be more stressful.
- Instead of life changes causing illness, it could be the other way round. Some life changes, like being sacked from work, might be an indication of an illness that is already developing.
- With the SRRS, each life change has a predetermined LCU score, but individuals may experience the same event differently. For example, the death of a friend could be less negative if that friend was suffering intense prolonged pain.

Daily hassles

Life changes can be extremely stressful, but are generally quite rare. Most life stress comes from daily hassles, those everyday irritations and annoyances that constantly infuriate, like queuing at the post office or being stuck in traffic. Daily hassles, due to their constant nature, are perhaps a better indicator of physical and mental states of well-being, because while critical life events can activate big stress reactions, daily hassles tend to build up, producing an overall elevated level of stress, which thus presents a serious risk of illness. Daily life also has its share of **uplifts** and these can neutralise the harmful effects of hassles.

Key terms

Daily hassles – everyday irritations that produce an overall elevated level of stress

Kanner *et al.* (1981) designed a **Hassles scale** of 117 negative items covering all aspects of daily life and an **Uplifts scale** of 135 positive items.

Figure 4.8 Daily hassles consist of irritations like traffic jams

Hassles were defined as:

'The irritating, frustrating, distressing demands that to some degree characterise everyday transactions with the environment. They include annoying practical problems, such as losing things or traffic jams and fortuitous occurrences, such as inclement weather, as well as arguments, disappointments, and financial and family concerns.'

Daily uplifts were defined as:

'Positive experiences, like the joy derived from manifestations of love, relief at hearing good news, the pleasure of a good night's rest, and so on.'

Research into daily hassles

- Kanner *et al.* (1981) performed a study of 100 men and women, aged 45–64 years, over a 12-month period. They confirmed that hassles are correlated with undesirable psychological symptoms and that hassles were a more powerful predictor of illness than life events. For instance, divorce creates stress by a number of hassles, like having to cook for oneself, handling money matters and having to tell people about it. This suggests that daily hassles intervene between critical life events and health, with the collective impact of such irritations proving harmful to health. However, the effect of uplifts was unclear.

- De Longis *et al.* (1988) studied stress in 75 married couples by giving them a life events questionnaire as well as the Hassles and Uplift scales. No relationship was found between life events and health or between uplifts and health, indicating that stress is not related to these factors, although hassles did seem to be associated with next-day health problems.
- Sher (2004) found that daily hassles were associated with increased cortisol levels in healthy individuals. They also found that increased cortisol secretion caused by daily hassles contributes to the development of depressive disorders in vulnerable individuals. This implies that it is increased levels of the stress-hormone cortisol, caused by the stress of daily hassles, which negatively affects health.

You are the researcher

Research into life changes and daily hassles generally uses the correlational method.

Design your own correlation into hassles and illness.

You will need to construct a list of daily hassles, like 'queuing in the cafeteria' or 'arguments with others'. For each hassle you will need to award a daily score, say 4 for extremely irritating, 3 for very irritating, 2 for irritating, 1 for slightly irritating.

Illness could be assessed by days absent.

How many participants will you need?

How long would you have to conduct the study to get sufficient data?

What type of graph would you need to construct to plot your data?

Evaluation

Evaluation of daily hassles

- Research has tended to concentrate on examining whether life changes or daily hassles are the greater contributor to stress-related illness. However, it is probably more valid to consider the mediating effect that the two influences have upon each other. For example, the effects of daily hassles may depend upon the impact that critical life events have had upon a given individual. A person who has recently experienced the death of a loved one may find daily hassles much more negatively impacting than usual.
- A practical application of research into daily hassles is the usefulness of findings and conclusions towards formulating effective stress-management and coping strategies to deal with the ever-rising number of stress-related illnesses.
- What actually constitutes daily hassles is somewhat vague and confusing, especially the difference between daily hassles, like finding a car parking space and chronic, long-term stressors, like lack of finance. This distinction is important, as they may be having totally different effects upon individuals.
- A methodological problem in studying daily hassles is that participants are commonly asked to remember retrospectively hassles they have experienced and this is dependent upon accurate and full recall. A solution to this is to ask participants to keep a diary, where daily hassles and feelings of well-being are recorded on a daily basis.

Contemporary research

Daily hassles reported by chronic fatigue syndrome and chronic organic disease sufferers – Boudewijn van Houdenhove *et al.*, 2002

Chronic fatigue syndrome (CFS), sometimes referred to as post-viral fatigue syndrome, is the collective name for a group of disorders characterised by extreme, persistent fatigue unrelated to exertion. National Health Service figures for 2009 show that there are over 250,000 sufferers in Great Britain. Primarily a recent phenomenon, the researchers were interested in investigating whether the illness was related in some way to the daily hassles of modern life.

Aim: To provide insight into the frequency, emotional impact and nature of daily hassles experienced by patients suffering from CFS compared with patients with a chronic organic disease.

Procedure: 177 CFS patients and 52 patients suffering from the chronic organic diseases rheumatoid arthritis (RA) and multiple sclerosis (MS) were investigated within 2–6 months after diagnosis.

All patients completed self-report questionnaires assessing daily hassles and associated distress, a measurement scale assessing pain and fatigue and a depression and anxiety questionnaire.

Findings: CFS patients showed a higher frequency of hassles, higher emotional impact and higher fatigue, pain, depression and anxiety levels compared with MS/RA patients. Three hassle themes dominated in the CFS group: dissatisfaction with oneself, insecurity and a lack of social recognition. In contrast, hassles reported by MS/RA patients showed a much larger diversity and were not focused on person-dependent problems.

Conclusions: Patients suffering from CFS are highly preoccupied and distressed by daily hassles that have a severe impact on their self-image, as well as their personal, social and professional functioning.

Evaluation:

- The seemingly minor hassles of modern living may actually be contributing to a large number of severe debilitating illnesses, such as CFS.
- Therapeutic approaches to CFS and similar disorders need to take account of, and address, the contribution of daily hassles to the onset and continuation of the illness.

Figure 4.9 Professor Boudewijn van Houdenhove

You are the researcher

The questionnaires used in van Houdenhove's research were ones that were reliable.

Compile your own questionnaire that measures participants' levels of depression and anxiety and then create a method of assessing your questionnaire's *external* reliability.

This would be a sensitive area to investigate. Explain how your research would ensure *confidentiality* and *anonymity*. How else would you ensure your research was conducted in an ethical manner?

If you would like to have a go at a simple test that calculates your personal stress level, go to http://www.texmed.org/Template.aspx?id=4481

Remember, though, this is a bit of fun, not a clinical measurement.

Workplace stress including the effects of workload and control

The modern workplace is a major and ever-increasing source of stress. This can negatively impact upon the health of those in stressful jobs, but also lead to poor performance at work, resulting in decreases in productivity, as well as increases in absenteeism, accidents and high-staff turnover levels. Workplace stressors can have a *direct* impact upon individuals' health and performance, as well as an *indirect* effect through the fostering of unhealthy lifestyles, like heavy drinking. This incurs a high financial cost for industry, and the health services, as well as a major cost in human terms to people's quality of life. The Confederation of British Industry estimates that the cost of absenteeism to industry in 2009 was around £19.9 billion.

Key terms

Workplace stressors – aspects of the work environment which have a negative impact on health

It is, therefore, to everyone's benefit that research should identify the important variables at play, in order to reduce the impact of workplace stress upon individuals and to society as a whole. A non-stressed workforce is a happy and productive workforce; a goal all would like to see achieved.

Major workplace stressors that have been identified include workload, predictability and controllability of work role, environmental factors and role conflict and ambiguity.

Classic research

Stress reactions in highly mechanised work – Geir Johansson *et al.*, 1978

Figure 4.10 A sawmill

The researchers chose the setting of a Swedish sawmill, which employed workers in a range of occupations with varying degrees of responsibility and job repetitiveness, to examine the effect of workplace stressors upon health.

Aim: To assess whether workplace stressors increase physiological arousal and lead to stress-related illnesses.

Procedure: A *high-risk* group of ten finishers, whose jobs involved repetitiveness and high levels of responsibility, was compared with a *low-risk* group of ten cleaners. Stress-related hormones in urine samples were recorded on work days and rest days.

Stress-related illnesses and amount of days absent from work were also recorded.

Findings: The high-risk group of finishers had higher stress hormone levels than the low-risk group of cleaners.

The high-risk group of finishers had higher stress hormone levels on work days than on rest days.

The high-risk group of finishers had more stress-related illnesses and had more days absent from work.

Conclusions: Work stressors, like repetitiveness and high levels of responsibility, create long-term physiological arousal, leading to stress-related illnesses and absenteeism.

Evaluation:

- Which workplace stressors were most stressful was not identified.
- Individual differences were not accounted for. It may be that people more vulnerable to stressors are attracted to demanding jobs with lots of responsibility.
- A practical application is that employers can reduce workforce illness and absenteeism by lessening workplace stressors.

Research into workplace stress

- Russek (1962) gave questionnaires to medical professionals, finding that those in high-stress jobs were more likely to develop cardiovascular diseases (CVDs) than people in low-stress jobs. This suggests a link between stress and heart disease, though it was not shown whether the link was direct or indirect.
- Marmot *et al.* (1997) performed a five-year study of London-based civil servants, using self-reports from questionnaires as well as health screenings for signs of heart disease. They found that employees with low job control were around three times more likely to have heart attacks than those with high job control. This suggests that high job control is desirable in order to reduce the costs of work-related stress disorders. However, Caplan *et al.*'s (1975) research contradicts this, finding that ambitious individuals, like those in Marmot's study, were more strongly affected by workplace stressors. Therefore the results may not be universally generalisable. Also, Marmot's study found no association between high workload and stress-related illnesses, contradicting Johansson's (1978) findings. However, Johansson's study focused on jobs with high levels of responsibility that were demanding in terms of requiring continuous concentration. Therefore Johansson's study may be a more valid measure of high workload.
- Kivimaki *et al.* (2006) performed a meta-analysis of 14 studies involving over 80,000 workers from Europe, Japan and the USA. They found that workers with high levels of job demand were significantly more at risk of developing coronary heart disease. This implies that workplace stressors are related to elevated health risks.
- Hobson and Beach (2000) examined relationships between working hours, perceived work stressors and psychological health in British managers. Managers at two factories completed questionnaires and work diaries. Hours of work were not directly related to psychological health, but were significantly associated with individual perception of work stressors which, in turn, were associated with measures of psychological health. This suggests that perceived workload is more important in determining psychological health than actual workload, implying a cognitive component to stress-related health risks.

Research in focus

Research into workplace stressors generally employs questionnaires, but when the alternative self-report method of interviews is used, different patterns of results are gained, with interviews identifying other stressors not included in questionnaires.

Why, therefore, might interviews be superior? (You may wish to refer to the Evaluation feature box on page 130 for guidance.)

How might this affect the results of research into workplace stressors?

Psychology in action

Quality circles

Originally a Japanese idea, the concept of quality circles was introduced to Britain by the Wedgwood Pottery Company in 1980. Quality circles consist of groups of workers given time away from their jobs to suggest and discuss ideas for improving their work tasks. Workers generally receive a share of any savings or boosts to profits.

Quality circles are an alternative to the dehumanising tradition of workers being treated like robots. They enrich and empower the lives of workers, creating harmony and improved performance in the workplace. Companies using quality circles find workers become happier, less stressed and therefore less prone to absenteeism through stress-related disorders.

From a psychological viewpoint, quality circles lessen workplace stressors by increasing employees' controllability of work role, reducing role conflict and ambiguity and improving environmental conditions, all by putting the emphasis for positive change under employees' control.

Evaluation

Evaluation of workplace stress

- Workplace stressors are not naturally harmful to health. In fact, the workplace can provide heightened opportunities to increase self-esteem, confidence and motivational levels and give individuals a sense of purpose and fulfilment; all factors which can contribute to positive physical and psychological well-being.
- Different research methods have produced different patterns of results. Traditionally questionnaires are used to assess the effects of workplace stressors, but interviews appear to identify other types of important stressors, like interpersonal clashes. It may be that questionnaires, by their very nature, are limiting the stressors respondents can comment on and interviews are superior, as they give a wider scope to report on individual experiences.
- Research into workplace stressors does not account for individual differences. Different people may experience the same stressors in different ways and in varying amounts. This may be related to each individual's perceived ability to cope with stressors, with those high in 'hardiness' more able to cope. (See Psychological methods of stress management, page 145.)
- The findings and conclusions drawn from studies of workplace stressors may be quickly redundant, owing to the ever-changing demands of the workplace and its associated stressors. For instance, the increasing use of technology, lower job security and changing job practices place completely new demands upon employees that previous research does not reflect.

Strengthen your learning

1. What is the difference between life changes and daily hassles?
2. a) What is the Social Readjustment Rating Scale?
   b) Holmes and Rahe found that people with higher LCU scores for the preceding year were more likely to experience what?
   c) Give two evaluative points of the SRRS.
   d) Outline two other pieces of research supporting the idea of a link between life events and stress-related illness.
3. a) Why might daily hassles be a better indicator of health than life events?
   b) Outline two pieces of research investigating the relationship between hassles and health.
   c) Give two evaluative points of daily hassles.
4. a) What are workplace stressors?
   b) Outline two pieces of research suggesting that workplace stressors are related to stress-related illnesses.
   c) Give two evaluative points concerning workplace stressors.
5. How might quality circles reduce stress levels?

Assessment Check

1 Copy and complete the following table by placing a letter W next to three of the following descriptions that concern factors in the workplace which can lead to stress-related illness. [3 marks]

Factors	Letter
Working long hours	
Being a high-grade employee	
Having a high degree of control over the demands of your job	
Being set achievable targets	
Having a repetitive job	
Working flexible hours	

2 Explain how life changes can be a source of stress in everyday life. [4 marks]

3 Research into life changes as a source of stress has tended to use correlational analysis.
   a) Explain what is meant by a correlational analysis. [2 marks]
   b) Explain one disadvantage of conducting a correlational analysis of life changes as a source of stress. [2 marks]

4 Spencer works in a factory. Recently he has been exhibiting symptoms of stress-related illness. His doctor believes that certain features of Spencer's workplace are contributing to his illness. Outline three factors of workplace stress that could be contributing to Spencer's stress-related illness. [2 + 2 + 2 marks]

5 Explain the relationship between daily hassles and stress. [4 marks]

6 Discuss how workplace factors may affect stress. [12 marks]

Examination guidance:

1 The first question is a selection question where you choose from the options available. This means the answers are there, but you must identify and place the correct letters in the boxes.

2 This question requires sufficient description of how life changes can be a source of stress in everyday life to gain four marks. This could be achieved by making several brief points or fewer, more detailed points.

3 This question requires knowledge of research methods, namely correlations, and the application of this knowledge to life changes as a source of stress.

4 Question four specifically asks for three factors. Giving fewer than three, even if detailed, will reduce access to the marks available and giving more will not earn extra credit.

5 This focuses specifically on daily hassles, so be careful not to offer material on life changes, as this would not be creditworthy.

6 In question six the command word 'discuss' means to describe and evaluate, with six marks available for describing how workplace factors affect stress and six marks available for an evaluation.

Personality factors

Personality is made up of characteristics, or traits, which give individuals unique identities, making them different from others. Research has shown that individual differences in the ways people perceive and respond to stressors are attributable in some part to differences in personality.

Psychologists refer to personality types, broad characterisations describing categories of people sharing similar characteristics. Much research into stress focuses on people categorised as having Type A personality, though other important stress-related personality types have also been identified and investigated.

Type A and type B personality

Friedman and Rosenman (1959) wanted to find evidence for the role of non-physiological factors in coronary heart disease (CHD). In particular the role of individual differences in the ways men deal with stressful situations (women had been found to be less vulnerable). They discovered that a certain pattern of

Key terms

Personality types – broad characterisations describing categories of people sharing similar characteristics

Type A personality – personality type characterised by time urgency, excessive competitiveness and generalised hostility, incurring risk of heart disease

Characteristic	Description
Time urgent	Does several things at once Constantly sets deadlines Has low boredom threshold
Excessive competitiveness	Achievement orientated Aggressive
Generalised hostility	Easily irritated/provoked Volatile Displays self-anger

Table 4.2 The key characteristics of people with Type A personality

behaviour, Type A, was linked to an increased risk of developing heart disease. The key characteristics of this type are given in Table 4.2.

Other traits include insecurity about status and a need to be admired by their peers in order to feel good about themselves.

The researchers simultaneously described the Type B personality. Type B men were described as having the same degree of ambition, but in a steady, non-competitive manner and being much more self-confident, relaxed and easy-going, not driven to achieve perfection and much less hostile. In essence, Type B man is the direct opposite of Type A.

Key terms

Type B personality – healthy personality type characterised by non-competitiveness, self-confidence and relaxation

If you want to know whether you have a tendency towards Type A personality, take the simple on-line test found at http://stress.about.com/lr/personality_tests/340468/2/

There are plenty of other personality tests here too, along with some tips for stress management. Remember, though, that these tests are just a bit of fun and do not form a clinical diagnosis.

Research into Type A personality

- Friedman and Rosenman (1974) assessed the personality types of over 3,500 healthy middle-aged men as part of a 12-year longitudinal study. Participants were asked questions relating to impatience, competitiveness, motivation for success, frustration at goals being hindered and their feelings towards being under pressure. High scorers were described as 'Type A' personalities while low scorers were described as 'Type B' personalities. More than twice as many of the Type A personalities developed cardiovascular disorders than did Type B personalities. This suggests that personality traits are a risk factor in developing stress-related illness and that psychological factors can have physiological effects, through the harmful physical effects of stressors being mediated through psychological personality factors. Therefore stressors are not harmful in themselves: it is how people perceive and react to them that is potentially dangerous for health.
- Hayes (2000) examined specific components and behaviours of the Type A personality, finding certain characteristics correlated more, or less, with specific forms of cardiovascular disorder. For example, angina sufferers were composed of Type A personalities who were impatient with other people and susceptible to feeling pressure at work, while those with heart failure tended to comprise Type A personalities with hasty personal habits and schedules. This suggests that it is particular traits of the Type A personality, rather than the personality type itself, which are related to specific heart conditions.
- Matthews and Haynes (1986) found that coronary heart disease was most associated with the hostility trait of Type A men, especially those who do not express their high levels of hostility.
- Forshaw (2002) also reported that the Type A characteristic of hostility was the best single predictor of CHD and a better predictor than Type A personality as a whole. This suggests that it is the specific trait of hostility, rather than Type A personality, which increases the risk of developing stress-related illness, though it does not mean that hostility causes CHD, just as we could not claim that a Type A personality did.

Evaluation

Evaluation of Type A personality

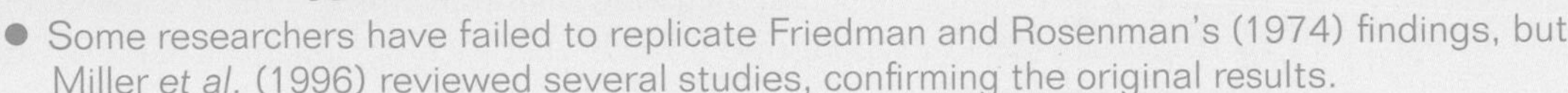

- Some researchers have failed to replicate Friedman and Rosenman's (1974) findings, but Miller *et al.* (1996) reviewed several studies, confirming the original results.
- Not all aspects of lifestyle were controlled in Friedman and Rosenman's study, so it may be other factors such as hardiness (see page 148) which affect vulnerability to heart disease.
- While Type A men are more at risk of developing CHD, the risk is only relative: the vast majority of Type As do not develop CHD, while many Type Bs do.
- Ragland and Brand (1988) found that 15 per cent of Friedman and Rosenman's original sample had died of CHD, with age, high blood pressure and smoking proving to be significant factors, but little evidence of Type A personality being a risk factor. This suggests the original conclusions are unsupported.
- The Type A personality is too broad a description and it is more useful to think in terms of specific personality traits as stress-related risk factors.

Research in focus

Many **replications** of Friedman and Rosenman's (1974) study have taken place.

Explain a) what a replication is and b) what the purpose of carrying one out is.

What features of how practical research is written up ensure that replications can take place?

Hardiness and other personality types

Apart from the identification of and research into Type A personality, other stress-related personality types have also been proposed and investigated. Friedman and Rosenman classified Type B personality as well as Type A, but this type was basically just the opposite of Type A.

Subsequent research has made the case for Type C personalities, Type D personalities and hardy personalities. As well as being a personality type hardiness is taught as a means of stress management. See page 148 for a more detailed look at hardiness.

Research into other personality types

- Kobasa (1979) proposed the hardy personality type. A hardy personality has *control* over their life, is *committed* to what they are doing and perceives stressors as enjoyable *challenges* to be mastered leading to self-improvement. Having such a personality results in lowered physiological arousal when in the presence of stressors, leading to a reduction in stress-related disorders. (See Stress management, psychological methods, page 145.)
- Morris *et al.* (1981) found that Type C women, who are pleasant, conventional, caring and helpful to others, often repress their emotions when stressed and are more likely to develop cancer. This was believed to be due to emotional suppression leading to a lowering of the immune system's effectiveness. This was supported by Greer and Morris's earlier (1975) finding that women diagnosed with breast cancer showed significantly more emotional suppression than those with non-life-threatening breast disease.

Key terms

Type C personality – personality type characterised by suppression of negative emotions, incurring risk of cancer

Type D personality – personality type characterised by distress, gloom, worry and lack of sociability, incurring risk of heart attacks

- Temoshok (1987) also found that Type C personalities were cancer prone, with such individuals having difficulty expressing emotion and suppressing or inhibiting emotions, especially negative ones like anger. This was backed up by Weinman (1995), who found it likely that such personality characteristics influenced the progression of cancer and the patient's survival time.
- Denollet *et al.* (1996) proposed the Type D personality as a 'distressed personality' characterised by worry, irritability, gloom and lack of sociability. Such individuals have the tendency to experience increased negative emotions and do not share these feelings with others, due to a fear of rejection or disapproval. Such people are more at risk of heart attacks, with up to 53 per cent of cardiac patients displaying this personality type. This was supported by Denollet *et al.* (1998) who found Type D associated with a four-fold increased risk of sudden cardiac death, independent of traditional risk factors, like heavy smoking.

Evaluation of personality types

- The studies into Type C women might be considered unethical, as they may cause further distress to seriously ill women. However, the findings could be used to formulate effective strategies to reduce the chances of Type C women developing harmful tumours.
- Chesney and Rosenman (1980) found that *control* was an important factor which interacted with personality type to determine responses to stressors. Type A managers experienced greater anxiety when they were not in control, while other managers experienced greater anxiety when they were in control. The issue of perception of control in moderating stress outcomes may be an important one worthy of further research.
- There is no real evidence that people divide easily into separate personality types. Individuals may have elements of many of these characteristics and indeed labelling people could lead to **self-fulfilling prophecies**, where individuals adopt the characteristics ascribed to the label put upon them.
- If aspects of such a personality are learnable, then teaching people hardiness could form an effective stress-management technique (see page 148). However, it may be that hardiness does not exist and it is negativity, not lack of hardiness, that leads to stressful experiences.

Key terms

Hardiness – healthy personality type characterised by control, commitment and self-improvement

Coping strategies – methods of adapting to stress involving cognitive and behavioural efforts to meet external and/or internal demands

Coping with stress

One form of stress management is what individuals do, spontaneously and often unconsciously, on a day-to-day basis to deal with stress. A major way of achieving this is through coping strategies. These are methods of adapting to stress in positive

Research in focus

The research carried out into Type C women (see above) might be considered unethical, as it may cause additional distress to women already ill with cancer. However, such research might be considered ethical by reference to a **cost–benefit analysis**.

Explain what is meant by a cost–benefit analysis and how it might be applied in this instance.

and constructive ways, involving cognitive and behavioural efforts to meet external and/or internal demands, which stretch our capacities and resources.

Roth and Cohen (1986) found that some people confront stressors in a direct fashion, this is **approach coping**, while others address stressors by finding ways of avoiding thinking about them or by reducing their importance, this is **avoidant coping**.

Approach coping works best with long-term stressors, while avoidant coping works better with short-term stressors. However, most people appear to use just one coping style, regardless of the type of stressor being faced.

A different approach was proposed by Folkman and Lazarus (1980), who identified two general styles of strategy used to cope with stressful events: emotion-focused strategies and problem-focused strategies.

Key terms

Emotion-focused strategies – methods of coping that make individuals feel positive about stressful situations

Problem-focused strategies – methods of coping that directly confront negative effects of stress

Emotion-focused strategies

Emotion-focused strategies aim to reduce the negative effects of stressors by making an individual feel positive about stressful situations. Such strategies include:

- looking for distractions
- preparing oneself for the worst possible outcome
- keeping active to avoid thinking about the stressor
- denying that the situation exists or is a problem
- distancing oneself from the problem
- altering the way a problem is perceived, for example seeing the humour in the situation.

Some emotion-focused strategies are positive ones, like perceiving stressful situations as opportunities for self-improvement, while other emotion-focused strategies are negative ones, like denying the stressful situation exists.

Problem-focused strategies

Problem-focused strategies reduce the negative effects of stressors by confronting them directly. Such strategies focus on dealing with the causes of stressful situations. This can be achieved by searching out information on the problem and learning new skills to manage it.

For example, using knowledge gained from previous experience to address stressors, getting advice from experienced others or creating alternative methods of addressing stressors.

There are three commonly used problem-focused strategies:

- Excluding other activities – not turning to alternative activities to put off dealing with stressful situations. For example, not going out with friends in order to put off revising for an exam.
- Being in control – taking personal charge/responsibility for stressful situations. For example, using the internet to research details of a dangerous illness.
- Assessing positives and negatives – weighing up the strengths and weaknesses of each possible means of dealing with stressful situations.

Research into coping strategies

- Desmond (2007) found that males using problem-focused strategies to deal with the stress of having a limb amputated fared better than those using emotion-focused strategies, suggesting problem-focused strategies to be superior.
- Epping-Jordan *et al.* (1994) reported that cancer sufferers who used problem-focused strategies maintained physical health better and for longer than those using emotion-focused strategies. This again suggests that problem-focused strategies are more efficient in helping people to cope with stressful situations.
- De Boer *et al.* (1999) found, however, that utilising emotional social support helped patients cope with cancer. This suggests that both forms of coping strategies are useful for those battling against the effects of cancer.
- Toda *et al.* (2007) found that stress levels decreased in people who viewed humorous films, suggesting that emotionally uplifting experiences and activities alone help to alleviate stressful symptoms.
- Rukholm and Viverais (1993) found that with stressors that people perceive as threatening, emotion-focused strategies are superior in addressing the anxiety caused by such stressors. However, when the resultant anxiety had been addressed, then problem-focused strategies could be utilised successfully. This implies that both types of coping strategy can be used in conjunction with each other to form a successful overall strategy.

Evaluation

Evaluation of coping strategies

- People tend to use both emotion-focused and problem-focused strategies, either collectively or individually, to address stressful situations. The type of stressful situation being faced and previous experiences of using different coping strategies will influence which type of coping strategy will be used by a given individual.
- In general, problem-focused strategies are superior, as they deal directly with the cause of the problem by attempting to remove the stressor. They also have less of a negative impact on health.
- Gender differences have been found in that women tend to use emotion-focused strategies more, though this may be because females are more able to do so, as they are socialised to express their emotions more openly and are therefore able to make more use of social support networks than men.
- Social support networks help to provide emotion-focused strategies, for example using the support of others to uplift emotions.
- Social support strategies also provide problem-focused strategies, like using knowledge from experienced others to address stressors.
- Sometimes problem-focused strategies cannot be used because they are inappropriate. For example, only emotion-focused strategies can deal with the negative emotional impact of the end of a romantic relationship.
- It is also not possible to use problem-focused strategies in situations where stressors cannot be eradicated, like having a terminal illness.

Figure 4.11 Social support networks can provide emotion- and problem-focused coping strategies and are more used by females

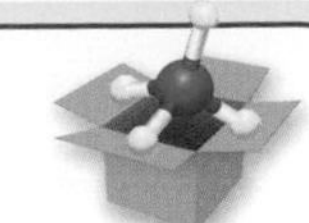

Contemporary research

Differences between males and females in use of cognitive emotion strategies against depression – Nadia Garnefski *et al.*, 2004

There is a higher incidence of stress-related depression in women than men. This could be because more females report and seek help for the condition, or women may be biologically more vulnerable or suffer more negative life events. However, another possibility is that the high rates of depression in women are due to their use of less-effective emotion-focused strategies.

Aim: a) To focus on the comparability of males and females in the extent to which they use specific cognitive emotion regulation strategies in response to the experience of life stress.

b) The extent to which the use of these strategies is related to the reporting of depressive symptoms.

Procedure: A volunteer sample of 251 males and 379 females ranging in age from 18 to 71 years of age was used. These were respondents to a direct mailing request, with addresses taken from the population of a doctor's general practice.

Participants filled out the Cognitive Emotion Regulation Questionnaire, which assesses what individuals think after experiencing threatening or stressful life events. The scale measures nine cognitive emotion regulation strategies:

1 **Self blame** – thoughts of putting the blame of what has been experienced onto oneself.
2 **Other blame** – thoughts of putting the blame of what has been experienced onto the environment or other people.
3 **Acceptance** – thoughts of accepting what has been experienced and resigning oneself to what has happened.
4 **Refocus on planning** – thoughts of what steps to take and how to handle the negative event.
5 **Positive refocusing** – thinking about joyful and pleasant issues instead of the actual event.
6 **Rumination** – thinking about thoughts and feelings associated with the negative event.
7 **Positive reappraisal** – thoughts of creating positive meaning to the event in terms of personal growth.
8 **Putting into perspective** – thoughts of diminishing the event in terms of comparison to other events.
9 **Catastrophising** – thoughts of emphasising the terror of what you have experienced.

Participants' depressive symptoms were also measured by use of the SCL 16-item scale depression questionnaire and a check list was used to collect data on the experience of negative life events, such as divorce, physical/mental illness, death of loved ones and so on.

Findings: In both males and females rumination, catastrophising and self-blame were strongly related to higher depression scores. Females used significantly more rumination and catastrophising strategies than males.

Conclusions: Certain emotion-focused coping strategies are maladaptive (harmful) in relation to depression – namely rumination, catastrophising and self-blame. The higher incidence of depression in females is not directly linked to gender, but instead to the use of different emotion-focused strategies by males and females. Women use more maladaptive emotion-focused strategies than men, suggesting that the higher incidence of depression in females is linked to their less effective ways of coping.

Evaluation:

- The findings suggest a practical application in that treatments should be focused on challenging maladaptive strategies like self-blame and encouraging more positive, beneficial strategies, like positive refocusing.
- The findings are based on self-report measures that may be prone to bias and therefore need validating by alternative methodologies.
- 2,029 people were approached to participate, of which 630 accepted (31 per cent). The sample may therefore be biased, for instance more severely depressed people may have been less willing to participate.

You are the researcher

Design a semi-structured interview assessing the types of coping strategies different sorts of people use (see page 134 for guidance).

What *sorts* of people would you interview?

How many of each sort would be required for a *representative* sample?

How would you go about getting a *self-selected* sample?

The success of such an interview would depend on the quality of your questions. Write some appropriate questions to ask.

In what way would this method be superior to a structured interview?

Strengthen your learning

1 Describe an individual with Type A personality.

2 What evidence is there that Type A personality is linked to stress-related illnesses?

3 Describe the following personality types:
   a) Type B
   b) Type C
   c) Type D
   d) Hardy personality
   and comment on their relationship to stress-related illnesses.

4 a) What are emotion-focused coping strategies?
   b) What are problem-focused coping strategies?
   c) Is there a best type of coping strategy?

Assessment Check

1 Paul's long-term girlfriend has just unexpectedly left him. Copy and complete the table below, putting a letter E in the box beside each emotion-focused coping strategy and a letter P next to each problem-focused strategy that Paul might employ. [6 marks]

2 Describe the features of someone with a Type A personality. [3 marks]

3 Explain how problem-focused coping strategies differ from emotion-focused ones. [4 marks]

4 Christian and Steve are finding preparing for their karate grading stressful. Christian has prepared a rigorous training schedule with plenty of rest periods. He also reads lots of recommended books on training methods.
Steve has left his preparation to the day before the grading. He has been argumentative with anyone who asks how his preparation is going and spends lots of time chatting on the phone trying to get friends to reassure him that everything will be okay.
Making reference to the information above, outline the differences between problem-focused and emotion-focused approaches to coping with stress. [6 marks]

5 Outline and evaluate how personality factors affect the ways people react differently to stress. [12 marks]

Strategy	Letter
Weeping	
Registering with a dating agency	
Writing sad poetry	
Sending his ex-girlfriend a spiteful letter	
Phoning his ex-girlfriend and begging her to have him back	
Deciding the relationship was going nowhere anyway	

continued ...

...continued

Examination guidance:

1 The first question is a selection question where you choose from the options available. This means the answers are there, but you must identify and place the correct letters in the boxes.
2 This question specifically requires a description of Type A personality. Any description of other personality types or evaluative material would not gain credit.
3 The easiest way to answer the third question is to demonstrate two ways in which problem-focused and emotion-focused strategies differ and provide brief, relevant elaboration of each point.
4 This is a scenario or stem question, requiring reference to information in the scenario to gain marks.
5 This is a long-answer question, with six marks available for outlining how personality factors affect the ways people react to stress and six marks for evaluation. Suitable evaluation could make use of relevant research evidence.

IN THE NEWS

Golf: O'Grady says players use beta-blockers. Drugs 'helped win majors'

Figure 4.12

According to Mac O'Grady, former US tour professional, at least seven of the world's top golfers take beta-blockers.

'You see these guys meandering around for years doing nothing and all of a sudden they're making all the putts and winning tournaments.'

O'Grady said he used beta-blockers for 6 months in 1985 and they helped his putting. 'The use of the drug is unethical; they give players an unfair advantage.'

Making or missing a putt can be measured, not just in terms of feet and inches, but in thousands of pounds. The pressure can lead to the dreaded 'yips', a manifestation of nerves, most spectacularly suffered by Bernhard Langer, former US Masters champion, who was physically unable to putt.

Top golfers Sam Torrance and Nick Price both admit to using the drug in the past.

Source: adapted from Tim Glover's article in the *Independent*, 6 April 1994. Copyright the *Independent*.

Beta-blockers are often used in precision sports, like archery and snooker, as they steady nervous twitches, thus improving accuracy. They reduce the heart rate, helping the players to remain focused and in control. Indeed Swedish sports scientists estimate that they improve performance in pistol shooting by up to 13 per cent. However, aside from the risk of serious negative health effects, many view their use as cheating. Indeed the International Olympic Committee has banned them, but golf, regarded by many as a 'gentlemanly' sport, does not have drug testing.

Stress management

Key terms

Stress management – physiological and psychological methods of reducing the negative effects of stress

Benzodiazepines – anti-anxiety drugs that dampen down the activity of the nervous system, creating a sensation of calm and relaxation

Beta-blockers – anti-anxiety drugs that block the transmission of nerve impulses, to reduce heart rate and alleviate the physical effects of stress

There are two general categories of stress management: *biological* methods, including drug therapy and biofeedback and *psychological* methods, including stress inoculation training (SIT) and hardiness training.

Biological methods of stress management

Biological methods are designed to focus directly on biological stress-response systems, such as hormones and the autonomic nervous system (see The body's response to stress, page 116). Being from the biological or medical model, methods directly address symptoms, as they are perceived as the causes of stress, rather than any underlying psychological factors.

Drug therapy

Drugs are generally taken in tablet form. They enter the bloodstream to reach the brain and affect the transmission of chemicals in the nervous system called **neurotransmitters** which facilitate communication between **neurons** (brain nerve cells). Drug treatment is therefore a very direct way of treating stress.

Anti-anxiety drugs are generally used to combat stress, slowing down the activity of the central nervous system and thus suppressing the physical symptoms of anxiety. They are often used as a starting point to address stress-related conditions, with psychological methods being added later on, when drugs have reduced symptoms sufficiently for psychological methods to have a positive impact.

Two of the most commonly used anti-anxiety drugs are the benzodiazepines and beta-blockers.

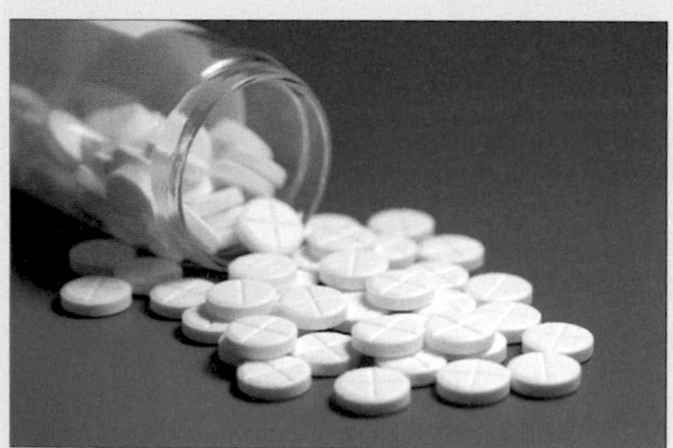

Figure 4.13 Valium is a benzodiazepine and is the world's most prescribed drug

Benzodiazepines (BZs), like Valium and Librium, work by increasing the effect of the neurotransmitter **GABA** which has a dampening, or quietening, effect on many neurons of the brain. GABA works by allowing an increase of chloride ions into the neurons, making it more difficult for other neurotransmitters to stimulate them. The net result is the slowing down of neural activity, creating a sensation of calm and relaxation. The effect of BZs is to permit an even greater increase of chloride ions, boosting GABA's soothing effect. BZs also dampen down the excitatory effect of the neurotransmitter **serotonin**, therefore further slowing down the activity of the nervous system and adding to the feeling of serenity.

BZs are recommended for short-term use only, due to possible side effects such as dependency, cognitive impairment and unsteadiness. They are a popular course of treatment, with over 2 million people treated with them in Britain alone.

Research into benzodiazepines

- Havoundjian *et al.* (1986) induced stress in rats by getting them to swim. They found that the stress resulted in rapid increases in the amount of chloride ions in the benzodiazepine–GABA receptor complex in the cerebral cortical membranes, thus demonstrating the mechanisms by which acute stress operates. Such changes represent the compensatory response of an organism to stress-provoking changes in the environment and it is this response that BZ drugs have a moderating effect upon.
- Zandstra *et al.* (2004) studied 164 short-term and 158 long-term users of BZs and found that it was older, less well-educated, lonely patients who tended to use avoidant-coping strategies to deal with stress, who were more likely to be long-term users. As long-term BZ usage is not seen as desirable, the findings suggest that patients with these characteristics should be treated with alternatives in the short-term or be closely monitored if BZs are prescribed.
- Davidson (1993) performed an assessment of BZ usage as a treatment for 75 patients diagnosed with social-anxiety disorder. Patients were randomly assigned to either the drug or placebo treatment (a 'dummy' treatment with no clinical effect) for 10 weeks and drug treatment was found to have an early and sustained positive effect, with 78 per cent of patients improving, compared to only 20 per cent of placebo patients. Many drug-treatment patients did report the side effect of unsteadiness, with some forgetfulness and loss of concentration. A two-year follow-up study found a significant advantage in function among those treated with BZ drugs than a placebo, suggesting BZs to be effective in the short- and long term.

Evaluation

Evaluation of benzodiazepines

- BZs, as with most drugs, are easy to take, cost-effective and popular with patients due to the familiarity of taking pills for a multitude of uses.
- BZs were first introduced to counteract high addiction rates in patients taking barbiturates. However, over time it became apparent that BZs too are addictive, even at low doses, with patients showing noticeable withdrawal symptoms when treatment ceased. The recommendation is that treatment with BZs should not exceed four weeks. However, there continues to be a sizeable minority of patients using BZs in a long-term fashion, with the resultant risks of addiction.
- BZs are only recommended as a short-term treatment, not just because of addiction risks, but also because the brain develops a tolerance, giving them only a brief effectiveness.
- A minority of patients taking BZs experience side effects. However, these can be quite debilitating and include unsteadiness and cognitive impairments, especially impairment of long-term memory and lapses in concentration. Some patients have even become aggressive and/or experienced sexual dysfunction. This can reduce the effectiveness of treatment, as patients experiencing side effects may stop taking the drugs before symptom reduction is achieved.

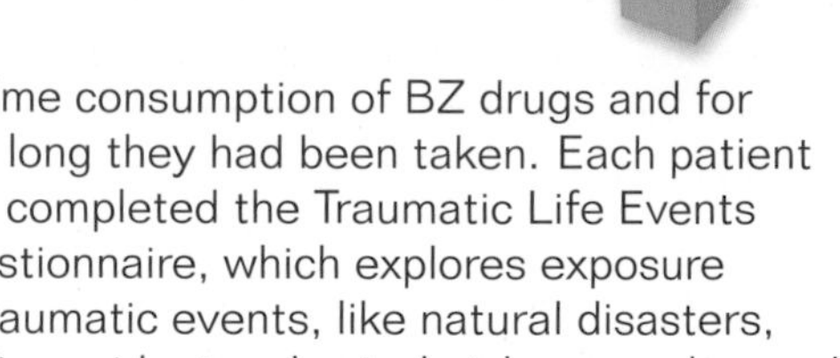

Contemporary research

Benzodiazepine exposure and history of trauma – Dr Randy Sansone *et al.*, 2003

In recent years medical practitioners have become concerned about patient abuse of BZ drugs. In this study, the researchers were interested in the use of BZs to 'blot out' painful memories, as there was evidence that BZ abuse was common among army veterans with post-traumatic stress disorder. The interesting conclusion that the researchers reached was that BZs might have a cognitive component protecting against the long-term effects of severe emotional trauma. However, there is the danger that long-term usage could lead to cognitive impairment.

Figure 4.14 Dr Randy Sansone

Aim: To investigate a possible relationship between benzodiazepine use and trauma.

Procedure: An opportunity sample of 40 female and 13 male participants aged between 20 and 82 years of age, who were being treated with BZ drugs for trauma, agreed to participate. Each patient completed a research booklet, recording lifetime consumption of BZ drugs and for how long they had been taken. Each patient also completed the Traumatic Life Events Questionnaire, which explores exposure to traumatic events, like natural disasters, traffic accidents, physical violence and sexual abuse. For each event recorded, participants had to record measures of fear, helplessness and horror.

Findings: The strongest positive correlation was found between the amount of BZ drugs taken and the number of *different* traumatic experiences, but there were also significant positive correlations found between the *number* of traumatic experiences and the amount of BZ drugs taken and the number of traumatic experiences associated with fear, helplessness and horror and the amount of BZ drugs taken.

Conclusions: The degree of benzodiazepine use is related to the amount and degree of trauma experienced. The cognitive characteristics of benzodiazepines offer protection against re-experiencing traumas that were particularly emotionally intense.

Evaluation:

- The data are correlational and therefore do not indicate a causal relationship. An alternative interpretation of the research might be that the data indicate doctors' willingness to prescribe BZ drugs according to the amount and severity of traumatic experiences encountered by patients.
- Amount and duration of BZ usage was recorded by patients' responses to a questionnaire, which is dependent on full and accurate recall.

Research in focus

Sansone *et al.*'s (2003) study gained data from questionnaires.

Explain why such data are vulnerable to:

a) demand characteristics

b) socially desirable answers.

What strategies do psychologists employ to try to reduce these effects? (For guidance, see Chapter 3, Research methods page 99.)

Beta-blockers (BBs) work by blocking the transmission of nerve impulses. Some nerve endings, when stimulated, release the neurotransmitter noradrenaline, which activates **beta-adrenergic receptors**, tiny structures occurring on cells in various body parts, including the heart, brain and blood vessels. One effect of this is an increase in the force and the rate of the heartbeat. Beta-adrenergic receptors are also stimulated by the hormone adrenaline which is released into the bloodstream from the adrenal glands in increased amounts when an individual is frightened or anxious, also resulting in an increased heart rate.

Beta-blockers 'sit' on beta-adrenergic receptors, thus blocking them from being stimulated. As a result, the force and rate of an individual's heartbeat are reduced, thus dampening down the physical effects of anxiety.

Research into beta-blockers

- Lau *et al.* (1992) performed a meta-analysis of studies assessing the effectiveness of beta-blockers, finding them effective in reducing high blood pressure. They were found to reduce the risk of death by 20 per cent in patients with heart disease, suggesting that they are a lifesaver in some instances.
- Lindholm *et al.* (2005) used data from 13 randomised trials involving 105,000 participants to compare the effectiveness of beta-blockers against other anti-hypertension drugs. They found that the risk of strokes was 16 per cent higher with beta-blockers. There was no difference between the drugs in relation to heart problems and beta-blockers alone reduced the risk of strokes by 19 per cent compared to no treatment at all. This suggests that beta-blockers are effective in treating heart complaints and reducing the risk of strokes, but that there are superior treatments for the prevention of strokes.
- Gates (1985) tested the effectiveness of beta-blockers against stage fright in musicians. Thirty-four singing students were given different amounts of the beta-blocker Nadolol or a placebo during end-of-term examinations. Low doses were found to improve performance minimally, while high doses hindered performance significantly. This research, therefore, does not offer much support for the use of beta-blockers in addressing performance anxiety.

Evaluation

Evaluation of beta-blockers

- Beta-blockers have an immediate effect, acting directly on the body to reduce heart rate and blood pressure. Therefore they can be seen as being a desirable treatment against possible fatal cases of stress-related hypertension.
- Unlike BZs, beta-blockers are not associated with dependency and addiction problems, but they can have serious side effects, like cold extremities, tiredness, nightmares and hallucinations.
- Beta-blockers have a purely physical action and are therefore more useful as an immediate, short-term treatment. They are not effective as a long-term treatment for stress conditions with more of a psychological element to them.
- Like many drug therapies, beta-blockers do not address the cause of a problem, merely its symptoms. Therefore the medication may only 'mask' effects and once treatment ends, symptoms return, suggesting drug treatments cannot be seen as a cure.

Supplementary learning

Biofeedback

Biofeedback provides a lasting remedy for harmful stressors by bringing involuntary behaviours into the conscious arena, with a view to assisting patients to develop personal control over their physiological activities.

Patients are attached to a machine which gives visual or auditory feedback about physiological activity, for instance whether heart rate is at the desired level.

Patients are also taught relaxation techniques that help to dampen the physical effects of stress and bring them under personal control.

Relaxation helps patients to achieve targets, like reducing muscle tension. This reinforces the behaviour making it likely to reoccur. This type of operant conditioning requires no conscious thinking to be learned.

Figure 4.15 Biofeedback uses relaxation techniques to combat the physical effects of stress

The patient then transfers these new skills to real-life situations.

Evaluation:

- Biofeedback has been used to successfully address a variety of physical disorders.
- Budzynski *et al.* (1973) found that biofeedback helps to counteract chronic muscle-contraction headaches.
- Curtis (2000) used biofeedback to address the constriction of blood flow to toes and fingers caused by Raynaud's disease.
- Biofeedback is not invasive and has no negative side effects.
- Relaxation strategies learnt can be continually applied in stressful situations.
- Attanasio *et al.* (1985) found that biofeedback works best with children. Children are more willing and try harder to achieve success.
- It is not fully understood how biofeedback works and it may be that its success is due to learning to relax, which leads to alleviation of stress symptoms, or it may be that patients acquire a greater sense of perceived control, which lowers stress levels.
- The treatment is relatively expensive, requiring specialist equipment and supervision. If the success of biofeedback is indeed due to relaxation, then such specialist equipment and supervision are unnecessary.

Psychology in action

Eustress

Most people think of stress in a negative sense, as something that irritates and aggrieves and which, in its worst forms, can make us dangerously ill. However, there is **eustress**, or good stress, which is the stuff of personal growth and development. You cannot get better, stronger, smarter, faster or more loving without it. Eustress is any stress that you are subjected to that causes positive adaptations.

First proposed by Hans Seyle in 1975, eustress is controlled stress which results in a top performance at high-stress activities, like giving a speech or a sports performance. Eustress stems from the challenge of taking part in something enjoyable and difficult to attain. It pumps you up, providing a healthy spark for any task undertaken. From a biological point of view it has been found that engaging in mildly stressful activities increases the levels of sigA, an antibody that improves the ability of the immune system to resist infection.

continued ...

...continued

Eustress is a form of self-stress management, attainable by anyone who assumes control of their life, takes on and relishes challenges and achieves and maintains a balance between life activities.

In essence it is a way of turning stress into a positive experience, where threats become challenges to be enjoyed.

Figure 4.16

Psychological methods of stress management

Psychological methods aim to identify and rectify underlying causes of stress-related disorders with the focus being on how individuals manage their perception of stress.

Psychological methods are drawn from different psychological approaches, with each method reflecting how different approaches perceive the causes of stress-related disorders.

Cognitive behavioural therapy

Cognitive behavioural therapy (CBT) is based on the cognitive approach, which sees stress-related disorders as resulting from irrational, maladaptive thought processes. The central idea behind CBT is that these irrational processes are replaced with rational, adaptive thought processes.

CBT is an umbrella term for a number of different therapies. For a more detailed view of these therapies and the cognitive approach upon which they are based, see Chapter 6, Cognitive therapies section, page 216.

Stress inoculation therapy

A major example of CBT that applies specifically to stress-related disorders is Meichenbaum's (1977) stress inoculation therapy (SIT), which has the central idea of applying the therapy before the stress-related disorders actually occur.

SIT is a form of **cognitive restructuring**. This term refers to various methods of changing the way people think about themselves and their lives, aimed at changing their emotional responses and behaviour. SIT is an attempt to reduce stress through changing cognitions. It assumes that people sometimes find things stressful because they think about them in **catastrophising ways** – they misperceive them in a way that makes them seem more threatening and distressing than they really are.

SIT is a cognitive behavioural method of stress management. The cognitive part involves individuals being trained to *recognise* stress symptoms and the behavioural part involves the use of certain skills to *act* upon the causes of stress.

Key terms

Cognitive behavioural therapy – psychological means of stress management based on replacing irrational, maladaptive thought processes with rational, adaptive ones

Stress inoculation treatment – type of cognitive behavioural therapy that cognitively restructures emotional and behavioural responses

SIT can be compared to the idea of a biological immunisation, in which a small, harmless dose of the infectious disease is given as a vaccine, which wards off any later infection the individual is exposed to. So, SIT is a way of enabling an individual to become resistant to a stressor by exposing them to a small 'dose' of it. In other words, the individual has an appropriate previous experience with the stressor. As Orne (1965) put it: 'If an individual is given the opportunity to deal with a stimulus that's mildly stressful and is able to do so successfully, by mastering it in a psychological sense, they'll be able to tolerate a similar stimulus of greater intensity in the future.'

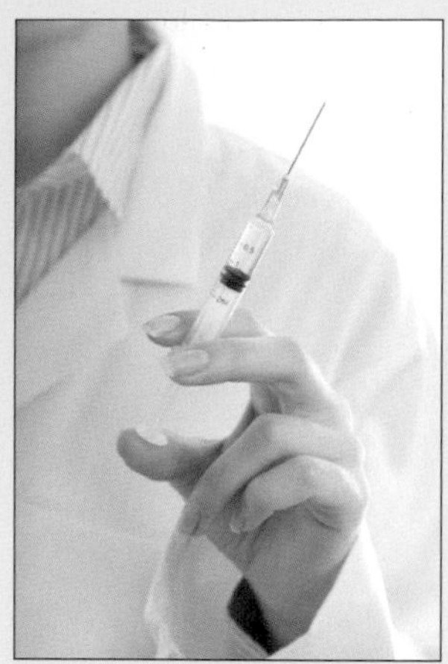

Figure 4.17 SIT works by 'vaccinating' people against stress

SIT has been employed successfully in the treatment of acute, short-term stressors like medical examinations, chronic long-term intermittent stressors like recurrent headaches, chronic long-term continual stressors like medical illnesses, as well as anger control.

SIT aims to restructure the way a person thinks. It has three phases:

1 **Assessment** – where the patient and therapist discuss the problem and consider how to deal with it by reducing it into individual components. The therapist explores with the patient how they think about and deal with stressful situations. They also discuss how successful these strategies have been. A common response to stressful situations is to make **negative self-statements**, like 'I can't handle this'. This is a **self-defeating internal dialogue**, making stressful situations even more stressful.

2 **Stress-reduction techniques** – where patients are taught skills to deal with stress, such as self-instruction where coping self-statements are practised. The therapist helps the patient to develop a variety of coping techniques, both direct actions and cognitive coping. **Direct action** might include arranging for escape routes and learning physical relaxation exercises that would help reduce physiological arousal. **Cognitive coping** might involve the use of **preparation statements**, like 'maybe what you think is anxiety is an eagerness to confront it'. These are positive, coping statements that are incompatible with the negative self-statements. The client practises these preparation statements.

3 **Application and follow through** – where patients visualise using stress-reduction techniques learned in the second phase and then use them in role play exercises and lastly in real-life situations. Once the patient can cope with a relatively non-threatening situation, a more threatening one is presented and the process is repeated.

Research into SIT

- Jay and Elliot (1990) developed a videotape for parents of 3–12-year-old children with leukaemia who were undergoing bone marrow treatment and lumbar punctures. One hour before treatment, parents are shown a film of a model parent employing self-statements, relaxation techniques and coping imagery rehearsal. The parents then practise these skills. Compared to parents receiving child-focused interventions, the SIT-treated parents showed significantly less anxiety and enhanced coping skills. This implies SIT to be an effective treatment for acute, short-term stressors. Meichenbaum (2001) reports that SIT modelling films have also been used successfully to control anger with alleged rape victims when preparing them for forensic examination.

- Holroyd *et al.* (1977) assigned 31 participants experiencing intermittent chronic tension headaches to either a SIT group, a biofeedback group (see Supplementary learning box on page 144) or a no treatment control group. They found that only the SIT group showed substantial improvements in daily reductions of headaches, suggesting SIT to be an effective treatment for chronic, long-term intermittent stressors and superior to physiological treatment.
- Holcomb (1986) assigned 26 psychiatric patients with severe stress and anxiety disorders to either a) SIT, b) a combination of SIT and drug treatment or c) just drug treatment, finding SIT superior to drugs in reducing symptoms of depression, anxiety and distress. A three-year follow-up study revealed that patients from the SIT alone group required fewer admissions for psychiatric problems than other patients, suggesting that SIT is superior in treating stress-related disorders and that drugs may actually hinder recovery.

An excellent, wide-ranging and detailed account of SIT, written by the therapy's founder Donald Meichenbaum, can be found at http://www.melissainstitute.org/documents/stress_inoculation.pdf

Evaluation

Evaluation of SIT

- Although some research shows SIT to be effective in treating combat-based stress in the military, many studies have found it ineffective. This surprising result may be due to the stigma associated with mental health issues in the military, with many soldiers only reluctantly undergoing treatment. Soldiers may hold the stereotypical view that psychological problems are the result of weaknesses in character and may hinder promotion chances. In addition, military SIT programmes tend to be delivered via an academic lecture format that is not appropriate or engaging for soldiers.
- SIT inoculates against future as well as current stressful situations, as it is effective over long periods and across different stressful situations. Patients continue to practise and apply skills they have learned to any type of stressful situations they come up against.
- SIT is not an easy option, requiring patients to be motivated and committed over long periods. This is not always an easy thing for individuals suffering from stress-related disorders to achieve.
- There are so many separate threads to SIT that it is difficult to work out which component – relaxation, cognitive appraisal, practical life skills and so on – is most important in addressing the negative effects of stress. It could just be relaxation.

Figure 4.18 SIT has met with mixed results as a means of treating combat-based stress in soldiers

Hardiness training

Kobasa (1986) believes that some people are more able to cope with stress as they have a hardy personality. (The material featured here is also relevant to the study of hardiness as a personality type. See page 133.) People may be able to develop the ability to cope better with stress by undertaking hardiness training.

There are three components to hardiness training:

1. **Focusing** – where people are shown how to concentrate on the physical symptoms of stress and to be aware of when action is necessary.
2. **Reconstruction of stress situations** – where previous stressful situations are revisited with a view to comprehending current stressors and coping strategies.
3. **Self-improvement** – where the patient learns to perceive stressors as challenges to be taken control of.

Evaluation of hardiness training

There is good research support for the link between hardiness and lowered stress that suggests that hardiness training should be successful. For example, Kobasa (1979) measured the stress levels of 800 business executives with the SRRS, finding that individuals with equal stress levels had different illness levels. This suggests that some people had hardy personalities that afforded them a degree of protection against the effects of stress. Further investigation revealed that individuals with high stress and low illness levels scored high on control, commitment and challenge, which suggest that these characteristics are the important components of hardiness. This implies that if people can be trained to be hardy, they will cope better with stress.

As Kobasa's research was mainly done on affluent executives, her results might not be generalisable to other sections of society.

Sarafino (1990) found that people who undertook hardiness training developed lower blood pressure and felt less stressed.

It could be that hardiness does not actually exist. Funk (1992) believes a low hardiness score just means that a person is negative and it is this that results in the debilitating effects of stress. It could be that commitment and challenge are not as important as control in alleviating the effects of stress.

Research in focus

Kobasa measured the stress levels of 800 business executives using the SRRS. This measuring scale produces quantitative data.

Explain what is meant by quantitative data and how it differs from qualitative data.

State one strength of quantitative data and one weakness.

How might you convert qualitative into quantitative data?

Strengthen your learning

1 a) How do benzodiazepines (BZs) work?
b) What side effects are associated with BZs?
c) Give details of two pieces of research associated with BZs.

2 a) How do beta-blockers work?
b) Outline two pieces of research assessing the value of beta-blockers.
c) Compile a concise evaluation of beta-blockers.

3 What is eustress and why is it beneficial?

4 a) Outline the three phases of SIT.
b) What types of stressors has SIT proven effective against? Give an example of each.
c) Give two evaluative points concerning SIT.

Assessment Check

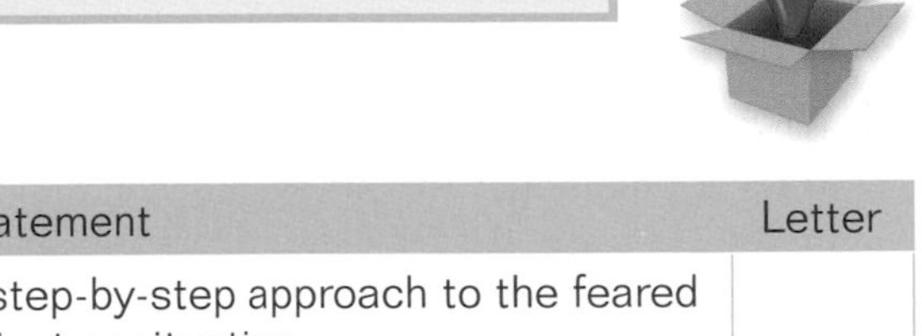

1 Copy and complete the table by placing a letter C next to the two statements that apply to cognitive behavioural therapy and a letter D next to the two statements that apply to drug treatments. [4 marks]

Statement	Letter
A step-by-step approach to the feared object or situation	
Replaces maladaptive thoughts with more positive, rational ones	
Goals are set so that realistic and rational beliefs can be achieved	
Alters the levels of neurotransmitters	
Affects the transmission of chemicals in the nervous system	

2 Outline the use of stress inoculation training (SIT) as a method of stress management. [4 marks]

3 a) Outline one psychological and one biological method of stress management. [3 + 3 marks]
b) Explain one limitation of each method of stress management outlined in a). [2 + 2 marks]

4 A local hospital has begun to offer stress-management treatments in response to rising levels of stress-related depression. One treatment that has proven effective is the prescription of anti-depressant tablets such as Prozac.
a) Identify the stress management treatment outlined above. [1 mark]
b) Explain one reason why this treatment might be effective. [2 marks]
c) Explain one limitation of this treatment. [2 marks]

5 Outline and evaluate biological methods of stress management. [12 marks]

6 'Stress is the key thing we have to cope with in the modern world and psychology will educate us in how to deal with it.'

What insights has psychology given us into the strengths and weaknesses of different methods of stress management? [12 marks]

Examination guidance:

1 The first question is a selection question where you choose from the options available. This means the answers are there, but you must identify and place the correct letters in the boxes. One option will be left over.

2 This question specifically requires a description of SIT, which must be orientated to its use as a method of stress management to gain access to all available marks.

3 With this question, ensure you outline one biological and one psychological method of stress management, for example drugs and SIT, and not two from the same category.

4 The answer to 4 a) can be gained from the description in the scenario provided. You need to get this right to be able to answer parts b) and c).

5 This is a long-answer question, with six marks available for outlining biological methods of stress management (the wording of the question means you need at least two) and six marks for evaluation. Suitable evaluation could make use of relevant research evidence or by contrast with psychological methods.

6 The quotation in question 6 is there purely to guide you. Six marks are available for outlining the strengths and limitations of different methods of stress management and you must refer to at two methods, which could be biological or psychological ones or both. Six marks are available for evaluation, with suitable evaluation possibly making use of relevant research evidence.

End of chapter review

- Stress is a general response to any demand made of the body, occurring when there is a lack of balance between the perceived demands of a situation and the perceived abilities to cope with those demands.
- Stressors are the sources of stress; anything causing stress is a stressor.
- The sympathomedullary pathway deals with acute (short-term) stressors and consists of the sympathetic nervous system and the sympathetic adrenal medullary system.
- The sympathomedullary pathway prepares the body for the fight-or-flight response, boosting the supply of oxygen and glucose to the brain and muscles and suppressing non-emergency processes like digestion.
- Acute stress produces the fight-or-flight response in men, but the tend and befriend response in women.
- The pituitary–adrenal system deals with chronic (long-term) stress by stimulating the release of stress-related hormones like cortisol, providing a constant source of energy.
- The immune system, which protects the body against infection, is weakened by chronic stress.
- Stress can also cause physical damage to the heart and blood vessels leading to cardiovascular disease.
- Life changes – occasional events incurring major adjustments to lifestyle – are linked to stress-related illnesses, with life change units (LCUs) predicting the chances of becoming ill.
- Daily hassles, perhaps a better indicator of physical and mental states of well-being, tend to build up, producing an overall elevated level of stress and present a serious risk of illness.
- Workplace stressors are a major and ever-increasing source of stress.
- Major workplace stressors include workload, predictability and controllability of work role, environmental factors, role conflict and ambiguity.
- Individual differences in the ways people perceive and respond to stressors are attributable in some part to differences in personality.
- Type A personality, with characteristics of time urgency, excessive competitiveness and generalised hostility, is linked to increased risk of developing heart disease.
- Coping strategies are methods of adapting to stress in positive and constructive ways, involving cognitive and behavioural efforts to meet external and/or internal demands.
- Emotion-focused strategies are methods of dealing with stressful events that aim to reduce negative effects of stressors by making an individual feel positive about stressful situations.
- Problem-focused strategies are methods of dealing with stressful situations that aim to reduce the negative effects of stressors by directly confronting them.
- Biological methods of stress management, like drugs, focus directly on biological stress-response systems.
- Benzodiazepine drugs have a dampening effect on the neurons of the brain, but can incur side effects and dependency problems.
- Beta-blockers stop the transmission of nerve impulses, reducing heart rate. They can also have serious side effects.
- Biological methods of stress management, like SIT, aim to identify and rectify the underlying causes of stress-related disorders.
- SIT is a form of cognitive behavioural therapy, aimed at changing emotional responses and behaviour.
- SIT is used to treat acute stressors, chronic intermittent stressors, chronic long-term continual stressors, as well as anger control.

5 Social psychology

Introduction

Social psychology studies how people's thoughts, feelings and behaviour are affected by the presence of others. This can occur with the focus on the individual or as a group occurrence. The particular social psychology topic looked at here is that of social influence: how we affect and are affected by others. In particular there are three areas of social influence focused upon:

1 types of conformity and factors influencing conformity
2 research studies and explanations of obedience to authority
3 ways in which people resist social pressures to conform and obey and how such resistance leads to social change.

Understanding the specification

- Internalisation and compliance are types of conformity that you must have knowledge of, because they are referred to directly in the specification and could be included explicitly in the wording of examination questions.
- Informational and normative social influences are also referred to directly as explanations of conformity and so again could feature in examination questions.
- There is a clear requirement for the work of Stanley Milgram to be studied, with the same being true of how people resist pressures to conform and obey authority.
- Another basic requirement is that locus of control, resisting pressures to conform and resisting pressures to obey must be included as explanations of independent behaviour, as again you may have to answer a question on it.
- These are the basic requirements to ensure you can answer any examination question thrown at you. However, other relevant material is included to help provide depth and detail to your understanding and hopefully help you to maximise marks gained in your AS examinations.

Social influence

Conformity (majority influence)

Conformity can be defined as yielding to group pressure. Conformity occurs when an individual's behaviour and/or beliefs are influenced by a larger group of people, which is why conformity is also referred to as **majority influence**. Conformity can be regarded as a negative thing, as it seemingly takes away from independence and can have harmful consequences (see Psychology in action, page 161). However, much human activity is socially based and therefore occurs in groups, so there is a need for individuals to agree in order that groups can form and operate efficiently. Conformity helps this to occur; indeed conformity can be regarded as a flag around which group members rally. Kelman (1958) made reference to three types of conformity. These vary in the extent to which they affect an individual's belief system.

1 Compliance – occurs when an individual alters their behaviour and opinions to those of a group to gain acceptance or avoid disapproval. Compliance, therefore, basically occurs because of a desire to fit in and involves public, but not private, acceptance of the group's behaviour and attitudes. It is a fairly weak and temporary form of conformity, only exhibited in the presence of the group. For example, you may profess a liking for dub-step, because many others of your age group do and you wish to be accepted and not ridiculed by them. However, privately you may have little interest in this style of music.

2 Identification – occurs when an individual alters their behaviour and opinions, both publicly and privately, to those of a group, because membership of that group is desirable. This is a stronger form of conformity, involving private as well as public acceptance, but this form of conformity is generally temporary and is not maintained when you leave the group. For example, when joining the army an individual may adopt the behaviour and beliefs of fellow soldiers, but on leaving the army for civilian life, new behaviours and opinions may be adopted again.

3 Internalisation – occurs when an individual truly alters their behaviour and opinions to those of a group. This involves the individual being exposed to the belief system of others and having to decide what they really believe in. If the group's opinions are validated as correct, then it leads to public and private acceptance of the group's behaviour and opinions, which is not dependent on the presence of the group or group membership for maintenance. For example, if an individual is influenced by a group's Buddhist beliefs to the extent that they truly convert to that faith, then the new religious way of life will continue without the presence or influence of the group. (Internalisation can also occur through minority influence. See Supplementary learning, page 154.)

Key terms

Conformity – yielding to group pressure (also known as majority influence)

Compliance – publicly, but not privately, going along with majority influence to gain approval

Identification – public and private acceptance of majority influence in order to gain group acceptance

Internalisation – public and private acceptance of majority influence, due to adoption of the majority's belief system

IN THE NEWS

The conformity of saggin'

Figure 5.1

It will cost you if you get caught with your pants down in one South Carolina county. The Jasper County council passed an ordinance Monday prohibiting sagging pants in public. It prohibits anyone from wearing pants more than three inches below the hips exposing skin or underwear. The Beaufort Gazette reports the ordinance carries fines of between $25 and $500. The vote was 2–1 in favour with two council members absent.

Source: adapted from the *Beaufort Gazette*, South Carolina, USA, 18 December 2008

The trend for wearing sagging trousers that reveal underwear has its roots in slavery. Male slaves were not allowed to wear belts, in order to degrade them. Sagging trousers were also enforced on prisoners, who were not allowed to wear belts due to their potential use as weapons or suicide aids. However, wearing sagging trousers has recently been adopted as a fashion statement and has become the uniform of trendy young males. Something which started off as a means of humiliating black people has become a conformist norm and is worn with pride in order to be accepted into hip-hop culture. There was even a hit record for Plies with his track Pants Hang Low. (You can watch a video of it at http://www.pliesworld.com/video/pants-hang-low/ but be aware that the video contains offensive language.) Perhaps the good citizens of Jasper County should take all this into account before dishing out fines to the underwear revealers.

If you would like to learn more about minority influence, especially the famous study by Moscovici *et al.* (1969) which, unusually for the time, used only female participants, then go to http://www.simplypsychology.pwp.blueyonder.co.uk/minority-influence.html

Supplementary learning

Minority influence

Minorities tend not to have status or influence and may be subjected to ridicule. However, they sometimes exert a powerful influence. If a minority is persistent and consistent in its opinions, it can create enough uncertainty within a majority group that, over time, social change can occur. The majority are compelled to examine the point of view of the minority and may ultimately convert to their viewpoint. This, therefore, is a form of internalisation and is the means by which **innovation** occurs. Majority influence is a force keeping things the way they are, that resists social change, while minority influence allows the adoption of new ideas and behaviours into mainstream society. For instance, in the 1950s a small minority of people who would be classed today as environmentalists first emerged. Their radical opinions about farming practices, pollution, recycling and so forth were completely against the norms of the time and such people were subjected to derision and disregarded as crackpots. However, this vocal, organised minority persevered in a consistent and reasoned fashion. Increasingly people came round to their way of thinking, to such an extent that 'green' attitudes and behaviours are now the majority viewpoint. A perfect example of how minority influence creates change and innovation in society.

Figure 5.2 Environmentalists are now the majority

Key terms

Minority influence – a type of social influence that motivates individuals to reject established majority group norms

Classic research

The role of discussion in changing opinion regarding a matter of fact – Arthur Jenness, 1932

Originally seen as an investigation into social facilitation (the effect of the presence of others on performance), Jenness's research is now regarded as a groundbreaking study into conformity, especially of informational social influence. Although the original focus was on how group discussion

Figure 5.3

...continued

influenced accuracy of judgement, the most interesting result concerned how majority influence caused group members' judgements to converge (move together). The task he gave his participants, estimating the number of jellybeans in a jar, was not an easy one; it was difficult to assess the amount. Therefore the conformity produced was motivated by informational social influence, where individuals in uncertain situations look to others for guidance as how to behave.

Aim: To investigate the effect of discussion in groups on the accuracy of individual judgements.

Procedure: Participants, as individuals, estimated the number of jellybeans in a bottle and then discussed the estimates either in a large group or in several smaller groups, learning in the process that individuals differed widely in their estimates. Group estimates were then arrived at and finally, individuals made a second post-group individual estimate.

Findings: A number of findings concerning how different types of groups affected the accuracy of judgement were found, but the interesting result from a conformity point of view was that 'typicality of opinion was increased'. Quite simply, when asked as individuals to make a second post-group estimate, there was a significant convergence towards the group estimate. Interestingly, the average change of opinion was greater among females.

Conclusions: The judgements of individuals are affected by majority opinions, especially in ambiguous or uncertain situations. Discussion is not effective in changing opinion unless the individuals who enter into discussion become aware of differences in opinion held by others.

Evaluation:

- Females are more affected by majority influence. This may be due to differences in gender roles where women are more interpersonally oriented than men, or may be because females are less sure of their judgements in uncertain situations.
- Unlike other classic social influence studies, there was no element of deceit and thus the research can be regarded as ethically sound.
- This was a laboratory-based experiment using an artificial, unusual scenario and as such may not reflect actual behaviour in real-life situations.
- The study tells us little, if anything, about majority influence in non-ambiguous situations (see Asch, 1955, below).

Classic research

Opinions and social pressure – Solomon Asch, 1955

Solomon Asch, a Polish immigrant to the USA, is regarded as a groundbreaking social psychologist who transformed the study of social influence. He was, in fact, a tutor of Stanley Milgram, who himself would achieve fame with his obedience studies.

Asch was critical of research like Jenness's that involved ambiguous tasks and uncertain situations. He was more interested in a stricter test of conformity, one that examined the tendency to conform to majority influence in unambiguous situations where the correct answer was obvious. Asch performed a series of experiments beginning in 1951, adding new data to his results as he progressed.

Aim: To investigate the extent to which individuals will conform to a majority who give obviously wrong answers.

Procedure: 123 American male student volunteers took part in what they believed to be a study of visual perception. Individual participants were placed in groups with between seven to nine others, sat either in a line or around a table, who in reality were pseudo-participants (confederates). The task was to say which comparison line, A, B or C,

continued ...

...continued

was the same as a stimulus line. On 12 out of 18 'critical' trials the pseudo-participants gave identical wrong answers, the real participant always answering last or last but one.

There was also a control group of 36 participants who were tested individually on 20 trials.

Findings: The control group had an error rate of only 0.04 per cent (three mistakes out of 720 trials), while on the 12 critical trials there was a 32 per cent conformity rate to wrong answers. Seventy-five per cent of participants conformed to at least one wrong answer (meaning also that 25 per cent never conformed). Five per cent of participants conformed to all 12 wrong answers.

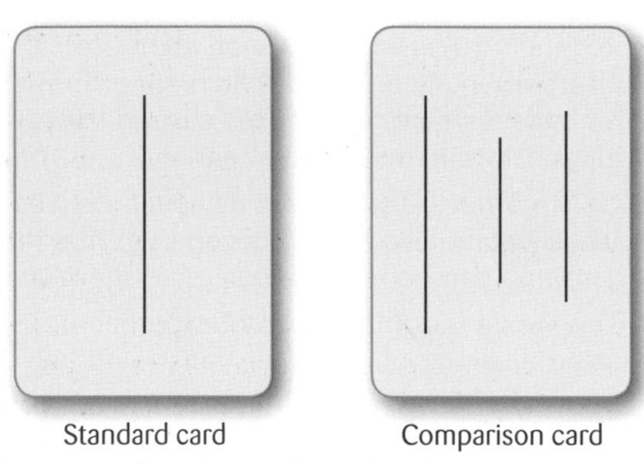

Figure 5.4 Stimulus cards used in Asch's experiment

Post-experiment interviews with participants found three reasons for conformity:

1 **Distortion of action** – where the majority of participants who conformed did so publicly, but not privately, as they wished to avoid ridicule
2 **Distortion of perception** – where some participants believed their perception must actually be wrong and so conformed.
3 **Distortion of judgement** – where some participants had doubts concerning the accuracy of their judgements and so conformed to the majority view.

Conclusions: The judgements of individuals are affected by majority opinions, even when the majority are blatantly wrong.

There are wide individual differences in the extent to which individuals are affected by majority influence. The fact that the majority of participants who conformed did so publicly, but not privately, indicates them to have been motivated by normative social influence, a form of conformity where individuals conform to gain acceptance or avoid rejection by a group.

Evaluation:

- Asch's method for studying conformity has been adopted by many other researchers. It is now the established way of performing conformity research – the basic procedure (or **paradigm**).
- The fact that only one real participant is tested at a time makes the procedure uneconomical and time-consuming. Crutchfield (1954) performed similar research, but improved on the procedure by testing several participants at once.
- The situation was unrealistic. It would be extremely rare to disagree so fundamentally with someone over the 'correct' answer.
- Asch's procedure is unethical, as it involves deceit; participants believed it was a study of visual perception. It also involved psychological harm, with participants under a lot of stress. Bogdonoff *et al.* (1961), using an Asch-type procedure, found elevated stress levels in participants when faced with a majority influence that was incorrect. Stress levels decreased if participants conformed, indicating conformity to be a healthy thing to do.
- As the overall conformity rate on the critical trials was only 32 per cent (one-third of the participants), the majority of people are independent rather than conformist.

Figure 5.5 A minority of one faces a unanimous majority in Asch's study

Supplementary learning

Variations and replications of Asch's paradigm

- Asch found that when there was one real participant and one confederate, the conformity rate was very low. With two confederates, conformity rose to 13 per cent and with three confederates it rose to 32 per cent, the same as in his original experiment. He found that adding in extra confederates had no further effect on the overall conformity rate. Some other researchers, such as Gerard *et al.* (1968), have questioned this, finding conformity rates do rise as more confederates are added, though the rate of increase declines with each additional confederate.
- Asch found that if there was one confederate who went against the others and gave correct answers, then the overall conformity rate declined to 5.5 per cent. This effect was similar if the rebel went against the other confederates and the real participant (conformity rate of 9 per cent), suggesting that it is the reduction of the majority's consensus that is the important factor.
- Asch found that if he made the task more difficult by making the comparison lines similar to each other, then participants were increasingly likely to conform to the wrong answer.
- When Asch got the participants to write down answers rather than saying them aloud, conformity declined to 12.5 per cent, suggesting fear of ridicule and disapproval are important factors.
- Levels of conformity vary over time. Larsen (1974), using the Asch paradigm on American students, found a lower rate of conformity and yet in a later study (1979), found a similar conformity rate to that of Asch, implying that social changes can increase and decrease conformity levels within society.
- Levels of conformity also vary across cultures, suggesting that different levels of social cohesion and independence affect conformity rates. For instance Perrin and Spencer (1981) used the Asch paradigm on British science students and found a conformity rate of only 0.25 per cent. However, a different interpretation might be that science students are taught to question things and be independent. In support of this, the same researchers found a similar conformity rate to Asch's when testing British young offenders, who could be said to be lacking in independent thought.

Research in focus

Have a look at the ethical guidelines in the Research Methods Chapter and then note down what features of the studies by Asch and Jenness may be unethical.

Is there any way in which such unethical features can be justified? You may wish to consider the idea of a cost–benefit analysis to help form your answer.

Was Asch's sample a representative one?

What measures of conformity were used in the studies of Asch and Jenness?

Were the tasks used by Asch and Jenness like ones encountered in everyday life? How could this affect the findings?

Listen to a BBC Radio 4 programme about Asch's research as part of the *Landmark Experiments in Psychology* series http://www.bbc.co.uk/radio4/science/mindchangers1.shtml

Contemporary research

Culture and conformity: A meta-analysis of studies using Asch's (1952, 1956) line judgement task – Bond and Smith, 1996

Various research studies have found both similar and dissimilar results to that of Asch. This could be due to whatever social climate was in place at time of testing, or possibly that different cultural groups are either more conformist or independent in nature. Rob Bond and Peter Smith from the University of Sussex conducted a meta-analysis (combination of many trial results) to investigate these claims, using cultures that championed independence, such as the USA, and ones that emphasised collectivism, such as Japan. Secondly the researchers analysed results from studies carried out at various times in the USA alone.

Aim: To compare conformity rates on the Asch-type paradigm across different cultures and also at different times within one culture.

Procedure: The researchers performed a meta-analysis of 134 published replications of the Asch conformity effect, conducted within 17 different nations. Subsequently a similar meta-analysis was conducted on the 97 replications conducted within the USA.

Findings: The within-USA studies showed a distinct negative correlation between time of study and level of conformity, with a steady decline in conformity rates from the time of Asch in the 1950s.

As predicted, independent cultures tended to show lower rates of conformity than collectivist ones.

A positive correlation was found between conformity rates and the size of the majority influence: the greater the size of the majority, the higher the conformity level found.

The more difficult or ambiguous the task, the higher were the conformity levels. Females conformed more.

Conclusions: Conformity rates can be predicted on the basis of the level of independence within a cultural grouping.

Conformity rates change over time within a culture, reflecting social changes within that cultural grouping.

Conformity rates increase with tasks with uncertain answers or solutions, suggesting more of an informational social influence.

Females are more interpersonally orientated than males and have a greater need for social agreement.

Evaluation

- Meta-analyses that look for moderator variables of effect size are correlational investigations and have methodological weaknesses, like not showing causality.
- A culture is not necessarily uniform in its composition and may not be similar in nature throughout the cultural grouping. So drawing conclusions from studies across different cultures may be an oversimplification.
- One strength of the study is that in applying the strict criterion of only including replications of Asch's study, the sample is very similar in composition, allowing for accurate analysis, increasing the validity of the findings.
- A potential weakness of the study is that the line judgement task and apparatus used may be more meaningful in some cultures than others and it is those differences rather than social influence affecting the results.

Research in focus

Smith and Bond performed a meta-analysis and found a positive correlation between conformity rates and the size of the majority influence.

What is a meta-analysis?

Explain how a positive correlation differs from a negative correlation.

Outline one strength and one weakness of correlations. If you need guidance, see the section on correlations in Chapter 3, Research methods (see page 77).

What is meant by a 'replication of Asch's study'? Why would psychologists wish to carry out such replications?

You are the researcher

Figure 5.6 Who conforms more?

Psychology is centred around the designing and carrying out of practical research. Can you design a simple study to compare the level of conformity in PE students with Science students? What would the independent variable (IV) be? What experimental design would you use? You will need a measure of conformity to form your dependent variable (DV).

Philip Zimbardo was a school friend of Stanley Milgram and Zimbardo's prison simulation participant observational study of 1973 is regarded as one of the most famous of all psychological studies. It contains elements of conformity and obedience, so care should be taken to only use the aspects of the study that relate to conformity to social roles, when answering examination questions on the topic.

A good outline and appraisal of the study can be found at

http://www.simplypsychology.pwp.blueyonder.co.uk/zimbardo.html

Strengthen your learning

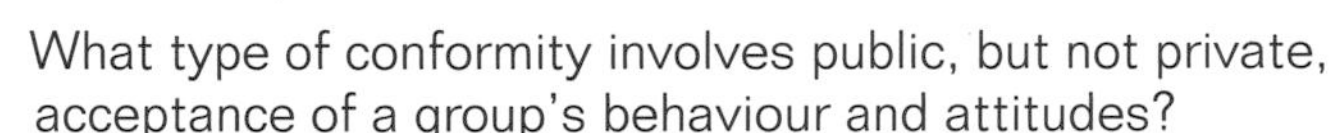

1 What type of conformity involves public, but not private, acceptance of a group's behaviour and attitudes?
2 What type of conformity involves an individual truly converting to the belief system of others?
3 Why does compliance occur?
4 What type of conformity is maintained without the presence or influence of the majority influence?
5 What type of conformity occurs because membership of the group is seen as desirable?
6 Why is identification seen as a stronger form of conformity than compliance, but a weaker form than internalisation?

Assessment Check

1 The following statements relate to conformity:
A Looking to the group for information as to the correct behaviour
B Going along with a group because we accept their belief system as our own
C Going along with a group, even though privately we do not agree with them
D Rejecting the established norm of the majority and moving to the position of the minority

Copy and complete the table below by writing which statement, A, B, C or D, describes which type of conformity. [2 marks]

Type of conformity	Statement
Compliance	
Internalisation	

2 Explain what is meant by compliance. Give a real-life example. [3 marks]
3 Outline what psychologists have learned about types of conformity. [5 marks]

Examination guidance:

1 The first question is a selection question where you choose from the options available. This means that the right answers are there, but you have to identify them and then place them in the correct statement box.
2 In the second question you get up to two marks for explaining what is meant by compliance – one mark for a correct explanation and another for elaboration of this point. The third mark is earned by selecting a relevant example; you would need to know what is meant by compliance to do this.
3 The third type of question gives an opportunity for choice in what material to use. Although the specification lists compliance and internalisation as types of conformity, you are not just limited to these and could, for example, use identification or minority influence (see page 154).

Key terms

Normative social influence – a motivational force to be liked and accepted by a group

Informational social influence – a motivational force to look to others for guidance in order to be correct

Explanations of conformity

We have looked so far at *types* of conformity; now we will turn our attention to *explanations* of conformity – what actually motivates people to conform.

Deutsch and Gerard (1955) distinguished between informational social influence (ISI) and normative social influence (NSI). They saw this distinction as crucial to understanding majority group influence.

Informational social influence

We have a basic need to feel confident that our ideas and beliefs are correct (a need for certainty). This makes us feel in charge of our lives and in control of the world. This is the motive underlying ISI. When we are unsure about something, we seek others' opinions: if we know what they think, we are in a better position to form our own opinions. This is more likely to happen in unfamiliar situations, like deciding who to vote for in your first election, or in ambiguous situations, like reading a book and not knowing what to make of it. Asking friends who *they are* voting for or what *they* thought, helps you to make up your mind.

The participants in Jenness's experiment were unsure how many jellybeans were in the jar. Similarly, when Asch made the comparison lines more similar, the situation became more ambiguous; the correct answer was much less obvious.

Figure 5.7 Which to use? We look to others for guidance in uncertain situations

If we conform because of ISI, it is likely that we believe the opinions we adopt. We are uncertain what to believe, so we look to the opinions of others and become 'converted' to their viewpoint.

When Jenness's participants were tested individually again, they tended to move towards the group estimate, showing that they genuinely (privately) believed what they said. This illustrates a type of conformity called internalisation or true conformity.

This is how others help us define 'social reality'. Abrams *et al.* (1990) thinks that we will only be influenced by others' opinions in ambiguous situations if we see ourselves as sharing characteristics with them. For example, you are more likely to internalise the views of friends than strangers.

Figure 5.8 Normative social influence occurs because of a need to be accepted

Normative social influence

The motive underlying NSI is the need to be accepted by others. We want others to like and respect us, and being rejected is painful. People have the power to reward or punish us, and one way of ensuring acceptance is to agree with them. This does not necessarily mean we truly believe what we say.

For example, many of Asch's participants who conformed on the critical trials *knew* the stooges' answer was wrong. But if they gave the correct answer, they risked being ridiculed by the majority. In the post-experimental debriefing, they said 'I didn't want to look stupid' or 'I didn't want to be the odd one out'. So, what they *said* (publicly) and what they *believed* (privately) were different. This illustrates a type of conformity called compliance; it represents a compromise in situations where there is a conflict between our opinions and those of others. Jenness's participants did not face this conflict.

However, we only experience conflict if we disagree with others whom we see as similar to ourselves in some relevant way (as in ISI: see Abrams *et al.*, 1990).

Cognitive dissonance

Cognitive dissonance is an unpleasant feeling that occurs when we hold two simultaneous contradictory ideas (cognitions). Festinger (1957) suggested that altering cognitions reduces cognitive dissonance and that this can be achieved by conforming. The fact that some examples of conformity cannot be explained by normative or informational social influence, but only by cognitive dissonance, lends support to the explanation. For example, Bogdonoff *et al.* (1961) found heightened stress levels in participants using an Asch-type procedure, which were then reduced by conforming.

Key terms

Cognitive dissonance – the unpleasant feeling of anxiety created by simultaneously holding two contradictory ideas

Psychology in action

Obedience, normative social influence and genocide

During the Second World War (1939–45), the Nazis carried out the genocide of millions of people, including the Jews and the Gypsies, and normative social influence may have played a role in this. The Nazis had contempt for inferior races, seeing them as '*Untermenschen*' (sub-human) and themselves as '*Ubermenschen*' (supermen). They believed inferior races were a threat to genetic purity and the natural superiority of the German Aryan race. Propaganda films of the time show Jews as hordes of filthy rats invading German homes and spreading disease. Normative social influence explains the tendency for group members to accept the legitimacy of the group's norms and therefore support behaviour maintaining such norms. The massacre of hundreds of thousands of Tutsis and Hutus in the Rwandan civil war of 1994 can be seen in similar terms. The Hutus established a norm whereby Tutsis were '*inyenzi*', or cockroaches, parasites that must be crushed. The resulting ethnic violence was 'justified' by the acceptance of this norm.

Figure 5.9 The Nazis dehumanised Jewish people, seeing them as sub-human

Evaluation

Evaluation of explanations of conformity

- ISI and NSI, as well as cognitive dissonance, can be used to explain and understand real-life examples of conformity, giving support to them as explanations.
- It is not always possible to identify a single explanation for a given example; sometimes more than one explanation is relevant. For instance in Asch's study, the conformity witnessed is partially informational, as well as being normative – participants looked to others for information concerning the right answer, as well as agreeing with them to avoid ridicule.
- NSI can be used to explain the degree of negative and positive attitudes to groups, as being related to how socially acceptable such groups are.
- The use of conforming behaviour to reduce cognitive dissonance is healthy, as it reduces stress levels.
- Conformity can sometimes have negative connotations, for example NSI leading to inter-group violence. However, it is only by understanding how and why conformity in such situations occurs that practical applications can be devised that reduce such conflicts or even stop them arising in the first place.

Strengthen your learning

1. In what way does normative social influence differ from informational social influence?
2. What type of conformity is associated with normative social influence?
3. What type of conformity is associated with informational social influence?
4. Can you think of real-life examples of your own of informational social influence and normative social influence?
5. How can examples of genocide be explained by reference to normative social influence?
6. What is cognitive dissonance? How can it be used as an explanation of conformity?

Assessment Check

1. Outline explanations of conformity. [6 marks]
2. Outline one ethical issue that researchers into conformity have to take into account. [3 marks]
3. Explain what is meant by informational social influence. [2 marks]
4. Asmah has recently moved to a new school and has started attending the youth club in the evenings. Asmah found it difficult to make new friends, but she noticed many youth club members had a strong liking for table tennis. She started showing enthusiasm for the game, even though she had little interest in it, and soon found people being friendly to her and including her in their activities.
   a) What kind of conformity is being exhibited in the above passage? [1 mark]
   b) Refer to features of the above scenario to justify your answer. [3 marks]

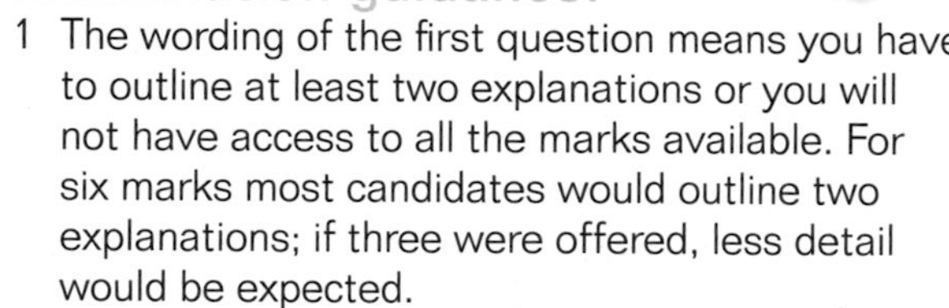

Examination guidance:

1. The wording of the first question means you have to outline at least two explanations or you will not have access to all the marks available. For six marks most candidates would outline two explanations; if three were offered, less detail would be expected.
2. The ethical issues of deceit and psychological harm have featured heavily in conformity research. Using actual examples from research studies would be a good way of illustrating your answer.
3. In this question, one mark is awarded for a correct explanation of informational social influence and a further mark for elaboration, in other words adding more relevant detail.
4. In this question only one of the four marks is available for identifying the type of conformity. To gain the extra three marks, reference should be made to information in the scenario that supports your answer.

Key terms

Obedience – complying with the demands of an authority figure

Obedience

Obedience is a form of social influence defined as complying with the demands of an authority figure. Obedience can be a good thing – it is difficult to imagine society functioning in a meaningful way unless there are rules and laws that are followed and recognition of which people hold authority positions and have the right to give orders.

Sometimes, however, obedience can be destructive. After the Second World War, psychologists focused their attention on the holocaust where, under the Nazis, German citizens unquestioningly followed orders that saw the mass murder of millions of people like the Jews, the Gypsies and the disabled. One such psychologist was Stanley Milgram, formerly a student of Asch, who greatly inspired the design of his classic obedience study. Milgram came from a working class, New York Jewish family that fled Europe for America and escaped the holocaust. Milgram was aware of this and became motivated to understand the reasons behind it. Did Germans have a personality defect leading them to obey blindly and commit horrific actions without question, or were people much more obedient than was realised?

JUST FOLLOWING ORDERS
JUST FOLLOWING ORDERS
JUST FOLLOWING ORDERS
JUST FOLLOWING ORDERS

Figure 5.10

Also topical at this time was the trial of Adolf Eichmann in 1961. He was the Nazi responsible for carrying out '*die Endlösung*' (the 'Final Solution'), the extermination of millions in the death camps. Kidnapped by Israeli secret service agents in Argentina, Eichmann was taken to Jerusalem to stand trial. In her book *Eichmann in Jerusalem*, Hannah Arendt (1963) famously reported on the '*banality* (ordinariness) *of evil*' – how instead of an inhuman monster, Eichmann was a mild-mannered, unobjectionable man, who had 'merely been doing his job'. His only defence for his actions was repeatedly to say 'I was just following orders.' A few days after Milgram's study was completed, Eichmann was hanged. Milgram originally intended to take his study to Germany after he had conducted his pilot study in Connecticut, but the results from this study at Yale University (see below) proved so shocking, there was no need.

Figure 5.11 Obedience is necessary for safe social interactions

Figure 5.12 Adolf Eichmann: monster or obedient servant?

Classic research

Behavioural study of obedience – Stanley Milgram, 1963

Figure 5.13 Stanley Milgram

Aim: Milgram set out to test the 'Germans are different' hypothesis, which claimed that Germans are highly obedient and that Adolf Hitler could not have exterminated the Jews in the 1930s and 1940s without the unquestioning cooperation of the German population.

Procedure: Forty American males aged 20–50 years responded to an advertisement and volunteered for a study of memory and learning to take place in the Yale University Psychology Department. On arrival, they were met by the apparent experimenter wearing a grey lab coat, actually a biology teacher, who introduced them to Mr Wallace, actually a confederate, a mild-mannered, harmless looking man in his late 50s. The experimenter told them that the experiment was about the effects of punishment on learning, with one playing the role of 'teacher' and the other the 'learner', with the roles determined quite randomly. In fact the situation was rigged, so Mr Wallace was always the learner and the participant was always the teacher.

The experimenter explained that punishments would be electric shocks. All three then went into an adjoining room, where the experimenter

continued ...

...continued

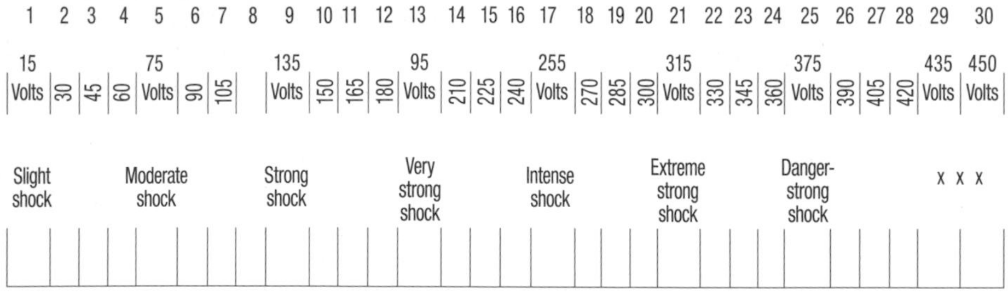

1 2 3 4 5 6 7 8 9 10 11 12 13 14 15 16 17 18 19 20 21 22 23 24 25 26 27 28 29 30

15 Volts | 30 | 45 | 60 | 75 Volts | 90 | 105 | 135 Volts | 150 | 165 | 180 | 95 Volts | 210 | 225 | 240 | 255 Volts | 270 | 285 | 300 | 315 Volts | 330 | 345 | 360 | 375 Volts | 390 | 405 | 420 | 435 Volts | 450 Volts

Slight shock — Moderate shock — Strong shock — Very strong shock — Intense shock — Extreme strong shock — Danger-strong shock — X X X

Figure 5.14 The levels of electric shock used in the Milgram experiments

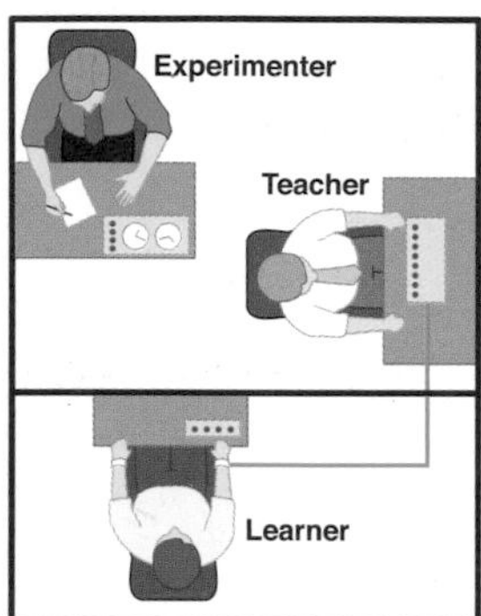

'I observed a mature and initially poised businessman enter the laboratory smiling and confident. Within 20 minutes he was reduced to a twitching, stuttering wreck, who was rapidly approaching nervous collapse. He constantly pulled on his ear lobe, and twisted his hands. At one point he pushed his fist into his forehead and muttered "Oh God, let's stop it". And yet he continued to respond to every word of the experimenter, and obeyed to the end.'

Figure 5.15 The Milgram experiment set up

strapped Mr Wallace into a chair with his arms attached to electrodes. The teacher would deliver shocks via a shock generator in an adjacent room. The generator had a series of switches each marked with a voltage level. The first switch had a level of 15 volts and was marked with the verbal description 'slight shock'. Each switch gave a shock 15 volts higher than the one before, going up to 450 volts, marked 'XXX'. The naïve participant received a genuine shock of 45 volts to convince him that everything was for real.

In the voice-feedback version of the study, participants hear a pre-recorded series of verbal responses from the learner, but the naïve participants believe these are real responses. The teacher was instructed to deliver a shock each time Mr Wallace made a mistake on a paired-associate word task; he indicated his answer by switching on one of four lights located above the shock generator. With each successive mistake, the teacher gives the next highest shock, 15 volts higher than the previous one.

The important point comes at 150 volts. Before this point, the victim is quite willing to participate, but now he starts to protest and demands to be released. His protests become increasingly vehement and at 300 volts he refuses to answer any more questions and says he has heart problems which are giving him cause for concern. After 315 volts he screams loudly and from 330 volts is heard no more. The teacher, through a series of verbal prods, such as 'the experiment requires you continue' and 'you have no choice, you must go on', was instructed to keep on shocking if Mr Wallace stopped answering.

Findings:

- **Quantitative results** – obedience was measured as the percentage of participants giving shocks up to the maximum 450 volts. In this version of the experiment the obedience rate was 62.5 per cent (25 out of 40 participants). An earlier 'remote victim' version with no pre-recorded responses, but the victim pounding on the walls, gained an obedience rate of 65 per cent (26 out of 40 participants), with 100 per cent of participants continuing up to at least 300 volts.
- **Qualitative results** – Many participants showed distress, such as twitching, sweating or giggling nervously, digging their nails into their flesh and verbally attacking the experimenter. Three participants had uncontrollable seizures. Some participants showed little if any signs of discomfort, instead concentrating dutifully on what they were doing.

Conclusions: The 'Germans are different' hypothesis is clearly false – Milgram's participants were 40 'ordinary' Americans. Their high level of obedience showed that people

continued ...

...continued

obey those regarded as authority figures. If we had lived in Nazi Germany in the 1930s, we might have acted just as obediently. The results suggest that obeying those in authority is normal behaviour in a hierarchically organised society. We will obey orders that distress us and go against our moral code.

Evaluation:

- The Milgram paradigm – Milgram established the basic method, or paradigm, for studying obedience. This is equivalent to Asch's paradigm for studying conformity.
- **Cross-cultural replications** – Milgram's paradigm has been used in many countries. Methodological differences between these studies make comparisons difficult, but varying obedience rates were found; for example only 40 per cent obedience in Australia, but 90 per cent in Spain. This may be a reflection of cultural differences towards authority.
- **It was intended as a pilot study** – it is more useful to consider the research stimulated by the 1963 study than the study itself. Milgram was astounded to find such high levels of obedience, so he conducted his variations to determine why people were so obedient.
- **Practical application** – it was hoped that Milgram's findings would help form strategies to reduce destructive blind obedience. Unfortunately, not much has changed since 1963; thousands are killed every day by people operating under the excuse of 'simply following orders'.

To read an account of what it was like to be one of the 40 original participants, go to

http://www.jewishcurrents.org/2004-jan-dimow.htm

where you will find the personal account of Joseph Dimow.
There is also an extensive review of Milgram-type studies, 35 years after the original study, compiled by Dr Thomas Blass who is Milgram's official biographer. Find it at

http://www.stanleymilgram.com/pdf/obedience.pdf

Key terms

Milgram paradigm – experimental procedure devised by Stanley Milgram for measuring obedience rates

Did you know?

- Milgram's 'shock machine' still exists. It is kept at the Archives of the History of American Psychology at the University of Akron. For many years it was part of a travelling psychology exhibit created by the American Psychological Association.
- In 1949, at James Monroe High School in the Bronx, a tough 'ghetto' area of New York, two boys sat next to each other in class. One was Stanley Milgram and the other was Philip Zimbardo. Both had dreams of escaping the ghetto and doing something worthwhile with their lives and both went on to become world-renowned psychologists – Milgram for his obedience study and Zimbardo (1973) for his prison simulation study.
- The man who played the learner in Milgram's original study suffered a heart attack three years later and was resuscitated by someone who had been a teacher in the study. Unfortunately, the man still died.

Figure 5.16 Milgram's original 'shock machine'

If you want to know more about the life and work of Stanley Milgram then visit Dr Thomas Blass's website at

http://www.stanleymilgram.com/

This site is dedicated to the famous psychologist and is a great source of accurate, detailed material.

Supplementary learning

Most people would presume that Milgram's study is an experiment, indeed Milgram referred to it as such. However, there is no independent variable and in reality it is more of a controlled observation. It can, however, be considered an experiment if you take into account Milgram's variations of his study (see below). The IV then becomes which particular variation a participant performs, for example, having the experimenter not present in the room, as opposed to him being in the room.

Milgram's variations

Milgram performed a series of variations of his study to identify the important factors in getting people to obey. In each variation only a single variable was changed (IV), to see its effect on the obedience rate (DV). In each case the basic procedure remained the same as in his original study (the 'remote victim' condition).

Variation	Percentage going to 450 V	Comments
Standard procedure	65%	The baseline figure to compare other results to
Victim is silent throughout	100%	The highest rate of obedience seen
Study performed in a run-down office block	48%	The prestigious setting of Yale University did have some effect in giving the study a sense of legitimacy
Victim in same room as teacher	40%	Increasing proximity decreases obedience
Teacher forces victims hand onto a shock plate	30%	Again, increased proximity decreases obedience, but 30% is still alarmingly high
Experimenter not present in room, but phones orders in	20.5%	Proximity to the authority figure is important
Teacher is paired with two confederate teachers who refuse to obey	10%	Disobedient models have a large effect
Teacher only reads out words, a confederate gives the shocks	92.5%	Obedience is high when responsibility for the actions is switched to someone else

Table 5.1

The variations are perhaps the most informative part of the study, as widely varying obedience rates are produced (from 10 per cent to 100 per cent), giving us evidence to discover the reasons why people obey.

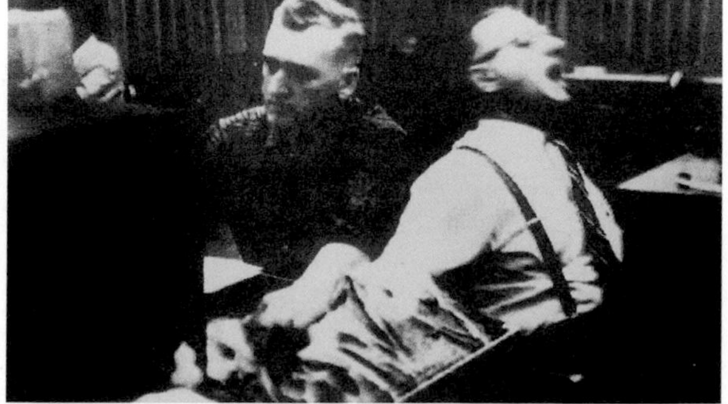

Figure 5.17 In one version of Milgram's experiment, the teacher forced the victim's hand onto a shock plate

Research in focus

There are several criticisms of Milgram's methodology:

- Orne and Holland (1968) criticised the internal validity of the study, as they believed participants only delivered the shocks as they knew they were not real. However, what percentage of participants in post-study interviews said they believed it to be real? How did the physical responses of many of the participants also suggest they believed it to be true?
- Why may giving electric shocks to people lack mundane realism?
- The research was **androcentric** as only males were used and the findings cannot, therefore, be generalised to females. However, what obedience rates have replications using females often found?
- The research was **eurocentric**. What does this mean? Does the fact that Milgram's paradigm has been used in many cultures, with widely varying obedience rates found, suggest that the criticism has value? Explain your answer.
- The research lacks historical validity, as it was performed a long time ago and does not necessarily reflect obedience levels now. However, Burger (2009) used an adaptation of the procedure. Do his findings suggest the criticism is valid (see page 169)?

Research in focus

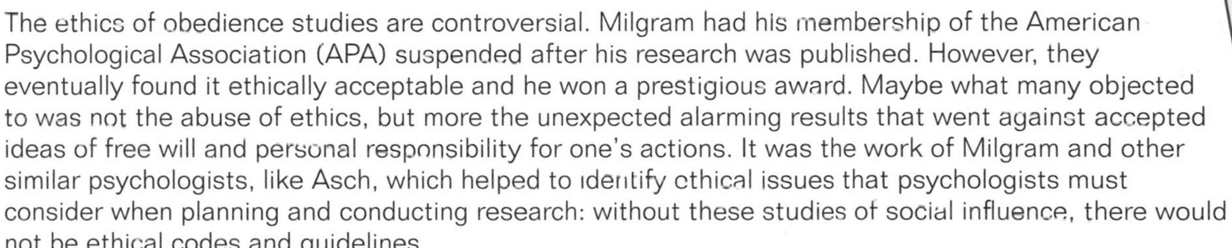

The ethics of obedience studies are controversial. Milgram had his membership of the American Psychological Association (APA) suspended after his research was published. However, they eventually found it ethically acceptable and he won a prestigious award. Maybe what many objected to was not the abuse of ethics, but more the unexpected alarming results that went against accepted ideas of free will and personal responsibility for one's actions. It was the work of Milgram and other similar psychologists, like Asch, which helped to identify ethical issues that psychologists must consider when planning and conducting research: without these studies of social influence, there would not be ethical codes and guidelines.

Psychological harm

Milgram is accused of exposing his participants to severe stress, which is supported by the extreme physical reactions many participants exhibited. However, only 2 per cent had any regrets about being involved and 74 per cent thought that they had learned something useful about themselves. A thorough debriefing was carried out where participants met the unharmed learner and a year later, all 40 participants received psychiatric assessments, none showing any signs of long-term damage. Therefore, the study can be justified by recourse to a cost–benefit analysis, where the short-term damage (stress reactions) is outweighed by the lack of long-term damage and the valuable results obtained. Baumrind (1964) accused Milgram of abusing his participants' rights and feelings, but Baumrind's criticism assumes that the experimental outcome was *expected*. In fact, Milgram was surprised by the high obedience rate. Prior to the experiment, Milgram asked 40 psychiatrists what percentage of people would obey up to 450 volts. Their prediction was only 1 per cent.

Deception and informed consent

Milgram did deceive his participants. He said that the study was concerned with memory and learning. Only after volunteers had agreed to take part were the electric shocks mentioned. Also, Mr Wallace was an actor who never actually received any electric shocks. Therefore participants could not give **informed**

consent – they volunteered without knowing the true purpose or procedure. Milgram defended his use of deception by debriefing his participants. Also, deception was necessary if participants were to behave 'realistically' – the participants had to believe they were real shocks, otherwise we could not generalise the results to real-life situations.

Right to withdraw

Milgram argued that participants did have the right to withdraw, as 35 per cent of them exercised this option and refused to carry on. However, the right to withdraw was not given explicitly before the study started and attempts to withdraw were met with the 'verbal prods' that tried to get them to continue.

Strengthen your learning

Make a list of the ethical issues contained within Milgram's study. Detail the evidence that supports these issues being violated and then detail any counter-arguments against such evidence. Using material in this way is a highly effective way of building elaboration into your answers, especially for the 12-mark essay questions.

Classic research

An experimental study into the nurse–physician relationship – Charles Hofling *et al.*, 1966

A major criticism of Milgram's study concerned how true to life the set up was and how externally valid his findings were. A number of naturalistic obedience studies in real-life settings have been carried out, but Hofling's study is significant because of its alarming findings.

Aim: To see whether nurses would obey orders from an unknown doctor to such an extent that there would be risk of harm.

Procedure: A confederate 'Dr Smith', allegedly from the psychiatric department, instructed 22 nurses individually by phone to give his patient 'Mr Jones' 20 mg of an unfamiliar drug called 'Astrofen'. Dr Smith was in a hurry and would sign the authorisation form later on. Astrofen was actually a sugar pill. The label on the box stated the maximum daily dose was 10 mg. So, if a nurse obeyed instructions, she would be giving twice the maximum dose. Also, hospital rules required doctors to sign authorisations before medication was given. Another rule demanded that nurses should be certain anyone was a genuine doctor.

Findings: Of the 22 nurses, 21 (95.4 per cent) obeyed without hesitation. A control group of 22 nurses were asked what they *would have done* in that situation: 21 said they would not have obeyed without authorisation, or exceeded the maximum dose.

Figure 5.18

Conclusions: Hofling *et al.* concluded that the power and authority of doctors was a greater influence on the nurses' behaviour than basic hospital rules. Also, what people *say* they would do and what they actually *do*, can be very different.

Evaluation:

- Hofling's study suggests that nurses and institutional staff should have special training in following rules rather than orders from authority figures.
- Hofling's study seems relevant to real-life settings. However, Rank and Jacobson (1977) reported that the drug was unfamiliar to nurses and that they had not been allowed to consult with each other, as was normal practice. When a familiar drug was used, Valium, and they were allowed to speak to their peers, only two out of 18 nurses (11 per cent) obeyed, suggesting that Hofling's study may not have external validity after all.

IN THE NEWS

Fatal injection was terrible mistake

Figure 5.19 Wayne Jowett

Eighteen-year-old Wayne Jowett, on remission from leukaemia, died in horrendous fashion when a cancer drug was wrongly injected into his spine instead of a vein. He died one month later from creeping paralysis after being in such pain it sometimes took six nurses to hold him down. A junior doctor correctly injected a first drug, Cytosine, into Wayne's spine and was surprised when passed a second syringe of Vincristine and told to inject it by a more senior doctor into the boy's spine, as he was aware this shouldn't occur. However, he didn't challenge the decision on the assumption the more senior doctor knew what he was doing. A Department of Health inquiry said staff had failed to question procedures and recommended an overhaul of training and safety procedures.

This is a terrible example of the negative consequences that can result from unquestioning obedience to authority figures, even though there was never any intention to harm Wayne. It bears a remarkable, though ultimately tragic, similarity to the findings of Hofling's hospital study.

Contemporary research

Replicating Milgram: Would people still obey today? – Jerry Burger, 2009

Milgram's study is one of the most famous psychology experiments ever undertaken, but would similar results be found today? Milgram's study would be unethical under present day guidelines, however Burger developed a version of Milgram's procedure that addressed ethical concerns, in order that a comparison could be made between obedience rates in the 1960s and now.

Aim: To develop a variation of Milgram's procedures allowing comparison with the original investigation while protecting the well-being of participants.

Procedure: Most of Milgram's procedure was followed, including the words used in the memory test and the experimenter's lab coat. However, important changes were made.

- No one with knowledge of Milgram's study was used and the maximum apparent shock was 150 volts, the level at which the learner first cries in pain, in order to protect participants from intense stress.
- A two-step screening process for participants was used to exclude any who might react negatively. No one with a history of mental problems or stress reactions was accepted. This excluded 38 per cent of potential participants.
- Participants were told three times they could withdraw at any time and received only a 15-volt real shock, as opposed to the 45 volts applied in Milgram's study.

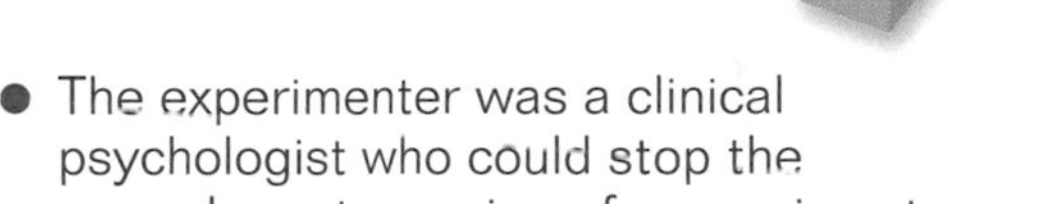

- The experimenter was a clinical psychologist who could stop the procedure at any sign of excessive stress.

Seventy participants of mixed gender were used. The relevant ethical monitoring body approved this procedure.

Findings: Burger found an obedience rate of 70 per cent, with no difference between male and female obedience rates. A second condition, where a defiant confederate teacher was introduced, failed to reduce obedience significantly, unlike Milgram's findings.

Conclusions: It is possible to replicate Milgram's study in a fashion non-harmful to participants. Obedience rates have not changed dramatically in the 40 odd years since Milgram's study.

Evaluation:

- Burger's technique permits obedience research to be conducted that has not been possible for decades.
- Burger's efforts to improve the ethics of the study are uncertain in their effectiveness and pose impractical demands.
- Different procedures used by Milgram and Burger do not allow a clear comparison of results.
- The study highlights the difficulties of extending research on destructive obedience in the context of contemporary ethical guidelines.

Explanations of obedience

Situational factors

According to Milgram (1974), most people would obey like his participants. So, the explanation for high levels of obedience must lie in aspects of the situation, rather than individual characteristics.

Perception of legitimate authority

Obedient participants accept the power and status of the experimenter: he was 'in charge'. Authority figures are visible symbols of power and status; these make it difficult to disobey. For example, the experimenter wore a lab coat.

The agentic state

When we obey, we see ourselves as the agent of the authority figure (in other words, we enter the agentic state). We give up personal responsibility, the autonomous state, and transfer responsibility onto the authority figure: remember 'I was only following orders' was the defence given by Nazi war criminal Adolf Eichmann.

Key terms

Agentic state – acting as an agent for another person who is therefore seen as responsible for the behaviour

Autonomous state – opposite side of the agentic state, where we see ourselves as personally responsible for our actions

Personal responsibility

The agentic and autonomous states are two sides of the same coin: anything detracting from the authority figure's power increases feelings of personal responsibility. This was demonstrated in Milgram's 'remote authority' variation. When the experimenter was not in the same room to give instructions, participants were more likely to disobey and when the learner's hand was forced onto a shock plate, obedience declined. It is more difficult to deny responsibility when you have to force the learner to endure the shocks. It is easier to disobey when you can see the effects of your behaviour. However, when someone else 'throws the switch' and the teacher merely reads out word pairs, it is easier to deny personal responsibility: 'He delivered the shock, not me'.

Gradual commitment ('foot in the door')

Participants got 'sucked into' a situation they found difficult to escape from. They had volunteered for a 'harmless' study of learning and memory; there was no mention of delivering electric shocks. This is only mentioned when they are in the experiment and then it becomes more difficult to leave. Once one shock of 15 volts is given, it becomes difficult not to give 30 volts and so on. The deeper in you are, the more difficult it is to escape.

You can watch an ABC News broadcast about Jerry Burger's Milgram study at

http://a.abcnews.com/Primetime/story?id=2765416&page=1

There are also press reports on the study:
A *New York Times* editorial

http://www.nytimes.com/2008/12/29/opinion/29mon3.html?r=1

The American Psychological Association Monitor
http://www.apa.org/monitor/2009/05/ethics.html

You are the researcher

Studies into obedience (as well as conformity) are difficult to carry out due to ethical concerns. For instance, if you reveal your hypothesis to your participants, then there is no point doing the study and yet you cannot get informed consent if you do. However, one way of overcoming these difficulties is to carry out the following study looking at peoples' obedience rates in everyday life. You will need two signs with the same wording '*please use other door*'; one sign should be printed professionally to give it an air of authority and the other should be poorly made with scruffy writing.

Place one sign on a door that is well used – there has to be an alternative door people can use – and count how many people obey/disobey the sign in a given time period. If several people approach the door simultaneously, you only count the behaviour of the first person, as the others may be influenced by this person's actions. Repeat the procedure using the scruffy sign. If people do obey authority, more people should obey the neat sign. If you have not got suitable doors, then use two adjoining benches where people congregate and have signs saying '*please use other bench*'.

PLEASE USE OTHER DOOR

PLEASE USE OTHER DOOR

Figure 5.20 Which of these signs are you more likely to obey?

Psychology in action

Obedience in the real world

One way in which psychologists can use knowledge they have gained about obedience is the training of staff, especially those in institutional settings, like a hospital. In such institutions there is a clear command structure and an expectation of unquestioning obedience, which can lead to terrible mistakes (see In the news section about Wayne Jowett on page 169). Staff members need to be trained to follow official procedures, not authority figures, and to have confidence to challenge authority figures' commands if they believe them to be wrong or potentially harmful.

Figure 5.21 Eighty per cent of aeroplane accidents result from people not challenging wrong decisions by authority figures

Tarnow (2000) investigated aeroplane accidents, finding that a major contributory factor in 80 per cent of accidents was the power stemming from the captain's absolute authority, which led to the co-pilots feeling unable to challenge wrong decisions.

Milgram's work into obedience can explain the abuses of Iraqi prisoners by US troops in the Abu Ghraib prison in Iraq in 2004. Several stages of abuse were involved. Firstly, *gradual commitment*, where initial abuses were minor, but paved the way for the acceptance of more serious abuse. Secondly, *senior role*, where low-ranking troops, like the teacher in Milgram's study, were given important roles in controlling prisoners. Thirdly, *dehumanisation*, where the prisoners were degraded, making it easier to suspend morality and abuse them. Fourthly, *justification*, where abuse was excused on the grounds of revenge for acts of violence carried out against American troops.

Assessment Check

1 Milgram's research has allowed insight into why people obey. Outline two reasons why people obey. [2 + 2 marks]
2 Outline one reason why people are obedient. [4 marks]
3 Describe one way in which Milgram's study can be considered unethical. [2 marks]
4 Explain one conclusion of Milgram's research. [3 marks]
5 Discuss Milgram's research into obedience to authority. [12 marks]

Examination guidance:

1 Question 1 requires two separate, relevant answers. Be careful you do not give the same answer twice using different words. Each relevant reason scores 1 mark, with an extra mark available for providing additional detail or elaboration.
2 Question 2 is similar to question 1, but only requires one reason, but this time for four marks. Therefore a more detailed answer is required.
3 This question calls for a relevant ethical issue to be described. Be careful you do not include any evaluation, as it will not gain extra credit. Deceit and psychological harm would be popular choices.
4 Students often get confused about the difference between findings and conclusions. A conclusion is the implications drawn from the findings. These should be expressed in terms of people in general, rather than the participants in a study.
5 The term 'discuss' means to outline and evaluate. Equal time should be devoted to each, as both are worth six marks. Milgram's study could be evaluated by the degree of research support, methodological and ethical considerations, as well as practical applications.

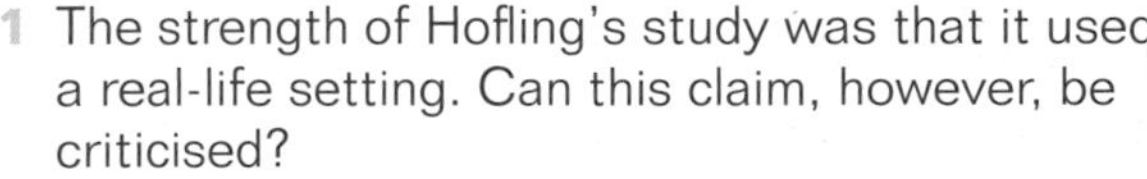

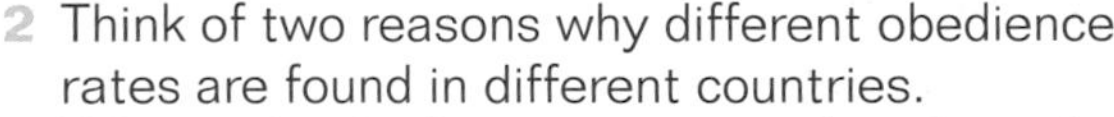

Strengthen your learning

1 The strength of Hofling's study was that it used a real-life setting. Can this claim, however, be criticised?
2 Think of two reasons why different obedience rates are found in different countries.
3 Why might obedience be generally a force for good?
4 What do Milgram's variations allow us to see?
5 Give one strength and one limitation of Burger's research.
6 Why is it difficult to conduct research into obedience and conformity?
7 Write two 50-word explanations for why people obey. Being able to write concisely, but informatively, will help you tremendously in your exams.

Social influence in everyday life

We have seen so far what social influence is in terms of conformity and obedience, now we turn to aspects of social influence occurring in everyday life.

Explanations of independent behaviour

Independent behaviour

Independent behaviour refers to resistance to conformity ('non-conformity') and to obeying authority figures ('disobedience'). Non-conformity can mean different things.

According to Willis (1963), two dimensions are necessary in order to construct representations of conformity and non-conformity, a) **dependence–independence** and b) **conformity–anti-conformity**. Taken together, these produce three major patterns of behaviour:

1 **Conformity**, which involves consistent movements *towards* social expectancy, for instance adopting the behaviour and norms of a reference group.

2 **Independence**, which involves a lack of consistent movement either towards or away from social expectancy (doing your own thing).

3 **Anti-conformity**, which involves a consistent movement *away* from social conformity, for instance adopting the behaviour and norms of a minority group.

Both 2 and 3 represent non-conformity, but differ in relation to the dimension of independence. Whereas 1 implies dependence on others, 2, as the word 'independent' implies, is free of such dependence; but 3 also involves dependence on others, in the sense of dependence on some minority group's norms which are adopted in opposition to the majority's.

Willis saw conformity and non-conformity not as fixed personality characteristics, but as outcomes of interaction in a particular situation. Also, in western cultures, anti-conformity has a more negative value than independence. As Hollander (1981) puts it, 'independence is probably seen as a more authentic, self-motivated, form of response than is the negativism of anti-conformity'.

Hollander and Willis (1964) found that participants responded differently to co-workers according to whether they behaved in a conforming, independent or anti-conforming way. Even when co-workers were presented as being more competent than the participant, participants were influenced more by the independent, competent co-worker than the anti-conforming co-worker, supporting Willis's claim that 2 and 3 are different kinds of non-conformity.

While 2 and 3 are forms of **dissent** (disagreeing with the majority), 3 seems to represent a refusal to conform, a way of expressing **individuality**. Dissent as self-expression is particularly likely in social influence situations where people have more options than simply agreeing or disagreeing with the majority, for example when there is a third option. According to Maslach *et al.* (1985), 'creative dissenters have high self-esteem, low anxiety in social situations and a strong tendency to be individuated', a willingness to act differently from others so as to stand out.

Resisting conformity

In Asch's study (see page 155), if naïve participants heard a dissenter disagreeing with the majority wrong answer on critical trials, conformity dropped sharply. Dissenters provide the participant with moral support, even if they give a different wrong answer from the majority, 'freeing' the participant to give the correct answer. The dissenter represents a form of social support. So, a major way of resisting conformity is to break the agreement of the majority – if they do not all agree, their impact is greatly reduced.

Conformity is reduced even when dissenters are not competent in particular situations. Allen and Levine (1971) found that conformity was reduced on a task involving visual judgements if there was a dissenter, even if the dissenting 'partner' wore glasses with thick lenses and admitted to having a sight problem. However, Baron and Byrne (1991) found that support that is received earlier is more effective than support received later: if you find yourself in a situation in which pressures towards conformity are increasing and you feel they should be resisted, try to speak out as quickly as possible. The sooner you do, the greater your chances of rallying others and resisting the majority.

Abrams *et al.* (1990) found that we do not conform with majorities simply because they are more numerous, they also have to be a group we regard as being similar to ourselves in some relevant respect.

Resisting obedience

Milgram's variations (see page 166) suggest that anything a) detracting from seeing the person giving orders as a legitimate authority and/or b) increasing the feeling of personal responsibility (in other words decreasing the *agentic state* and increasing the *autonomous state*) makes obedience less likely.

In Milgram's study, when the experimenter gave instructions by phone and when the participant could see, as well as hear, the effects of the shocks, obedience rates were reduced. Participants had to accept responsibility for their actions. When the experimenter said 'You have no choice, you must go on', many participants stopped obeying: they realised they did have a choice and were responsible.

Conformity also plays a role in helping to resist an experimenter. Milgram performed a variation with two other confederate teachers who refused to obey; participants witnessed this, making it easier for them to follow suit. The disobedient stooge teachers demonstrated that it is possible to disobey and how to do it.

Key terms

Reactance – rebellious anger produced by attempts to restrict freedom of choice

Ironic deviance – the belief that other people's behaviour occurs because they have been told to do it lowers their informational influence

Supplementary learning

Other factors in independent behaviour

Conformity

Gender

Eagly and Carli (1981) found that women are more conformist than men, suggesting that males display more independent behaviour. But females may only be more conformist in experimental situations, because they involve face-to-face scenarios, rather than in real-life situations, which often do not. Eagly and Chrvala (1986) found that older women are more conformist than older males, with younger women no more conformist than younger males. This suggests that it is not just gender, but other personal factors affecting conformist behaviour.

Reactance

When the freedom of choice of individuals is restricted, they may react with reactance (rebellious anger). Younger people often rebel against conforming to adult rules. Hamilton *et al.* (2005) found that adolescents in a low-reactance condition, who were told it was normal to experiment with drugs as long as they were aware of health risks, were less likely to smoke than those in a high-reactance condition who were told to never smoke.

Ironic deviance

Conway and Schaller (2005) found that office workers conformed and used a software product if other employees recommended it, but were less likely to conform if the colleagues had recommended it after being ordered by the office manager to use that particular software, rather than alternatives. This trait is known as ironic deviance. In this instance, they attributed fellow office workers' behaviour as being determined by the boss's order. This suggests that if individuals believe the source of informational influence is not genuine, conformity to that influence will be resisted.

continued ...

Figure 5.22 Those in high-reactance conditions are more likely to smoke

Status

People of low status within a group, like newcomers, are motivated to attain higher status by exhibiting conformist behaviour. (See Contemporary research section on Richardson, 2009 below.)

Obedience

Systematic processing

People are less likely to obey if they can consider what they have been ordered to do. Martin *et al.* (2007) found that when participants were encouraged and allowed to consider the content of an unreasonable order, they were less likely to obey.

Morality

Individuals making decisions based on moral considerations are more resistant to obedience than those who do not. Kohlberg (1969) gave moral dilemmas to participants from the Milgram study, finding that those who based decisions on moral principles were less obedient, supporting the theory.

Personality

Certain personality factors seem more orientated at resistance to obedience. Milgram (1974) identified the **authoritarian personality**, where people are prejudiced against minorities, are rigid and inflexible and are servile to higher-status individuals. People with opposite characteristics are more able to resist obedience.

Contemporary research

Distinction defeats group member deviance. The unlikely relationship between differentiation and newcomer conformity – Erika Richardson, 2009

Status affects conformist behaviour, as people of lower status within a group are motivated to attain higher status by exhibiting conformist behaviour.

Aim: To test the effects of information on newcomers' willingness to cooperate with group strategies.

Procedure: 84 male and female students were assigned randomly to same-sex groups comprising three people. Two of each group were confederates and one was a naïve participant. The naïve participants were led to believe that they were newcomers to the teams. Within each team the group members introduced themselves, with the confederates always going first. In each team the confederates described biographical details (level of education, amount of experience and so on) as of high or low status. The teams then looked at some information about two stock companies and decided which one to invest money in; one stock company was clearly superior to the other.

Team members gave their opinion, with the real participant always answering last. The two confederates chose the weaker of the two stock companies.

Findings: In the teams where the confederates are believed to be of high status, participants conformed to the group decision. The reverse was true where confederates were believed to be of low status.

Conclusions: People of perceived lower status conform to the decisions of those group members of perceived higher status, even when they believe those decisions are suspect, in order to attain higher status. People use competence-based clues about the status of other group members to determine the level of their conformist behaviour.

continued ...

...continued

Evaluation:

- The research has practical applications for the formation of groups. New group members should not be made to feel inferior, if they are to give honest opinions.
- The implication is that bad decisions made by people of high status are given additional support by the conformity to such decisions of junior group members. This is, therefore, similar to the findings of Tarnow (2000, see page 171) that aircraft accidents are often caused by junior co-pilots not questioning the wrong decisions of higher-status pilots.
- The study is unethical, as it involved deceit. The confederates were not who they claimed to be, therefore informed consent could not be given.

Figure 5.23 If we perceive others as of higher status, we are more likely to conform

To read a fuller account of the role of ironic deviance in conformity behaviour and of Lucien Conway and Mark Schaller's study go to http://www2.psych.ubc.ca/~schaller/ConwaySchaller2005.pdf

Research in focus

In what ways could Richardson's (2009) study be considered unethical? Can such breaches of ethical principles be justified?

Richardson's study was an experiment. What kind of experimental design was used?

What were the IV and DV?

What is the advantage of having mixed-gender samples?

Participants in Richardson's study were randomly assigned to teams. What is random sampling? How is it achieved? Does it guarantee a representative sample?

You are the researcher

Design a study to investigate a factor influencing resistance to conformity or obedience. You will have to choose your factor first, then decide what experimental design to use, what your IV and DV will be and create a hypothesis.

If you choose gender as a factor, you could perform a replication of Jenness's study (see page 154) to see whether females conform more. The experimental design would be the independent groups design; the IV would be gender and the DV would be the difference between the two individual estimates and the group norm. As previous research indicates that females are more conformist, you would have a directional hypothesis, like, 'female individual estimates of the number of beans in a jar will move significantly closer to a group norm than those of males'. Choose a factor of your own and have a go.

Strengthen your learning

1. Teachers often tell students how to improve performance. However, even though capable, some students do not follow their teachers' instructions. Can you explain such behaviour using reactance? (See page 174.)
2. Explain the difference between conformity, independence and anti-conformity?
3. How does the presence of a dissenter reduce the likelihood of conforming?
4. How does increasing personal responsibility and lowering legitimate authority increase resistance to obedience?
5. How many other factors of independent behaviour are there? Outline each one in no more than 50 words each.

Assessment Check

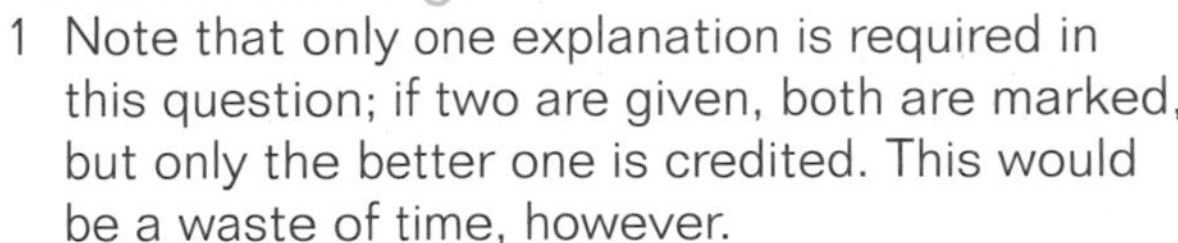

1. Explain one way in which people resist pressures to conform. [3 marks]
2. Outline ways in which people resist pressures to obey. [6 marks]
3. a) Describe one explanation of how people resist pressures to obey. [3 marks]
   b) Give one criticism of this explanation. [2 marks]
4. Research studies show that some people are able to resist pressures to conform and obey, despite the social pressures put on them. Outline and evaluate explanations of independent behaviour in social influence research. [12 marks]

Examination guidance:

1. Note that only one explanation is required in this question; if two are given, both are marked, but only the better one is credited. This would be a waste of time, however.
2. Question 2 calls for an outline of at least two ways in which people resist pressures to obey. If more than two are given, less detail is expected.
3. This is an example of a parted question. You need to give a relevant explanation in part a) to gain access to the marks in part b).
4. In question 4 there are six marks available for the outline and six marks for the evaluation. Ensure you dedicate equal amounts of time to both parts.

Locus of control

Locus of control (LOC) was identified as a personality dimension by Rotter (1966). It concerns the extent to which people perceive themselves as being in control of their own lives. Individuals with *high internal* LOC believe they can affect the outcomes of situations. Individuals with *high external* LOC believe things turn out a certain way regardless of their actions.

Internal LOC refers to the belief that things happen as a result of an individual's choices and decisions, while external LOC refers to the belief that things happen as a result of luck, fate or other uncontrollable external forces. Rotter (1966) believed that having an internal LOC makes individuals more resistant to social pressure, with those seeing themselves in control of a situation more likely to perceive themselves as having a free choice to conform or obey.

Key terms

Locus of control – an individual's beliefs about the causes of successes and failures

Attributional style – the meanings an individual attributes to people's behaviour and the way they experience life events

Attributional style

In attribution theory, behaviour is said to be caused externally by the situation one is in or internally by dispositional factors like personality. The high obedience rates observed in Milgram's study are attributed to behaviour being under external (situational) control, as most participants' behaviour was determined by the orders of the authority figure, an external/situational factor, rather than by morality, an internal/dispositional factor.

When individuals experience successes or failures they make **causal attributions**; in other words, they try to make sense of them and develop, from experience, particular attributional styles that they can apply to future situations. Therefore attitudes and behaviour become pre-determined. Those who blame others for failures will see failures as temporary events and do not let such negative occurrences affect the way they view events. Such people have a **positive explanatory style** and exhibit independent behaviour; they are more able to resist conformity and obedience. Conversely, those who have a **depressed attributional style** see themselves as incapable of turning failures into successes and have a fatalistic view of the world (what will happen, will happen). Such people are not independent and are more likely to conform and obey.

Have a go at measuring your own LOC at www.psych.uncc.edu/pagoolka/LocusofControl-intro.html

Supplementary learning

Research studies into locus of control and attributional styles

- Shute (1975) exposed undergraduates to peers who expressed either conservative or liberal attitudes to drug taking. He found that undergraduates with internal LOC conformed less to expressing pro-drug attitudes, supporting the idea that having internal LOC increases resistance to conformity.
- Moghaddam (1998) found that Japanese people conform more easily than Americans and have more of an external LOC. This suggests that differences in conformity across cultures can be explained by differences in LOC.
- Avtgis (1998) performed a meta-analysis of studies involving LOC and conformity, finding that individuals with external locus of control were more easily persuadable and more likely to conform, supporting the idea of differences in LOC being linked to differences in conformist behaviour.
- Twenge *et al.* (2004) found that Americans are developing increasingly external LOC, seen as a result of increased divorce, mental illness and suicide. Americans have, therefore, become less independent in their behaviour.
- Jones and Kavanagh (1996) investigated the link between moral disengagement and individual differences in LOC. They found that those with high external LOC were more likely to obey unethical authority figures. This is a possible explanation for corporate fraud, where junior staff members comply with immoral/criminal directives given to them by more senior managers (see Psychology in action section, page 179).

Figure 5.24 Japanese people conform more readily than Americans. Perhaps we can explain this by reference to locus of control

Psychology in action

Corporate fraud

Increasingly, corporate fraud is in the news, with large financial corporations, like Enron, found to have misappropriated billions of pounds. These frauds involve large groups of people working together within hierarchical structures. Evidence suggests that such frauds are only possible where lower-status staff have external LOC, increasing the possibility of them complying with illegal orders given by authority figures within the hierarchy. Chiu (2004) suggests that 'whistle blowing' – where individuals within a hierarchy report illegal activities at the risk of losing their jobs – is performed by individuals with high internal LOC.

Figure 5.25 Whistle blowers who report illegal actions tend to have high internal locus of control

You are the researcher

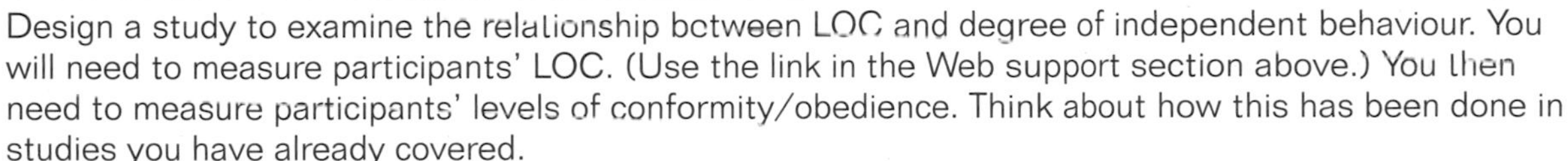

Design a study to examine the relationship between LOC and degree of independent behaviour. You will need to measure participants' LOC. (Use the link in the Web support section above.) You then need to measure participants' levels of conformity/obedience. Think about how this has been done in studies you have already covered.

Research in focus

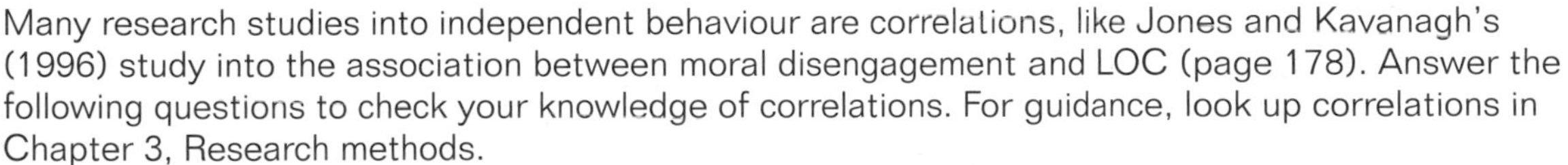

Many research studies into independent behaviour are correlations, like Jones and Kavanagh's (1996) study into the association between moral disengagement and LOC (page 178). Answer the following questions to check your knowledge of correlations. For guidance, look up correlations in Chapter 3, Research methods.

- How do correlations differ from experiments?
- What is the difference between positive and negative correlations?
- Give one advantage and one disadvantage of correlational studies.
- What is a correlation coefficient?

Evaluation

Evaluation of locus of control and attributional style

- LOC is assessed using general scales of measurement, like the Rotter scale. However, these may not be suited for purpose in examining independent behaviour in specific situations.
- One weakness of attribution theory is that it sees external (situational) factors as leading to conformist/obedient behaviour and, conversely, internal (dispositional) factors as leading to independent behaviour. However, there are situational factors associated with independent behaviour and dispositional ones associated with conformity/obedience.
- It is too simplistic to suggest that behaviour is caused by either internal or external LOC. What is more likely is that behaviour in a given situation is dependent upon whether internal or external factors are dominant.

Strengthen your learning

1 What is meant by locus of control?
2 What is the difference between those with internal LOC and those with external LOC?
3 Why are individuals with internal LOC more able to be independent?
4 Attribution theory sees behaviour as caused by two possible factors. What are they?
5 How can we link the results of Milgram's study to attributional style?
6 What is the difference between having a positive explanatory style and a depressed attributional style?
7 Does research support the idea of a link between LOC/attributional style and likelihood of conformity/obedience?

How social influence research aids understanding of social change

Social change occurs continually, but at a gradual pace, as minority viewpoints crossover and become the majority opinion. For instance, Greenpeace started life in Canada in the early 1970s and was originally regarded as a bunch of cranks attracting ridicule and legal action. However, slowly at first, the group attracted more members and popular support, until finally becoming the mainstream, accepted, legitimate voice for environmental issues. Such social change is explained by reference to minority influence.

Some social change can be regarded in positive terms, like increased rights for women. However, social change can also be negative, like the genocide inflicted upon millions by the Nazis.

Assessment Check

1 a) Explain what is meant by locus of control. [2 marks]
   b) Outline the influence of locus of control on independent behaviour. [4 marks]

2 The following statements are either true or false. Copy and complete the table by placing a T or an F in the box alongside each statement to indicate whether it is true or false. [4 marks]

Statement	True or false
Individuals with a high internal locus of control believe they can affect the outcomes of situations	
An external locus of control makes individuals more resistant to social pressure	
An internal locus of control refers to the belief that things happen due to uncontrollable external forces	
Individuals with a high external locus of control believe that things occur in certain ways regardless of their behaviour	

3 Outline and evaluate the influence of locus of control on independent behaviour. [12 marks]

Examination guidance:

1 This is a parted question. Part a) calls for an explanation of locus of control. Do not wander off into outlining how locus of control affects independent behaviour; you do that in part b).

2 This is a choice question. The choice is to decide whether each statement is true or false. Do not make the mistake of thinking that there will be two false and two true statements; there is no way of knowing in advance how many will be true/false.

3 This is an 'essay' question. Six marks are available for outlining the influence of locus of control and six marks are available for an evaluation, like the degree of support from research studies, practical applications and methodological considerations.

The role of minority influence in social change

Minorities can change attitudes and behaviour over time. This incurs a strong, long-lasting form of conformity, involving fundamental changes in belief systems. In this way **innovation** occurs and new ideas and behaviours become adopted as mainstream practices. This requires minorities to be consistent, flexible, committed and relevant. The gradual process by which minority opinions become majority ones is called **social cryptoamnesia** (the 'snowball effect'). At first, converts to the minority viewpoint are few, but as more and more people change their attitude, the pace picks up and the minority gains status, power and acceptability.

Key terms

Minority influence – a type of social influence that motivates individuals to reject established majority group norms

Research studies of minority influence

Moscovici *et al.* (1969) found 8 per cent of participants in groups containing a minority of confederates who consistently called blue slides green agreed with this wrong answer, compared to only 1 per cent in groups containing confederates who inconsistently did so indicating consistency to be the important variable.

Consistent minorities have even greater influence on private attitudes, as in another consistent condition where participants gave their answers privately, there was even greater agreement. This demonstrates how minority influence, unlike majority influence, affects thinking, leading to changes in beliefs systems and eventually social change.

Research studies generally support Moscovici. Meyers *et al.* (2000) found minority groups successful in affecting majorities were more consistent than those that were not.

Martin *et al.* (2003) found messages supported by a minority group were more resistant to change than if they were supported by a majority group. This suggests that cognitive processing of minority opinions leads to attitudes resistant to counter-persuasion and illustrates how minority opinion is a strong enough force to lead to social change.

Moscovici (born 1925) is a Romanian-born French Jew, with an event-filled, inspirational life. His experience of totalitarian governments, with their negative attitudes towards social change and innovation, inspired him to research minority influence. Read more about him at http://en.wikipedia.org/wiki/Moscovici

Supplementary learning

Other research studies of minority influence

- Nemeth and Kwan (1987) found that in tasks requiring divergent thinking (thinking simultaneously in different ways), minority influence leads to better performance than majority influence.
- Petersen and Nemeth (1996) found the opposite to be true with convergent thinking (focusing on one aspect), as better performance came from majority rather than minority influence. This suggests that it is the nature of a task that determines whether minority or majority influence is best.
- Martin and Hewstone (1996) found that minority influence leads to more creative and novel judgements than majority influence, supporting the idea of minority influence being a social force for innovation and change.

Strengthen your learning

1 What is meant by social change?
2 Give an example of positive and negative social change.
3 Explain in no more than 50 words how minority influence can bring about social change.
4 What is the snowball effect?
5 What was Moscovici's main conclusion?
6 In Martin *et al.*'s (2003) study, why did minority influence lead to resistant attitudes?
7 How can findings from social influence research be used to promote positive social change and resist negative social change?

Psychology in action

Resistance to destructive forces

Research studies show that it is often minority influence that provides the catalyst for social change, while majority influence and obedience merely reinforce existing social norms. However, sometimes conformity and obedience can lead to social changes with destructive consequences, like the Tutsi/Hutu massacres in Rwanda (see page 161). Practical applications assisting resistance to such destructive forces can be created from what we have learned about such events.

Morality

People taught to base decisions on moral principles are able to resist destructive conformity and obedience. Such people who are able to resist are more likely to become agents for social change. Dimow (2004), a teacher in Milgram's study who refused to obey, believes that his resistance came from his socialist upbringing where he was taught that authority figures would often have different views of morality and he should behave according to his own moral code, not others.

Systematic processing

People are less likely to obey or conform if they have time to consider what they have been told to do. Martin *et al.* (2007) found that when participants were encouraged and given time to consider the content of an unreasonable order, they were less likely to obey.

Locus of control

Shute (1975) found that individuals with internal LOC conformed less, suggesting that providing individuals with experiences fostering the creation of internal LOC would help more people to resist and thus be agents for social change.

Support

Asch (1955) found that when participants had a supporter, conformity dropped dramatically. Indeed this person did not even have to support the viewpoint of the participant, just merely disagree with the viewpoint of the majority. This suggests that people need to seek out a dissenting voice, in order to find the conviction to resist.

Figure 5.26 Sometimes conformity and obedience can lead to destructive consequences, as in the Rwandan civil war of 1994

Assessment Check

1 Outline the role of minority influence in social change. [4 marks]
2 Critically discuss the implications of research into social influence for social change. [12 marks]
3 Explain two implications for social change of research into social influence. [3 + 3 marks]

Examination guidance:

1 Outlining anything other than the role of minority influence will not be creditworthy. Remember, outline means to give brief details, so make sure you do not include any evaluation.
2 The term 'critically discuss' in this question means to outline and evaluate. Six marks are available for each of these, so ensure that there is a balance between the two parts of your answer.
3 This question is really in two parts, as each explanation is worth three marks. One mark is given for each relevant explanation, with a further two marks for elaboration of each explanation.

Key terms

Social change – the process by which society changes beliefs, attitudes and behaviour to create new social norms (expected ways of behaviour and thinking)

End of chapter review

- Conformity involves yielding to group pressure. Kelman (1958) proposed three types of conformity: compliance, identification and internalisation, which differ in the degree to which they affect belief systems.
- Conformity is regarded as a form of majority influence, with minority influence regarded as a form of internalisation.
- One motive for conformist behaviour is informational social influence, where individuals yield to majority influence in order to be correct. This was demonstrated in Jenness's (1932) study.
- Another motive for conformist behaviour is normative social influence, where individuals yield to majority influence to be accepted/avoid rejection. This was demonstrated in Asch's (1955) study.
- Another explanation of conformist behaviour is cognitive dissonance, where conformist behaviour reduces the unpleasant feelings created by simultaneously holding two contradictory cognitions.
- Obedience involves complying with the demands of an authority figure. It is generally a force for good, helping society to function in a constructive way. However, destructive obedience can have negative consequences.
- Milgram's (1963) obedience to authority study was inspired by the unquestioning obedience to Nazi directives to exterminate millions of people. Unexpectedly large obedience rates were found.
- Milgram's variations identified the key variables at play. Perception of legitimate authority was one important factor. Another was the agentic state, where an individual sees themselves as an agent of the authority figure. Further factors were the degree of personal responsibility perceived and gradual commitment, where obedience to initial orders makes disobedience to later orders more difficult.
- Milgram's study raised serious ethical concerns and attracted criticism over the validity of the findings.
- Independent behaviour refers to resistance to conformity ('non-conformity') and to obeying authority figures ('disobedience').
- Non-conformity consists of independence, where there is neither movement towards or away from social expectancy, and anti-conformity, where there is movement away from social expectancy.
- Conformity is resisted by the presence of a dissenter, while obedience is resisted by reducing the status of the authority figure and/or increasing the perception of personal responsibility.
- Other factors involved in independent behaviour towards conformity include gender, reactance, ironic deviance and status.
- Other factors involved in independent behaviour towards obedience include systematic processing, morality and personality.
- Locus of control (LOC) concerns the degree of control individuals believe they have over their lives. Those with high internal LOC are more resistant to pressures to conform and obey.
- Attributional style can affect levels of independent behaviour. Individuals with a depressed attributional style have a fatalistic view of the world and exhibit less independent behaviour.
- Social change can occur via minority influence. Minority groups that are consistent, flexible, committed and relevant are more able to affect individual's belief systems, to such an extent that over time the minority viewpoint becomes the majority one.
- Minority influence allows innovation to occur, where new ideas and behaviours become adopted as mainstream practices.
- Minority influence provides the catalyst for social change, while majority influence and obedience reinforce existing social norms. However, sometimes majority influence and obedience lead to destructive consequences.

6 Individual differences

Introduction

As a science, psychology formulates a generalised view of the mind and behaviour to discover what humans have in common. This can include research into how memory functions or the ways in which cognitive abilities develop. Indeed most psychological research tests large numbers of participants and averages out the results to establish 'truths'.

However, some psychological topics focus more upon how individuals differ from each other. The particular topic scrutinised in this chapter is abnormality, with its various definitions, explanations and treatments.

Understanding the specification

- There are three definitions of abnormality you should be able to describe fully: deviation from social norms, failure to function adequately and deviation from ideal mental health. You also need to understand the limitations of each definition.
- There are two approaches to psychopathology you need to know: the biological approach and the psychological approach, which sub-divides into three parts – the psychodynamic, behavioural and cognitive approaches.
- There are two broad categories of treatments that need to be studied: biological therapies, including drugs and electro-convulsive therapy (ECT), as they are specifically referred to, and three psychological therapies: psychoanalysis, systematic desensitisation and cognitive behavioural therapy.

Psychopathology (abnormality)

Definitions of abnormality

Abnormality is difficult to define, as psychologists disagree about its causes and how it displays itself. Some say that abnormality results from defective biology, some that it stems from 'incorrect' learning or faulty thought processes, while others see it resulting from problems of the mind and personality. These different views are dominant at different times and across different cultures. Rosenhan and Seligman (1995) argue that normality is merely an absence of abnormality. This means that by defining abnormality, we also make decisions about what is normal.

Various criteria for defining abnormality are proposed, each with its own strengths and weaknesses.

Key terms

Abnormality – a psychological or behavioural state leading to impairment of interpersonal functioning and/or distress to others

Deviation from social norms – behaviour violating accepted social rules

If you would like to learn more about Stephen Gough's naked rambles then visit his official website at http://nakedwalk.org/

IN THE NEWS

Naked rambler faces life in prison

The naked rambler, Stephen Gough, has been told he'll spend the rest of his life behind bars if he continues refusing to wear clothes in public.

The former Royal Marine, notorious for his naked hike from Land's End to John O'Groats in 2003, has spent much of the past seven years in prison for repeatedly appearing nude in public.

He was yesterday found guilty of breaching the peace when he walked naked from Perth prison in December after finishing a 12-month sentence for the same offence. Mr Gough was warned he will continue to be jailed every time he steps out of prison without any clothes on.

Source: adapted from the *Daily Telegraph*, 13 January 2010. © Telegraph Media Group Limited 2010.

Stephen Gough's persistence in appearing naked in public and undergoing repeated imprisonment for stripping off would be considered abnormal behaviour by many definitions of abnormality. Others might argue that he is quite sane and just behaving according to his individualistic principles.

Figure 6.1 The naked rambler, Stephen Gough

The deviation from social norms definition

Society sets norms, or unwritten rules, for acceptable behaviour. According to the deviation from social norms definition, behaviour that deviates from these norms is abnormal and abnormal behaviour is, therefore, whatever violates social norms. This definition allows a distinction between desirable and undesirable behaviours and identifies those behaving undesirably as **social deviants** and permits intervention to help them. This can be beneficial to such individuals as sexual deviants, as they may be unable to seek help themselves.

The definition gives a social dimension to the concept of abnormality, with Szasz (1962) arguing that a main function of psychiatry is to exclude from society those perceived as behaving in socially unacceptable ways.

Limitations of the definition

- **Subjective** – social norms are not real, but are based instead on the opinions of elites within society rather than majority opinion. These are then used to 'control' those perceived as a threat to social order. A true definition of abnormality should be objective and free from subjective factors.
- **Change over time** – the norms defined by society often relate to moral standards that vary over time as social attitudes change. As an example, homosexuality was not removed from the ICD classification of mental disorders until 1990.
- **Individualism** – those who do not conform to social norms may not be abnormal, but merely individualistic or eccentric and not problematic in any sense.
- **Human rights abuse** – the definition permits abuse of human rights. Szasz (1962) sees the term 'mental illness' as a form of social control. Those labelled as abnormal are discriminated against. Some countries label political opponents as abnormal and confine them to mental institutions.
- **Situational and developmental norms** – deviation from social norms does not necessarily have mental health consequences. The situation or context in which norms are broken is important. Naturists break social norms, but are not perceived as having mental problems. Indeed there are beaches where nudity is the prevalent social norm and remaining clothed appears odd. There are also developmental (or age) norms to consider. If a 2-year-old child wears a nappy, that is considered normal behaviour. The same is not true for a 40-year-old adult.
- **Conforming neurotics** – these are people who conform strictly to social norms. They have such a fear of rejection that they conform rigidly to society's norms and worry excessively about them. However, such individuals are not included within this definition.
- **Ethnocentric bias in diagnosis** – western social norms reflect the behaviour of the majority 'white' population. Deviation from these norms by ethnic groups means that ethnic minorities are over-represented in the mental illness statistics. Cochrane (1977) found that black people were more often diagnosed as schizophrenic than white people or Asians. However, while this high rate of diagnosis for black people is found in Britain, it is not found in such countries as Jamaica where black people are the majority, suggesting a cultural bias in diagnosis among British psychiatrists.
- **Value of breaking social norms** – it can be beneficial to break social norms. Suffragettes broke many social norms, but this led to votes for women. Should such people be classified as abnormal?
- **Cultural differences** – social norms vary within and across cultures and so it is difficult to know when they are being broken. If a teacher has a plastic duck on his head does it indicate abnormality? Would the same be true of an art student? Therefore this definition of abnormality is culturally relative.

Research in focus

One problem with interpreting behaviour from different cultures is that of imposed etics.

What is an imposed etic and what effect can it have?

Key terms

Failure to function adequately – an inability to cope with day-to-day living

The failure to function adequately definition

The failure to function adequately definition perceives individuals as abnormal when their behaviour suggests that they cannot cope with everyday life.

Such people do not experience the usual range of emotions or behaviours. Behaviour is considered abnormal when it causes distress leading to dysfunction, like disrupting the ability to work and/or conduct satisfying interpersonal relationships.

The definition focuses on individual suffering, thus drawing attention to the personal experiences associated with mental disorders.

Rosenhan and Seligman (1989) suggest that personal dysfunction has seven features. The more an individual has, the more they are classed as abnormal (see Table 6.1).

Features of personal dysfunction	Description of a feature
Personal distress	A key feature of abnormality. Includes depression and anxiety disorders.
Maladaptive behaviour	Behaviour stopping individuals from attaining life goals, both socially and occupationally.
Unpredictability	Displaying unexpected behaviours characterised by loss of control, like attempting suicide after failing a test.
Irrationality	Displaying behaviour that cannot be explained in a rational way.
Observer discomfort	Displaying behaviour causing discomfort to others.
Violation of moral standards	Displaying behaviour violating society's moral standards.
Unconventionality	Displaying unconventional behaviours.

Table 6.1 Rosenhan and Seligman's features of personal dysfunction

Figure 6.2 According to Rosenhan and Seligman, displaying unconventional behaviours is a sign of abnormality

Figure 6.3 Harold Shipman

Sue *et al.* (1994) found that most people seeking clinical help believe that they are suffering from psychological problems that interfere with the ability to function properly. This supports the definition.

Limitations of the definition

- **Abnormality is not always accompanied by dysfunction** – psychopaths, people with anti-social personality disorders, can commit murders and still appear normal. Harold Shipman, the English doctor who murdered at least 215 of his patients over a 23-year period, maintained the outward appearance of a respectable member of his profession. Such people are certainly abnormal despite not exhibiting many features of dysfunction.
- **Subjective nature of the features of dysfunction** – there are problems in defining the features. For example, how is distress measured? People differ in their subjective experiences. What is normal behaviour for eccentrics, like wearing flamboyant clothes, is abnormal for introverts.
- **Normal abnormality** – there are times in people's lives when it is normal to suffer distress, like when loved ones die. Grieving is psychologically healthy to overcome loss.
- **Distress to others** – behaviour may cause distress to other people and be regarded as dysfunctional, while the person themselves feels no distress, like Stephen Gough, the naked rambler (see page 186).
- **Personally rewarding abnormality** – an individual's apparently dysfunctional behaviour may actually be rewarding. For example, a person's eating disorder can bring affection and attention from others.
- **Cultural differences** – what is considered 'normal functioning' varies from culture to culture and so abnormal functioning of one culture should not be used to judge people's behaviour from other cultures and sub-cultures.

The ideal mental health definition

This definition perceives abnormality in a similar way to the perception of physical health and looks for an absence of well-being.

Marie Jahoda (1958) devised the concept of **ideal mental health**. She identified six characteristics that individuals should exhibit in order to be normal (see Table 6.2). An absence of these characteristics indicates individuals as being abnormal, in other words displaying deviation from ideal mental health.

Key terms

Deviation from ideal mental health – failure to meet the criteria for perfect psychological well-being

Characteristics of ideal mental health	Description of characteristics
Positive attitude towards oneself	Having self-respect and a positive self-concept.
Self-actualisation	Experiencing personal growth and development. 'Becoming everything one is capable of becoming.'
Autonomy	Being independent, self-reliant and able to make personal decisions.
Resisting stress	Having effective coping strategies and being able to cope with everyday anxiety-provoking situations.
Accurate perception of reality	Perceiving the world in a non-distorted fashion. Having an objective and realistic view of the world.
Environmental mastery	Being competent in all aspects of life and able to meet the demands of any situation. Having the flexibility to adapt to changing life circumstances.

Table 6.2 Jahoda's characteristics of ideal mental health

The more criteria individuals fail to meet and the further they are away from realising individual criteria, the more abnormal they are.

Like the deviation from social norms and the failure to function adequately definitions, this definition focuses on behaviours and characteristics seen as desirable, rather than what is undesirable.

A positive aspect of the definition is that it emphasises positive achievements rather than failures and distress.

Limitations of the definition

- **Over-demanding criteria** – at a given moment, most people do not meet all the ideals. For example, few people experience personal growth all the time. Therefore, according to this definition, most people are abnormal. Thus the criteria may actually be ideals (how you would like to be) rather than actualities.
- **Subjective criteria** – many of the criteria are vague and difficult to measure. Measuring physical health is more objective, using well-established methods like X-rays and blood tests. Diagnosing mental health is more subjective, relying largely on the self-reports of patients who may be mentally ill and not, therefore, reliable.
- **Contextual effects** – as with other definitions, mental health criteria are affected by context. Spitting while out for a run is quite normal, but this behaviour is not considered normal in the college cafeteria.
- **Changes over time** – perceptions of reality change over time. In thirteenth-century Europe seeing visions was a positive sign of religious commitment, now it would be perceived as a sign of schizophrenia.
- **Cultural variation** – the criteria used to judge mental health are subject to cultural relativism and should not be used to judge others of different cultures and sub-cultures. Some types of abnormality only exist in certain cultures. For instance, one culture-bound syndrome is Koro, found only in South-east Asia, China and Africa, where a man affected with the condition believes that his penis is fatally retracting into his body. Western cultural definitions of abnormality, like the ideal mental health definition, are equally not culture free.
- **Non-desirability of autonomy** – collectivist cultures emphasise communal goals and behaviours and regard autonomy as undesirable. Nobles (1976) believes that Africans have a sense of 'we' which differs from the western 'me' view. Western cultures are more concerned with individual attainment and goals.

Key terms

Cultural relativism – definitions of what is 'normal functioning' vary from culture to culture and are equally valid

You are the researcher

Design a questionnaire to measure Jahoda's characteristics of ideal health. Include questions that produce both *qualitative* and *quantitative* data.

Demonstrate how you would you use *content analysis* to analyse your qualitative data.

Strengthen your learning

1 Explain what is meant by abnormality.
2 a) Outline the definition of abnormality which concerns deviation from social norms.
  b) What does this definition allow us to distinguish between?
  c) Explain three limitations of the definition.
3 a) Outline the definition of abnormality which concerns failure to function adequately.
  b) Outline Rosenhan and Seligman's features of personal dysfunction.
  c) How does Sue's (1994) research support the definition?
  d) Explain three limitations of the definition.
4 a) Outline the definition of abnormality which concerns deviation from ideal mental health.
  b) Outline Jahoda's (1958) characteristics of ideal mental health.
  c) Explain three limitations of the definition.
  d) What does the definition share with our other two definitions of abnormality?
5 a) What is meant by cultural relativism?
  b) How can all three definitions of abnormality be seen as culturally relative?

Assessment Check

1 The following statements relate to definitions of abnormality.
  A Abnormal behaviours are ones that are statistically rare.
  B People who cannot cope with everyday activities are abnormal.
  C People displaying behaviours regarded as non-acceptable to society are abnormal.
  D Abnormal behaviours are those that prevent a person from reaching self-actualisation.

Copy and complete the table below by inserting the statement, A, B, C or D, which describes each definition of abnormality. [3 marks]

Definitions of abnormality	Descriptions of abnormality
Failure to function adequately	
Deviation from ideal mental health	
Deviation from social norms	

2 Explain one limitation of each of the following:
  a) The deviation from social norms definition of abnormality.
  b) The failure to function adequately definition of abnormality. [2 marks]

3 Every time Betty leaves home she has a tendency to check several times that all doors are locked. This makes her anxious and generally results in her being late to work.
Using the failure to function adequately definition of abnormality, explain why Betty's behaviour may be regarded as abnormal. [2 marks]

4 Outline and evaluate two or more definitions of abnormality. [12 marks]

Examination guidance:

1 The first question is a selection question where you must choose from the options available. This means the correct answers are there, but you must identify and place them in the correct order. One description will be left over.
2 This question requires a relevant limitation of the two definitions quoted. Any outlining of these definitions would not be creditworthy.
3 This is a scenario or stem question, requiring reference to information in the scenario to gain marks.
4 This is a long-answer question with six marks available for outlining definitions and six marks for evaluating them. Limitations of the definitions, including reference to cultural relativism, could be a good way to create an evaluation.

Key terms

Biological approach – a model of abnormality perceiving mental disorders as illnesses with physical causes

Psychiatry – a branch of medicine dealing with the study, diagnosis and treatment of mental illness

Neurotransmitters – chemicals facilitating communication between brain nerve cells

The biological approach to psychopathology

The biological approach is the most widely used method of treating abnormalities in the western world. Developed by the medical profession, it is also referred to as the medical model and is the approach most favoured by psychiatrists (doctors specialising in the study of psychiatry). It perceives psychological abnormalities as similar to physical illnesses, caused by abnormal biological processes, specifically in the structure and workings of the brain.

The model assumes that mental disorders have physiological causes related to the physical structure and/or functioning of the brain. Distinctions are made between **organic disorders** and **functional disorders**. Organic disorders involve physical brain damage and/or disease, like a brain tumour, whereas functional disorders have no obvious physiological causes, like depression.

In medicine, physical illnesses have clear-cut symptoms, with doctors able to diagnose conditions using well-established criteria. Psychiatrists also use diagnostic criteria for mental illness, comparing symptoms with classifications of illnesses. In Britain, psychiatrists use the *International Classification of Diseases, 10th edition* (ICD-10) (1992), while American psychiatrists use the *Diagnostic Statistical Manual, 4th edition* (DSM-IV) (1994), which differs slightly.

Brain scans are used to help with diagnoses, particularly of organic disorders.

Biological factors

There are four ways in which biological factors are seen as causing mental impairments. There is some overlap between them.

Bacterial infections and viruses

Bacterial infections and viruses can damage the brain, causing malfunctions. One example is **general paralysis of the insane**, a neuropsychiatric disorder caused by syphilis (a sexually transmitted disease). With this disorder, the bacterium *Treponema pallidum* enters the body, causing ulcers in the genital region. In the latter stages of the illness, tumour-like masses develop in the brain. Memory and intellect are impaired, and personality and mood are greatly affected, with delusions and bizarre behaviour commonly occurring. Eventually, spastic paralysis sets in, the patient becomes bed-ridden and death occurs over a period of about 3–5 years.

Figure 6.4 Tertiary syphilis

Research studies into bacterial infections and viruses

- Brown *et al.* (2000) found a link between respiratory infections in the second trimester of pregnancy and the subsequent development of schizophrenia when the affected foetus reaches adulthood. This implies that infections from bacteria and viruses can cause mental illness.
- Gaskell *et al.* (2009) found that the toxoplasmosis parasite, transmitted to humans through eating food contaminated with cat faeces, is associated with developing schizophrenia and manic depression. The parasite affects levels of dopamine, a neurotransmitter that relays messages in the brain, which was previously linked to the development of schizophrenia. This furthers support the idea that infections and viruses cause mental illnesses.

Classic research

A demonstration of *Treponema pallidum* in the brain in cases of general paralysis – Noguchi Hideyo and J.W. Moore, 1913

Figure 6.5 Noguchi Hideyo (1876–1928)

As a child, Noguchi Hideyo suffered terrible burns to his hands and feet. Motivated by the donations of others which allowed him to receive treatment, he trained as a doctor. Moving to the USA in 1900, he worked at the Rockefeller Institute and here, in 1913, he performed groundbreaking research, proving that the syphilis bacterium Treponema pallidum led to 'paralysis of the insane'. Hideyo had established a crucial link between biological factors and mental illness.

Nominated for the Nobel Prize nine times and credited by many with discovering the causes of polio, rabies and yellow fever, Hideyo travelled to Africa to research a cure into yellow fever, but died himself of the illness in 1928. His last words were 'I don't understand.'

Aim: To establish a link between the syphilis bacterium and the deadly neuropsychiatric disorder general paralysis of the insane.

Procedure: Brain tissue samples were taken from 70 individuals aged between 33 and 60 years who had died in the Central Islip State Hospital from paresis (general paralysis of the insane). These tissues were silver stained, an established method for detecting the bacteria.

Findings: The syphilis bacterium was found in 12 of the 70 samples, ten males and two females. All samples were taken from individuals whose post-mortems had revealed that they had definitely died of paresis.

Conclusions: Syphilitic infection is essential for the later appearance of paresis, demonstrating that brain infections can cause mental illness.

Evaluation: The patients in whose brains the syphilis bacteria were found, were those whose illness had run a fairly rapid course, therefore the bacteria may have been easier to find in such cases.

The presence of the bacteria may not have been found in other tissue samples as the disease was often confused with other diseases, especially in its later stages.

Hideyo's work was pioneering in establishing a link between biology and mental illness.

This revolutionary research assisted the search for effective treatments of the disorder, something Hideyo was heavily involved in.

Brain damage

Brain damage can cause abnormal behaviour through physical damage or disease, for instance Alzheimer's disease, which leads to memory loss through destruction of cells within the nervous system.

Research studies into brain damage

- Tien *et al.* (1990) reported that drug abuse through heavy and persistent use of cocaine and/or amphetamines can lead to organic brain damage, resulting in psychosis. Symptoms included experiencing hallucinations, delusional beliefs, thought disorders and personality changes.

Figure 6.6 Heavy and persistent use of cocaine can result in brain damage and psychosis

- Brooks *et al.* (1986) interviewed close relatives of 42 brain-damaged patients five years after injury, finding that the patients were suffering from severe, long-term mental damage. Bizarre, puzzling, violent and inappropriate behaviours were reported, along with memory loss, language difficulties and concentration problems.

Biochemical factors

Biochemistry can lead to mental illness by affecting levels of neurotransmitters and hormones. For instance, elevated levels of the neurotransmitter dopamine have been associated with schizophrenia.

Research studies into biochemical factors

- Janowsky (2009) reported a link between abnormal neurotransmitter levels and the development of depression and manic depression. High levels of acetylcholine were associated with depression and low levels with mania, suggesting that biochemical imbalances may lead to mental illness.
- Zubieta *et al.* (2000) used PET scans to discover that people with bipolar disorder (manic depression) had 30 per cent higher levels of the monamine brain chemicals dopamine, serotonin and norepinephrine. This result suggests a specific biological cause for the disorder with genetic origins.

Genetic factors

Genetics are associated with increased risks of developing certain mental disorders. The rate of schizophrenia among the general population is 1 per cent, but for children of schizophrenics it is 10 per cent, implying a genetic link.

Research into genetic factors

- Sousa *et al.* (2010) analysed the genomes of nearly 1,000 autistic individuals, comparing their DNA to that of 1,200 non-autistic people. They found substantial differences in copy number variations (CNVs), genetic material distinguishing one person from another, which are known to affect brain development. Autistic individuals carry 20 per cent more CNVs than non-autistic individuals, suggesting a genetic cause to the disorder.
- Weinberger *et al.* (2002) reported that a particular gene on chromosome 22 was associated with a near doubled risk of developing schizophrenia. When abnormal, the gene, COMT, depleted the frontal lobes of the brain of the neurotransmitter dopamine, leading to hallucinations and impairment in the ability to discern reality. This implies a biological link to schizophrenia.

Key terms

Biochemistry – the study of chemical processes in living organisms

Genetics – a branch of biology dealing with the transmission of inherited factors

Evaluation

Evaluation of biological factors

- **Humane approach** – the model considers that patients are not responsible for their actions, they are merely unfortunate in the same way that someone contracting measles is unfortunate. Szasz (1972), however, argues that the approach is not humane, as those diagnosed as abnormal carry an irremovable stigma that people fear. Szasz argues that mental disorders are 'problems with living' rather than physical diseases.
- **Effective treatments** – the approach has contributed greatly to the formation of effective treatments, like drug therapies that suppress the effects of schizophrenia. If biological treatments are effective, along with ECT and psychosurgery in certain instances, then it lends support to the idea of abnormal conditions having a biological cause. However, the concept of **treatment aetiology fallacy** believes that it is a mistaken notion that the success of a treatment reveals the cause of a disorder.
- **Well-established scientific principles and evidence** – the biological approach is based upon well-established scientific principles, such as medicine and biochemistry. It focuses upon physiological features, like genetics and brain chemistry, which can be objectively measured. Advancements in scanning techniques and post-mortems have added to the credibility of the model.
- **Reliability of diagnosis** – there are two types of reliability (consistency of diagnosis): **inter-rater reliability**, where different psychiatrists agree separately on the diagnosis of a patient (in other words, they both agree on what disorder the patient has), and **test–re-test reliability**, where a psychiatrist gives the same diagnosis to a patient at different periods in time. Both types have improved, lending support to the idea that mental disorders are separate from one other, each having different diagnosable symptoms.
- **Validity of diagnosis** – research shows that diagnosis is valid for the general categories of mental disorders, but not for sub-categories (which is similar to the diagnosis of physical illnesses). This implies that diagnosis is measuring what it claims to measure, in other words there actually are separate mental illnesses like schizophrenia, as predicted by the biological model.
- **Reductionist approach** – the biological approach is impoverished as it over-focuses on physical symptoms, at the expense of the psychological element of emotional experience.
- **Animal studies** – support for the model comes from animal studies, but researchers cannot be sure that animals displaying abnormal behaviour are experiencing mental disorders in the same way as humans. Also, from an ethical viewpoint, is it reasonable to exploit animals for the possible benefit of humans?
- **Reliance on self-reports** – unlike physical illnesses where doctors diagnose via visible signs of illness, with mental disorders psychiatrists rely on less reliable patient self-reports. This leads to people pretending to be mentally ill.
- **Causality** – it is not clear whether some physical abnormalities, like elevated dopamine levels found in schizophrenics, are the cause or the effect of a disorder.
- **Culture-bound syndromes** – some mental disorders exist only in certain cultures. According to the biological model, this should not be the case; mental disorders should be universal to all cultures.
- **The myth of mental illness** – Szasz (1962) argued that the mind does not exist in a physical sense and so cannot be diseased. He believes that the diagnosis of mental illness is a means of 'social controlling' undesirable elements of society.
- **Labelling and self-fulfilling prophecies** – with mental illness terms, the whole person is labelled (for example, we say 'schizophrenic', rather than 'person suffering from schizophrenia'). You would not call a person suffering from measles 'measly'. Labelling can lead to self-fulfilling prophecies, where a person grows into their label and acts the part.
- **Diathesis–stress model** – concordance rates are never 100 per cent, which they would be if biological factors were solely responsible for mental disorders. The **diathesis–stress model** proposes that individuals have genetic susceptibilities to disorders, but only develop them in the presence of environmental stressors.

Dr Thomas Szasz is a critic of the moral and scientific foundations of psychiatry and its social control aims. His book *The myth of mental illness* (1960) sets out his anti-psychiatry views. To read an informative debate about Szasz, go to http://www.thenewatlantis.com/publications/the-myth-of-thomas-szasz

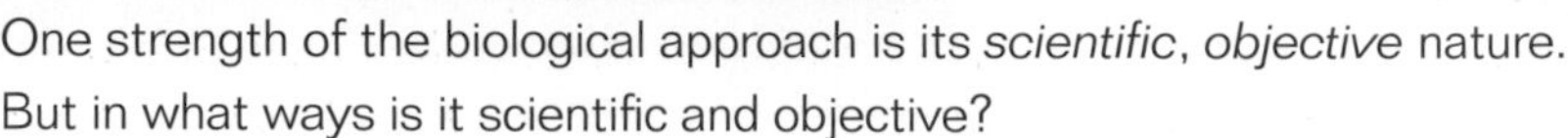

Research in focus

One strength of the biological approach is its *scientific*, *objective* nature. But in what ways is it scientific and objective?

Strengthen your learning

1 Outline the biological model of abnormality.
2 What evidence is there that the following factors can cause mental illness:
a) infections/viruses
b) brain damage
c) biochemistry
d) genetics?
3 Why might the biological model be regarded as humane?
4 Why does the concept of treatment aetiology fallacy oppose the idea that biological treatments support the biological model?
5 Explain three limitations of the model.

Assessment Check

1 Which two of the following statements, A, B, C, D and E, relate to the biological approach to psychopathology? [2 marks]

A	Abnormal behaviours can be learned and unlearned
B	Abnormal behaviours occur through irrational thought processes
C	Abnormal behaviours result from brain damage
D	Abnormal behaviours develop from unresolved childhood traumas
E	Genetics are associated with the development of mental disorders

2 Outline key features of the biological approach to psychopathology. [6 marks]
3 Mhairi has been hearing voices and experiencing frightening thoughts. Her behaviour has been increasingly bizarre and she has been diagnosed as suffering from schizophrenia. During diagnosis it was discovered that several of Mhairi's relatives have also experienced schizophrenic episodes.
With reference to the stimulus material above, explain how the biological approach could explain Mhairi's abnormal behaviour. [2 marks]
4 Outline and evaluate the biological approach to psychopathology. [12 marks]

Examination guidance:

1 Answers should be identified from the options available.
2 This question requires sufficient description of key features of the biological approach to gain six marks. Any evaluation of the approach is not creditworthy.
3 This question requires reference to relevant material from the scenario described to gain credit. Elaboration is required to earn both marks on offer.
4 This is a long-answer question, with six marks available for outlining the approach and six marks for evaluation. Suitable evaluation could consist of points in favour of and against the model.

The psychological approach to psychopathology

Psychological approaches see the origins of mental problems in abnormal thought patterns, emotional responses and behaviours, rather than in biology. Psychological models can be reduced to three broad perspectives: psychodynamic, behavioural and cognitive, each with a different explanation for the causes of abnormality. Different types of treatments have been developed in line with the central beliefs of each approach.

The psychodynamic model of abnormality

The psychodynamic approach is associated with Sigmund Freud, although subsequently others developed the psychodynamic model. This model attempts to explain the motivating forces determining behaviour. The psychodynamic approach suggests that abnormality occurs as a result of psychological problems; Freud argued that mental disorders emanated from unresolved, unconscious traumas from early childhood.

He saw personality (the psyche) as having three parts: the id, ego and super-ego. These three parts place conflicting demands upon each other, leading to anxiety.

The id is present at birth and is governed by the **pleasure principle**, an innate drive to seek immediate satisfaction. By the age of 2 years, as a consequence of experiencing reality, the ego develops. This is controlled by the **reality principle** and, although still pleasure-seeking, allows for the demands of the real world (in other words, what is and is not allowed). At 5 years of age the super-ego develops, governed by the **morality principle**, containing our conscience of what is morally right and wrong.

The conflicting demands of the id and super-ego are balanced out by the ego. When this balance is not achieved, abnormal behaviour results. For example, anxiety disorders may occur from an over-developed super-ego. To reduce this anxiety, the ego uses defence mechanisms, like repression, where threatening thoughts are hidden in the unconscious mind where people are not aware of them. They may later emerge as abnormal adult behaviours. Other defence mechanisms are **displacement**, where anger is directed elsewhere, **projection**, where someone else is blamed, **denial** and **regression**, where an individual acts like a child.

Freud saw children developing through psychosexual stages. He believed that the unresolved conflicts occurring during these stages affected later behaviour.

1 **Oral stage (0–1 year)**: pleasure gained from the mouth and sucking.

2 **Anal stage (1–3 years)**: pleasure gained from evacuating the bowels.

3 **Phallic stage (3–6 years)**: pleasure gained from the genitals.

4 **Latency stage (6–12 years)**: the development of other activities means less concentration on sexual areas.

5 **Genital stage (puberty onwards)**: pleasure gained through heterosexual relationships.

Freud believed that people could become 'fixated' at any stage, thus affecting later behaviour. For example, a smoker has an 'oral' personality, since they gain pleasure through the mouth. An excessively tidy and obsessive person has an 'anal' personality.

Key terms

Psychodynamic model – a psychological approach perceiving mental disorders as arising from unresolved, unconscious childhood traumas

Id – the irrational, pleasure-seeking, selfish part of personality present at birth

Ego – the rational, conscious part of personality developing due to environmental interactions

Super-ego – the moralistic part of personality seeking to block unacceptable urges of the id

Defence mechanisms – tactics developed by the ego to protect against anxiety

Repression – the unconscious exclusion of painful desires, fears and memories

Figure 6.7 Sigmund Freud (1856–1939)

Research into the psychodynamic model

- Williams (1994) interviewed 129 women who were sexually abused in childhood, finding that 38 per cent could not recall the abuse reported 17 years earlier. This was particularly so for those molested by someone they knew. This suggests repression of traumatic events, in line with Freud's theory.
- Solms (2000) used PET scans on non-brain-damaged people to back up Ito's (1998) claim that the id is based in the limbic system, while the ego and super-ego are found in the frontal lobes of the cerebral cortex. This provided clinical evidence supporting this element of Freud's theory.
- Massie and Szajnberg (2002) performed a longitudinal study that assessed 76 participants' parental relationships in childhood and recorded any traumatic life events up to the age of 30. They found a positive correlation between poor-quality parental relationships and childhood traumatic events, lending support to the theory.

Research in focus

Massie and Szajnberg performed a *longitudinal study*. Why is this the direct opposite of a *snapshot study*?

Give one advantage and one disadvantage of a longitudinal study compared to a snapshot study?

Evaluation

Evaluation of the psychodynamic model

- The model was the first to explain abnormal behaviour by psychological means. It inspired a wealth of research and was very influential in psychology and mainstream society, for example in art, films and literature. Freudian terminology is still found in everyday language and conversation.
- The model removes responsibility for abnormal behaviour from the patient, as behaviour is seen as emanating from the unconscious mind, over which the patient has no conscious control.
- Empirical evidence confirms that many patients with mental illnesses endured traumatic experiences in childhood.
- The theory has remained influential for over a century, with many patients experiencing successful psychoanalytic therapies. Most psychologists would agree that unconscious processes affect human behaviour.
- The theory lacks falsifiability and is impossible to test scientifically. If someone recalls painful childhood memories, this is seen as causing later abnormality and validates the theory. However, if trauma is not recalled, this is also seen as validating the theory, as the traumatic experiences have been repressed into the unconscious mind. Scodel (1957) tested Freud's hypothesis that men who encountered unresolved conflicts during the oral stage preferred large-breasted women, due to being more orally dependent. However, the opposite was true, with men who preferred small-breasted women showing more oral dependency. This refutes Freud's theory, though Freudians might argue that the men are in denial of their preference, demonstrating the non-testable nature of the theory.
- The original model over-emphasised childhood influences at the expense of adult ones and over-emphasised sexual factors, due to the sexually repressed times Freud lived in. Current psychoanalytic theorists acknowledge this and recognise the role inadequate interpersonal relationships and everyday problems play in abnormality.

continued ...

...continued

- Freud used poor methodology, relying upon case studies, a method notoriously ungeneralisable. Essentially a theory of childhood sexuality, only one case study, that of 'Little Hans', was carried out on children and that was conducted by the boy's father, an avid supporter of Freud. This is a good example of the researcher bias present in Freud's research. His research was additionally non-representative, being conducted mainly on middle-class, neurotic, Viennese, Jewish females.
- The theory puts the blame for mental disorders on poor parenting, with child abuse cases being used to validate this claim. However, **false memory syndrome** illustrates how 'recovered, hidden' memories of abuse are often false, generated by suggestive techniques of therapists when questioning patients. The use of recovered memories in psychotherapy is now banned.

The behavioural model of abnormality

The behavioural model concentrates on observable behaviour. It focuses on maladaptive (abnormal) behaviour, which it perceives as occurring through the learning processes of classical conditioning, operant conditioning and social learning. The emphasis is on observable and measurable behaviours, rather than hidden mental processes.

Classical conditioning

Classical conditioning works on reflex actions where a neutral stimulus acquires the properties of another stimulus through association. (See Classic research section on 'The case of Little Albert', page 200.) It is claimed that phobias (irrational fears) are learned in this manner, by an object or situation becoming paired with a fear response. Similarly, sexual fetishes can develop if an object or situation becomes paired with an arousal response.

Psychology in action

Stopping wolves attacking sheep

Gustafson *et al.* (1976) developed a practical application of learning phobias by classical conditioning. They used the behavioural technique to demonstrate a humane method of stopping wolves and coyotes attacking sheep.

Wild wolves and coyotes were fed mutton wrapped in sheepskins dosed with lithium chloride. This made them vomit and the predators quickly learned to associate sheep with the nauseous chemical and instead of attacking sheep, they began to show submissive behaviour towards them.

Key terms

Behavioural model – a psychological approach perceiving mental disorders as abnormal behaviours

Classical conditioning – a method of learning where innate reflexes become paired with other stimuli through repeated association

Operant conditioning – a method of learning where the likelihood of a behaviour occurring is increased or decreased through the use of rewards

Social learning – a method of learning occurring through the observation and imitation of others

Research into classical conditioning

- Coleman (1986) found that individuals receiving low rates of positive reinforcement for social behaviours become increasingly non-responsive, leading to depression.
- Krafft-Ebing (1886) reported on a man who developed masochistic sexual tendencies (gaining sexual pleasure through being punished), as a result of accidental friction on his penis while being spanked across an adult's lap as a child. This suggests that the tendency was acquired through associating arousal with physical punishment.

Classic research

'The case of Little Albert' – John Watson and Rosalie Rayner, 1920

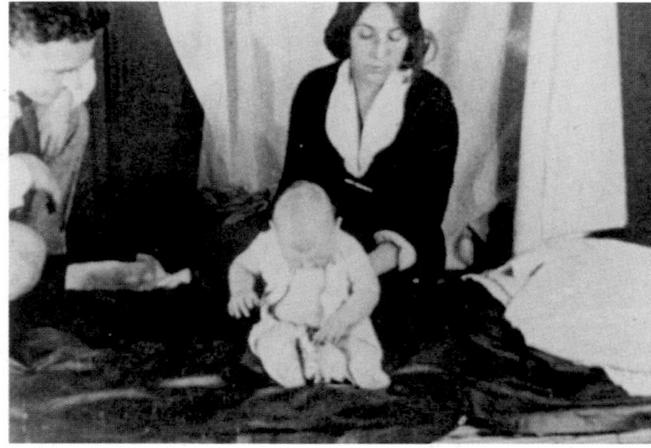

Figure 6.8 A rare photograph of John Watson and Rosalie Rayner during the conditioning of Little Albert

The researchers developed the idea, from real-world observations, that fear could be conditioned into children through the use of loud noises. Their participant was an 11-month-old boy, 'Little Albert', and the study took place at Johns Hopkins University, Baltimore USA.

Aim: To provide empirical evidence that human emotional responses could be learned through classical conditioning.

Procedure: A laboratory experiment was conducted with one participant, an 11-month-old boy who lived in the hospital where his mother was a nurse. Albert was presented with various stimuli, including a white rat, a rabbit and some cotton wool, and his responses were filmed. He showed no fear reaction to any stimuli.

A fear reaction (**unconditioned response**) was then induced into Albert by striking a steel bar with a hammer behind his head (**unconditioned stimulus**). This startled Albert, making him cry. He was then given a white rat to play with (**conditioned stimulus**), of which he was not scared. As he reached to touch the rat, the bar and hammer were struck to frighten him. This procedure was repeated three times. Variations of these conditioning techniques continued for 3 months.

It was intended that Albert's fear reactions would be 'de-conditioned', but he was removed from the hospital by his mother before this could occur.

Findings: Subsequently, when shown the rat, Albert would cry, roll over and crawl away. He had developed a **conditioned response** towards the white rat, which he also displayed to similar animals with less intensity and to other white furry objects, like a white fur coat and Santa Claus beard.

Before learning: hammer and bar (UCS) ⇨ fear (UCR)

During learning: hammer and bar (UCS) + rat (CS) ⇨ fear (UCR)

After learning: rat (CS) ⇨ fear (CR)

Conclusions: Conditioned emotional responses, including love, fear and phobias, are acquired as a direct result of environmental experiences, which can transfer and persist, possibly indefinitely, unless removed by counter-conditioning.

Evaluation: The extent of Albert's fear response is disputed. There are mentions in the original paper that Albert's fear reactions were only 'slight'. By today's standards the study was unethical, being performed without his mother's knowledge or consent and the participant was subjected to unnecessary distress. It would not, therefore, be possible to replicate the study to verify the findings.

(Footnote: It is believed that the real 'Little Albert' died of illness at only 6 years of age.)

Research in focus

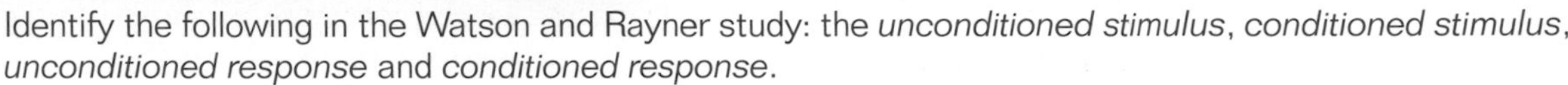

Identify the following in the Watson and Rayner study: the *unconditioned stimulus*, *conditioned stimulus*, *unconditioned response* and *conditioned response*.

Operant conditioning

Operant conditioning concerns learning through the consequences of behaviour. If behaviour is rewarded (reinforced), then it will be maintained or increased. If it is punished, then it ceases. Operant conditioning can apply to abnormal behaviour. For example, losing weight leads to praise from others (positive reinforcement), motivating the individual to lose further weight and this can result in an eating disorder. Abnormal behaviours could develop similarly, through reinforcement, by the attention the behaviour brings from others.

Research into operant conditioning

- Wikler (1973) reported that although drug taking can be initiated by classical conditioning, addiction is maintained via operant conditioning. The drug taking is reinforced through termination of negative withdrawal symptoms (negative reinforcement).
- Frude (1998) reported that operant conditioning, through seemingly minor events, could act as a positive reinforcement for the continuation of the dieting process into anorexia. For instance, clothes that previously would not fit, which now do. Also negative reinforcement can occur, as the anorexic feels less dissatisfaction, because they are experiencing fewer self-critical feelings.

Figure 6.9 Positive reinforcements can act as a continuation of dieting into anorexia

Social learning theory

Social learning theory explains the development of abnormal behaviour through **vicarious learning**. This involves observation and imitation of a role model exhibiting a behaviour and being reinforced by it. Social learning can explain how young people acquire an eating disorder by observing and imitating the maladaptive eating behaviour of a highly regarded person. A descent into drug addiction could similarly be initiated through imitating the drug-taking behaviour of peers, who are seen to gain favourable attention from others by their behaviour.

Research into social learning theory

- Mineka *et al.* (1984) found that young monkeys learned snake phobias by watching older monkeys display fear in the presence of snakes. This lends support to the idea of abnormal behaviours being acquired via social learning. Merckelbach *et al.* (1996) supported this, finding evidence that small animal phobias and blood- and injection-type phobias occur through social learning.
- Becker (1999) studied young Fijian women. Before 1995, Fiji did not receive western television. By 1998, 74 per cent of young Fijian women surveyed said they were 'too big or fat' and eating disorders, previously unknown on the island, had begun to appear. This

Figure 6.10 Young monkeys learn snake phobias from older monkeys

phenomenon is best explained by social learning and is supported by Nasser (1986) who compared Egyptian women studying in Cairo with similar Egyptian women studying in London. Twelve per cent of those living in London developed eating disorders, compared to 0 per cent in Cairo.

Research in focus

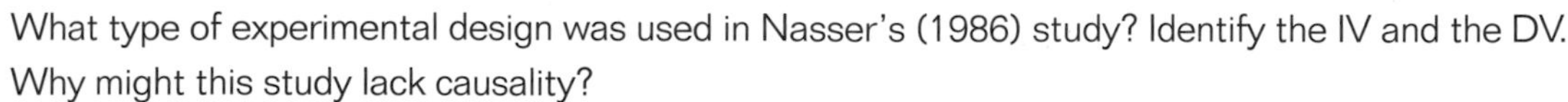

What type of experimental design was used in Nasser's (1986) study? Identify the IV and the DV. Why might this study lack causality?

Evaluation

Evaluation of the behavioural model

- The behavioural model allows clear predictions that can be tested and measured objectively. Such research demonstrates how certain abnormal behaviours can be learned via environmental experience, giving the model support.
- The model does not label people with the stigma of being 'ill'. Such labels are damaging via self-fulfilling prophecies and, because they tend to 'stick', can be difficult to remove. Instead the model is a positive one, perceiving mental disorders as maladaptive responses, which can be altered to become adaptive and desirable ones.
- The model encompasses individual differences and social and cultural contexts because it perceives the patient's individual behavioural history as having shaped their maladaptive behaviour.
- The model focuses on the present rather than the past. This is advantageous since many people do not know the past causes of their abnormal behaviour and it might be beneficial for the patient to concentrate on present symptoms.
- The behavioural approach is **reductionist**, explaining behaviour purely as the result of conditioning. Much human behaviour is more complex than this, and may have a cognitive element to it that this model does not consider. The model suggests that humans are simple mechanisms at the mercy of environmental stimuli. This is a somewhat dehumanising approach.
- Behaviourists consider mental disorders as consisting solely of observable symptoms. However, the model may be guilty of ignoring the more important underlying causes.
- The model is accused of over-emphasising the importance of environmental factors at the expense of biological and internal psychological factors. This model therefore finds it difficult to explain mental disorders with clear biological elements, like schizophrenia.
- Much of the theory, and evidence supporting it, is drawn from studies of simple animals, which may not be applicable to understanding the complexities of human mental disorders.

Key terms

Cognitive model – a psychological approach perceiving mental disorders as due to negative thoughts and illogical beliefs

The cognitive model of abnormality

Founded by Aaron Ellis (1962) and Albert Beck (1963) as a challenge to the behavioural approach, the cognitive model concentrates on thought processes and behaviour. Cognitive psychologists maintain that between a stimulus and a response there are mental processes – cognitions, appraisals and thoughts – and that it is these that inform the way individuals feel about stimuli. The explanation resembles the behavioural model as both acknowledge the role of maladaptive learning, but the cognitive model also considers the role of internal mental processes.

The model perceives mental disorders as being due to distorted and irrational thought processes, like negative thoughts and illogical beliefs, which Beck referred to as **cognitive errors**. These exert influence over emotions and behaviour, leading to abnormal behaviour.

The model sees individuals as making sense of their world through cognitive processes. **Automatic thoughts** are thoughts that occur without thinking. People with psychological problems have more negative automatic thoughts. **Attributions** refer to attempts to make sense of and explain the behaviour of oneself and others. People with psychological problems may make more inaccurate attributions, for example, attributing failed relationships to a lack of social skills. People suffering from psychological problems may also have inaccurate expectations. For example, they may expect relationships to end in failure. Such expectations make this likely to happen in reality, a self-fulfilling prophecy. In effect, people with psychological problems lack confidence in their ability to achieve life goals. Their illogical thoughts do not actually reflect reality, but do affect behaviour.

The cognitive explanation sees mental disorders as occurring when faulty thought processes lead to maladaptive behaviour. For instance, Beck (1963) explained depression as occurring through three illogical thought processes (the cognitive triad), resulting in irrational, negative feelings and leading to depression. For example:

1 **Negative feelings about themselves** ('nobody loves me')

2 **Negative feelings about the future** ('I will always be useless')

3 **Negative views about oneself** ('I have no value')

Key terms

Cognitive triad – the three types of illogical thought processes which result in irrational, negative feelings about oneself and lead to depression

Research into the cognitive model

- Gustafson (1992) found patients suffering from depression, sexual problems and anxiety disorders often showed evidence of maladaptive thinking, supporting the idea of a cognitive component to abnormality.
- Abela and D'Alessandro (2002) found that students identified as at risk of depression due to dysfunctional attitudes, who did not get into their university of choice, then doubted their ability and these thoughts led to depression. This suggests a cognitive cause to depression.
- Armfield (2007) got participants to visualise a spider. The participants were then assigned to different conditions of how dangerous/non-dangerous the spider was, how much control they had over removing themselves from the spider's presence and how predictable/unpredictable the spider's movements were. It was found that participants who believed they could not remove themselves from the spider's presence, plus those told the spider was dangerous and those told that the spider's movements were unpredictable, scored more highly on fear of spiders. This implies that it is our beliefs that determine how cognitively vulnerable we are to anxiety, thus supporting the cognitive model.

Figure 6.11 Our beliefs determine how cognitively vulnerable we are to anxiety

Evaluation

Evaluation of the cognitive model

- The model has been influential, especially when used in conjunction with the behavioural model to form the cognitive–behavioural model.
- Research evidence supports the idea that many people suffering from anxiety disorders and depression do report having irrational thought processes.
- It is a positive approach, because it empowers individuals by perceiving them as having the ability to change their own cognitions.
- As with the behavioural approach, the cognitive model focuses on the present rather than the past. Research suggests the concentration on current thought processes is more beneficial.

continued ...

...continued

- It is not clear whether irrational thought processes are the cause or the effects of mental disorders.
- According to the cognitive model, individuals are responsible for their own maladaptive thoughts and behaviour. This ignores the important roles that situational factors, like the life events surrounding an individual, and biological factors, like genetics, play in the creation of some mental disorders. The approach is therefore somewhat reductionist and mechanistic.
- As thoughts cannot be observed or measured, it is claimed the approach is unscientific.
- As mental disorders result from faulty thinking, the blame rests with the individual. This can make the disorder worse and is unfair, since factors beyond the individual's control might contribute to the disorder.
- Depression may not be irrational, but rather a logical response to negative life events.
- Many believe depressives have a more realistic view of life than 'normal' people. Viewing the world through rose-coloured spectacles might be irrational, but psychologically healthy.

Strengthen your learning

1. How does the psychodynamic model see mental disorders as arising?
2. What research evidence is there to support the psychodynamic model?
3. Explain two strengths and two weaknesses of the psychodynamic model.
4. How does the behavioural model see mental disorders as arising?
5. Give one piece of research evidence supporting each of the following as an explanation of abnormal behaviours:
   a) classical conditioning
   b) operant conditioning
   c) social learning.
6. Explain two strengths and two weaknesses of the behavioural model.
7. How does the cognitive model perceive mental disorders as arising?
8. What research evidence is there to support the cognitive model?
9. Explain two strengths and two weaknesses of the cognitive model.

Assessment Check

1 The following descriptions relate to psychological approaches to explaining abnormality.
Copy and complete the table by putting a letter C in the box after the two descriptions that relate to the cognitive approach, a letter P in the box after the two descriptions that relate to the psychodynamic approach and a letter B after the two descriptions that relate to the behavioural approach. [6 marks]

Descriptions	Psychological approach
Mental disorders occur due to negative thoughts	
Unresolved childhood traumas can lead to abnormal behaviours	
Abnormal behaviours can occur through classical conditioning	
Mental disorders are the result of learning processes	
Mental disorders can be explained by the influence of unconscious processes	
Abnormal behaviours can occur through irrational beliefs	

2 Outline the key features of the cognitive approach to psychopathology. [6 marks]

3 Lucas has a phobia of dogs. Explain one way in which Lucas's fear can be explained by the behavioural model of psychopathology. [4 marks]

4 Outline and evaluate the psychodynamic approach to explaining psychological abnormality. [12 marks]

continued ...

...continued

Examination guidance:

1 This involves working out which descriptions relate to the three psychological approaches and placing the correct letter in the correct box.
2 This requires description of the key features of one specific psychological approach to psychopathology, namely the cognitive approach. Outlining other approaches or providing evaluation will not gain credit.
3 This question requires an explanation of Lucas's phobia in terms of the behavioural model. This could be achieved by reference to classical conditioning, operant conditioning or social learning.
4 With this question, six marks can be gained by describing the psychodynamic explanation of abnormality and a further six marks by evaluating it. This could be achieved by proving a balance of points for and against the model.

The treatment of mental disorders

IN THE NEWS

Tranquillisers putting children's lives at risk

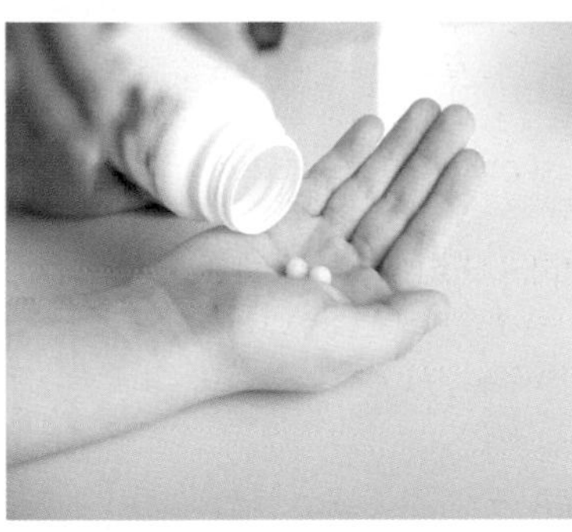

Figure 6.12
New evidence shows children's lives are put at risk by a surge in the use of controversial tranquillising drugs prescribed to control behaviour.

Anti-psychotic drugs are being given to youngsters under the age of six even though the drugs aren't licensed for use in children except in certain schizophrenia cases.

The number of children on the drugs has doubled since the early 1990s as the UK follows a trend started in the US, but critics say they are a 'chemical cosh' that could cause premature death.

Source: adapted from Sarah Boseley, the *Guardian*, 7 April 2008. Copyright Guardian News & Media Ltd 2008.

This news item highlights the accusation that anti-psychotics are often used as a form of control against 'difficult' individuals and incur serious health risks, rather than being used as a valid therapeutic tool.

If you want to read more about the use of antipsychotic drugs to control the behaviour of so-called 'problem' children, go to http://www.ahrp.org/infomail/04/09/02.php

Biological therapies

As the biological model is based on the belief that mental illnesses have physiological causes, it believes that cures emanate from rectifying these physical problems. The two main biological therapies are drug therapy and electro-convulsive therapy (ECT).

Drugs

Approximately 25 per cent of the drugs prescribed by the NHS are for mental health problems. In 1992/1993, spending on psychiatric drugs was £159 million, or 5.2 per cent of the NHS drugs budget. Psychiatric drugs modify the working of the brain and affect mood and behaviour. People suffering from mental disorders are frequently prescribed more than one drug.

Key terms

Biological therapies – treatments of abnormality based on the biological model

Drug therapy – treatment of mental disorders with medicines

ECT – treatment of mental disorders by applying an electrical voltage to the brain

Drugs enter the bloodstream to reach the brain and affect the transmission of chemicals in the nervous system called neurotransmitters, which have a variety of effects on behaviour. The main neurotransmitters are dopamine, serotonin, acetylcholine, noradrenaline and GABA. Psychiatric drugs essentially work by either increasing or decreasing the availability of these neurotransmitters, thus modifying their effects on behaviour. Drugs blocking the effects of neurotransmitters are called **antagonists**, while drugs mimicking or increasing the effects of neurotransmitters are called **agonists**. There are five main groups of drugs:

1. **Anti-manic drugs** (mood stabilisers), like lithium, are used to treat bipolar affective disorder (manic depression) and severe depression. It is believed they work by calming over-stimulated brain areas.
2. **Antidepressant drugs**, like Prozac, relieve persistent low moods and other symptoms of depression. They work by increasing production of the neurotransmitter serotonin. There are three types of antidepressant:

a) Tricyclic antidepressants (TCAs), which increase levels of the neurotransmitter noradrenaline.

b) Monoamine oxidase inhibitors (MAOIs), which increase noradrenaline levels, though by a different method.

c) Selective serotonin re-uptake inhibitors (SSRIs), which increase serotonin levels.

3. **Anti-anxiety drugs** (anxiolytics), like Valium, are minor tranquillisers used to treat stress-related symptoms and for short-term management of phobias. They slow down the activity of the central nervous system.
4. **Anti-psychotic drugs** (neuropleptics), like Chlorpromazine, combat the symptoms of schizophrenia by lowering dopamine activity. They have proven effective in treating mania and other psychotic symptoms. Anti-psychotics are divided into two types:
   a) First generation (typical), which arrest dopamine production.
   b) Second generation (atypical), which act upon serotonin and dopamine levels.
5. **Stimulants,** like methylphenidate, improve mood, alertness and confidence by triggering the release of the neurotransmitters noradrenaline and dopamine. They are often used to combat narcolepsy and Attention Deficit Hyperactivity Disorder (ADHD).

Contemporary research

Effectiveness of anti-psychotic drugs in the treatment of schizophrenia – John Geddes, Nick Freemantle, Paul Harrison and Paul Bebbington, 2008

First-generation, or typical, anti-psychotic drugs introduced in the 1950s allowed many schizophrenics to live relatively normal lives. They do not, however, work for everyone and can have serious side effects, resulting in patients discontinuing treatment. Second-generation, or atypical, anti-psychotics were introduced in the 1990s on the basis that they were more effective and incurred fewer side effects. The researchers set out to investigate these claims.

Aim: To develop recommendations for the use of antipsychotic drugs for patients with schizophrenia.

...continued

Procedure: A meta-analysis was performed of 52 randomised clinical trials involving 12,649 schizophrenic patients, comparing the effectiveness of the typical anti-psychotics Haloperidol and Chlorpromazine, against the atypical anti-psychotics Amisulpride, Clozapine, Olanzapine, Risperidone and Sertindole. Drop-out rates were recorded as a measure of tolerability of side effects and measures of symptom reduction were taken, as an indicator of effectiveness. Types of and severity of side effects were also recorded.

Findings: Atypical drugs were slightly more effective than typical drugs in reducing schizophrenic symptoms. No one atypical drug was superior to another.

Atypical drugs incurred significantly fewer side effects involving movement disorders (such as **akathisia**, where patients cannot remain still), but incurred other side effects, like weight gain.

Overall tolerability of anti-psychotics, measured by drop-out rates, was fairly equal between typical and atypical drugs.

It was also noted that anti-psychotics are significantly more expensive.

Conclusions: There is no clear evidence that atypical anti-psychotics are more effective or better tolerated than typical anti-psychotics.

Conventional anti-psychotics should be used in the initial treatment of schizophrenia unless the patient has previously not responded to these drugs, or has unacceptable movement disorder side effects.

Evaluation: Atypical anti-psychotics are not proven to be superior to typical anti-psychotics. Although reducing some side effects, they incur serious ones of their own and are no more favoured by patients than the more conventional drugs.

The results provide support for those who see promotion and use of anti-psychotics as a profit-making venture by the influential drug companies (see Psychology in action section, page 208).

Research into drugs

- Slaap *et al.* (1996) treated 30 social phobics with the antidepressant SSRIs Brofaromine and Fluvoxamine, finding that 72 per cent of patients had reductions in heart rate and blood pressure. This suggests that drug treatments are effective in decreasing physical symptoms of the disorder.
- Bergqvist *et al.* (1999) investigated the effect of low doses of the anti-psychotic drug Risperidone in treating obsessive-compulsive disorder, finding that the treatment was effective due to the drug's dopamine-lowering effect.
- Kahn *et al.* (2008) compared first generation with second generation psychotics for effectiveness in treating first-instance schizophrenia. They found that anti-psychotics are effective for at least one year, but that second generation drugs are no more effective than first generation ones.
- Furukawa *et al.* (2003) reviewed 35 studies, finding that antidepressants are more effective than placebos (see Supplementary learning section, page 216). This suggests that antidepressants are an appropriate treatment for depression.

Psychology in action

The drug company conspiracy

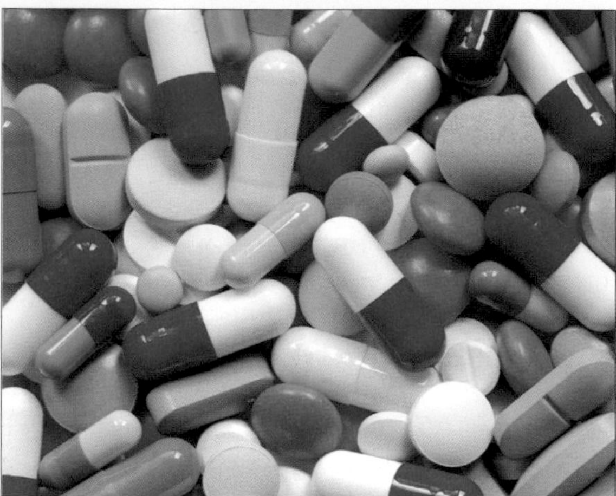

Figure 6.13

Drugs have been used to treat mental illness for many years and there is much research suggesting that they are safe and effective. All, therefore, seems rosy in the garden of mental health, with new, supposedly improved, drugs being manufactured and the public reassured that should loved ones fall victim to mental illness, then the drugs will return them to mental well-being.

There is, however, a growing body of evidence to suggest that the drugs are not effective and can even be unsafe. The drug companies are accused of suppressing evidence that their products are dangerous and non-effective, paying doctors and public health figures to promote their wares and having an unhealthy influence over politicians who create policies governing public mental health.

Sales of anti-psychotic drugs topped £10 billion globally in 2008. In the USA in 2003, 3.21 million patients received anti-psychotics of which two-thirds were new generation drugs costing on average £75 compared to £17 for the older ones. The number of prescriptions for children and adolescents doubled to 4.4 million between 2003 and 2006, due mainly to increased diagnosis of bipolar disorder.

However, recent research evidence suggests that newer atypical drugs are not significantly more effective or safer (see Contemporary research section on Geddes *et al*. (2008) on page 206).

Also of interest is the tale of Dr David Healy, a leading expert on antidepressant drugs. He was given a prestigious job at the Center for Addiction and Mental Health, North America's top research centre. But before starting he was sacked, as the centre, which is heavily financed by the drug companies, said he held 'unscientific views about a number of psychiatric drugs'. The truth was that Dr Healy reported evidence that SSRIs, like Prozac, can cause some people to have suicidal urges. An ardent supporter of SSRIs, Dr Healy was merely interested in finding ways of identifying those unsuitable for such treatment. His research suggests that up to 50 per cent of individuals prescribed Prozac should not be, but that would mean halving the profits of the drug companies. Dr Healy reports that he was warned his career would be destroyed if he kept on producing such research results.

Whatever the truth, the accusation remains that he was sacked because the drug companies did not want a leading authority drawing attention to the dominating role of pharmaceutical companies in shaping medical research.

Evaluation

Evaluation of drugs

- Drug treatments are cost-effective compared to other treatments, are easy to administer and are favoured by patients, as they are familiar with and have confidence in taking pills.
- There is much clinical evidence supporting the effectiveness of drugs in the treatment of mental disorder. For example, anti-psychotics work for two-thirds of psychotic patients and 80 per cent of schizophrenics.
- Although drugs often do not cure a disorder, but merely reduce its symptoms, such symptom reduction can improve patients' lives. About 75 per cent of depressives placed on the correct medication remain free of depression for extended periods of time.
- Most patients develop a tolerance to side effects during treatment, and the risks of side effects can be minimised by taking a low dose of medication for a short period.
- Drugs may address the effects of mental disorders, but not the cause. Therefore once the drug treatment stops, mental disorders may recur.

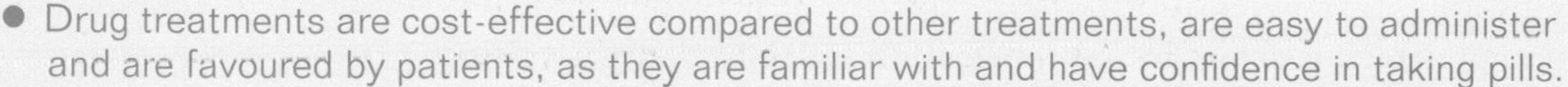

continued

- Drugs can have side effects. These occur as drugs interfere with brain mechanisms other than those causing mental disorders. First generation anti-psychotics often cause movement disorders, like tremors, slowing of body and facial features, and abnormal body movements. Second generation anti-psychotics have fewer side effects. Some minor tranquillisers are addictive and it is essential to monitor patients' tolerance and dependence levels. Some drugs are poisonous and an overdose can cause death. Other side effects can involve nausea, diarrhoea, headaches and sleeping difficulties. Anti-psychotics can also damage the immune system.
- With antidepressants, side effects can occur immediately after taking the drug, but the relief of symptoms often only becomes apparent after 2–4 weeks. Some patients thus stop taking the drugs before they have started to work. It is unclear why this effect is delayed, since the effect on the neurotransmitters is immediate.
- It is claimed that in mental institutions, drugs like major tranquillisers are used to control patients, rather than treat them. Indeed, they have been nicknamed 'pharmacological straitjackets' or a 'chemical cosh'.

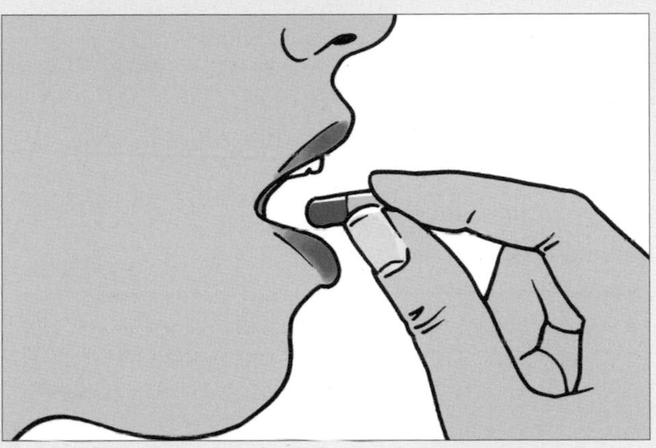

Figure 6.14 Drugs are favoured by patients as they are familiar and easy to take

To read a full account of the CBC news interviews with all concerned parties regarding the story of Dr David Hcaly go to http://www.pharmapolitics.com/cbcnational.html

Electro-convulsive therapy

Electro-convulsive therapy (ECT) is a medical treatment used with drug-resistant depressive disorders. It has also recently been reintroduced as a treatment for schizophrenia. It is mainly used when drugs and psychotherapy have failed or cannot be tolerated. Approximately 22,000 people receive ECT in Britain every year.

A patient receives ECT several times a week for about 6–12 treatments. A general anaesthetic and a muscle relaxant are given to ensure that the patient does not feel pain or convulse and incur fractures. Brain stimulation occurs through electrodes placed on the head, with a brief controlled series of electrical pulses. This causes a seizure within the brain, lasting about a minute. After 5–10 minutes, the patient regains consciousness.

There are two types of ECT: **unilateral ECT** occurs when only the non-dominant hemisphere of the brain is stimulated, while **bilateral ECT** involves stimulation to both hemispheres. Debate continues about how ECT works. It has been suggested that ECT induces changes in neurotransmitter levels, including increased sensitivity to serotonin in the hypothalamus and an increase in the release of GABA, noradrenaline and dopamine.

Research into ECT

- Tharyan and Adams (2005) reviewed studies of ECT as a treatment for schizophrenia, concluding that it was an effective treatment in the short term, but not as effective as anti-psychotic drugs.
- Tang *et al.* (2002) found ECT effective in treating schizophrenics who do not respond positively to treatment with anti-psychotic drugs, suggesting the treatment provides relief to such patients.
- Pagnin *et al.* (2008) performed a meta-analysis of studies to compare the effectiveness of ECT, placebos and antidepressant drugs in treating depression. ECT proved superior, implying that it is a valid therapeutic tool, for treatment of both severe and resistant forms.
- Levy (1968) compared bilateral with unilateral forms of ECT as a treatment of depression, finding that unilateral treatments incurred less memory loss, but bilateral treatments provided better relief of depressive symptoms.

Research in focus

Why might it not be possible for individuals with severe disorders to give informed consent for psychotherapeutic treatments?

Who could give consent in such circumstances?

Who else cannot give informed consent?

Evaluation

Evaluation of ECT

- There is no evidence that ECT damages the brain; indeed epileptics who have many seizures do not demonstrate brain damage and ECT-induced seizures take place under far more controlled conditions than epilepsy. Coffey (1991) used MRI scans, finding no indication of brain damage after ECT.
- ECT generally has an immediate positive effect. In contrast, drug treatments often take considerable periods of time before improvements are noticeable, by which time the occurrence of side effects may mean patients have discontinued the treatment.
- ECT has proven an effective treatment for severe depression and schizophrenia where other treatments have failed.
- ECT saves lives, as without it, depressives who do not respond to other treatments are at risk of committing suicide.
- It has been argued that ECT should not be used, because it is not understood how it works.
- Despite the fact that ECT should be used only after other treatments have failed, up to 18 per cent of patients are offered no other treatment. Also UKAN (1995) reports that 78.5 per cent of patients surveyed said they would never have ECT again.
- The side effects of ECT are more severe with children, adolescents, the elderly and pregnant women, and therefore the treatment should not be used with such people, unless as a last resort.
- Sackheim *et al.* (2001) found that 84 per cent of patients relapsed within six months. In addition, it was reported that up to 50 per cent of schizophrenics who respond favourably to ECT also relapse within six months. This suggests that it is not a long-term solution.

Strengthen your learning

1. How do drugs affect behaviour?
2. Outline two pieces of research evidence suggesting that drug therapies are effective.
3. Explain two strengths and two weaknesses of drug therapies.
4. What mental disorders does ECT treat?
5. Outline the procedure for delivering ECT.
6. Outline two pieces of research evidence suggesting that ECT is effective.
7. Explain two strengths and two weaknesses of ECT.

Assessment Check

1 The following is a list of descriptions of biological therapies for treating psychological abnormality:

A A therapy applied for a brief period to one or both sides of the brain.

B A therapy involving the irreversible destruction of brain tissue

C A therapy increasing or decreasing the release of neurotransmitters

D A therapy affecting the transmission of chemicals in the nervous system

E A therapy involving the use of a general anaesthetic and a muscle relaxant

Copy and complete the table below by using the appropriate letter, A, B, C, D or E, to indicate which two descriptions relate to ECT and which two to drug therapy. [4 marks]

Type of therapy	Letter
ECT	
ECT	
Drug therapy	
Drug therapy	

2 Describe the use of drug therapy in treating psychological abnormality. [6 marks]

3 Iona has suffered for some time with severe depression. Her condition has not responded to various treatments and she has been experiencing persistent suicidal thoughts. Her doctors have decided to give Iona ECT.

a) Explain why ECT might be an appropriate therapy for treating Iona. [3 marks]

b) Outline one or more possible limitations of administering ECT to Iona. [3 marks]

4 Discuss the biological approach to the treatment of psychological abnormality. [12 marks]

Examination guidance:

1 Two of the statements relate to ECT and two to drug therapies, meaning that there will be one description left over fitting neither of these therapies.

2 This question focuses on outlining drug therapies, therefore any description of other therapies or any evaluation would not gain credit.

3 Question 3 involves using information supplied in the scenario to explain why ECT might be an appropriate treatment. The second part of the question can be answered by giving one detailed limitation of ECT or several limitations in less detail.

4 The term 'discuss' means to describe and evaluate. Therefore six marks are available for outlining the biological approach to treating abnormality, with a further six marks for evaluation. One possible way to achieve this could be by reference to supportive and non-supportive research evidence. Another way would be to use ethical considerations.

Psychological therapies

The three psychological therapies, psychodynamic, behavioural and cognitive, each have their own means of treating mental disorders, based upon their viewpoint of what causes abnormal behaviours. Collectively they offer alternatives to the dominant biological treatments. No single treatment or approach is regarded as best; rather each has its strengths and limitations and is more effective in particular instances.

Key terms

Psychological therapies – treatments of mental disorders based on psychological rather than biological explanations

Key terms

Psychoanalysis – a psychodynamic treatment of mental disorders, seeking to give patients insight into the origins of their disorders

Psychoanalysis

Psychoanalysis is derived from Freud's psychodynamic model (see page 197). As the model assumes that mental disorders result from unresolved conflicts, the treatments are therefore orientated at identifying the nature of the conflict and then resolving it. As the conflict is unconscious, the patient may not be aware of it, therefore various methods are used to draw out information, allowing the therapist to identify and resolve the patient's issues. The central aim is for the patient to gain insight into the origins of their disorder, so they can achieve an understanding of the repressed events occurring in their past.

Various psychoanalytical techniques, like **dream analysis** and **free association**, are used by therapists to help the patient recover and gain insight into repressed conflicts.

Dream analysis

Freud believed that dreams were 'the royal road into the unconscious', and that images and events of dreams, if analysed by trained psychoanalysts, could, through symbolism and deeper meaning, reveal truths about inner conflicts. Freud believed that during dreams, ego defences are lowered, allowing repressed thoughts and desires, like those too traumatic or forbidden to be considered consciously, to 'bubble up' in disguised, symbolic forms and, through dream analysis, be scrutinised.

Figure 6.15 Dream analysis might see a collapsing bridge as actually representing a failing relationship

These thoughts and desires occur in disguised, symbolic forms, in order to stop unacceptable thoughts from waking us, for instance dreaming of a lollipop rather than a penis.

Therefore anxieties and concerns are 'hidden' in the **latent content** of dreams (the deeper meaning of the dream), whereas the **manifest content** is what the dream appears to be about on the surface. The analyst guides the patient in recalling and analysing dreams, the goal being to reveal the latent (hidden) meaning. For example, the manifest content could appear to be a collapsing bridge, but the latent content might actually symbolise the patient's anxiety about their failing marriage.

Free association

Free association is another way in which the unconscious mind can be revealed. It involves the patient lying on a couch and talking about whatever comes to mind, regardless of whether it seems unimportant, does not make sense or appears embarrassing, shameful or obscene. The therapist listens, taking care not to react in a negative manner, and relieves the patient of any responsibility for what they say. It is assumed that using this technique, the internal 'censor' of the unconscious relaxes, so unconscious material emerges, at least symbolically.

The patient's revelations provide clues to help the therapist to understand the unconscious conflicts. Another technique, **word association**, involves single words being presented to the patient, who responds as quickly as possible with the first word that comes to mind. Words thought to be emotionally significant

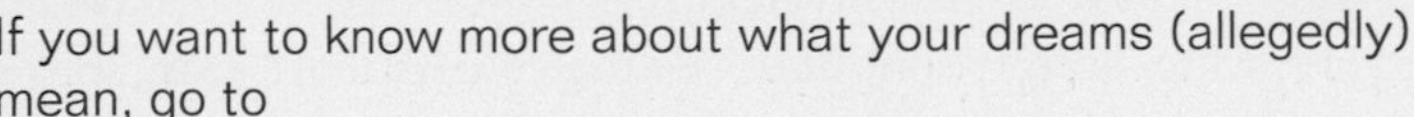

If you want to know more about what your dreams (allegedly) mean, go to http://dreammoods.com/cgibin/dreamdictionarysearch.pl?method=exact&header=dreamsymbol&search=bridge

where you can find information on common dreams and a search engine to interpret your dreams.

to the patient are included among neutral words. The analyst interprets the patient's responses, with significance being attached to how long it takes to respond. A long delay in responding suggests **resistance** or **censoring** of thoughts is occurring.

There are a number of therapeutic stages occurring during dream interpretation and free association:

1. **Resistance** – involves anything preventing progress of the therapy. Resistance can be conscious, like deliberately changing the subject, or unconscious. Resistance provides clues about the unconscious conflict experienced by the patient.

2. **Transference** – involves the patient transferring past attitudes towards the therapist. Patients respond to the analyst as if they were an important person from their past. Transference helps the patient understand the childhood origin of their anxieties. Analysts encourage transference by remaining in the background and revealing little about themselves and their views.

3. **Interpretation** – involves the analyst pointing out and interpreting hidden meanings in what the patient says and does. The analyst only offers interpretations that the patient is on the verge of making. Interpretation helps the patient to re-examine how their present behaviour has evolved from conflicts originating in childhood. The patient may show resistance or denial of interpretations and the analyst points out why this resistance/denial is occurring, with the resistance/denial taken as evidence that the interpretation is correct.

4. **Insight** – occurs when patients gain self-knowledge and understanding of the nature and origin of their problems and realise how the unconscious conflicts they have faced relate to present-day problems. This process develops gradually.

Research into psychoanalysis

- Andreoli *et al.* (1999) found psychodynamic psychotherapy, where patients are encouraged to relive childhood experiences, an effective treatment for depression if delivered by skilled, well-trained practitioners. This suggests that the treatment's effectiveness is dependent upon the quality of the clinician administering it.
- Leichsenring *et al.* (2004) found brief dynamic therapy, a simplified version of psychoanalysis, as effective as cognitive behavioural therapy (CBT) in treating depression. As CBT is regarded as the prime treatment for depression, this lends considerable support to the therapy.

- Klein *et al.* (1983) reported psychotherapy as effective as behavioural treatments for treating simple phobias, where individuals fear specific objects or situations, implying psychodynamic treatments to be of clinical value.
- Knijnik *et al.* (2004) gave psychodynamic group therapy (where patients receive treatment collectively rather than as individuals) for 12 weeks to patients with social phobias (fear of social situations), finding their condition improved. This lends support to the treatment.

Evaluation

Evaluation of psychoanalysis

- Although psychoanalysis seems an inappropriate treatment for disorders with a biological component, like schizophrenia, research suggests psychoanalysis is an effective treatment for certain abnormalities, like anxiety disorders.
- Modern forms of psychoanalysis are conducted over a shorter time-scale and concentrate more on current than past issues. These types of psychoanalysis produce swifter improvements and are more cost effective.
- Barton (1976) argues that psychoanalysis has an advantage, as it can be administered outside hospitals, reducing the risk of institutionalisation.
- The psychoanalytic approach to treating phobias works well in conjunction with cognitive, humanistic, behavioural and social therapies, demonstrating its flexibility and range of use.
- Eysenck (1952) famously claimed that psychoanalysis did not work and that receiving no treatment was more effective. He found that 44 per cent of patients improved with psychoanalysis, but 66 per cent improved through **spontaneous remission** (no treatment). In essence this means psychotherapy is harmful. However, Eysenck included patients who dropped out of psychoanalysis in his analysis. Bergin (1971) did not include such patients and arrived at a 91 per cent success rate.
- There is a difficulty in measuring the effectiveness of psychoanalysis. Some studies use patients' self-reports while others use analysts' judgements of success. This can lead to demand characteristics or self-serving bias, where the success of the treatment is exaggerated. There are also problems with a lack of standardised diagnoses and control over sampling procedures. In addition, it is claimed that the success of psychoanalysis may only become apparent some years after treatment.
- Psychoanalysis is based on Freudian theory, which is criticised for its lack of scientific evidence. Free association and dream analysis cannot be scientifically tested and are based on the analyst's subjective speculation.
- There are ethical concerns with psychoanalysis, as its usage can produce distressing emotional insights and even false memory syndrome, where patients 'recall' repressed memories that later prove to be false and which occur as a result of 'suggestion' by the therapist.

Behavioural therapies

The behavioural model sees mental disorders as maladaptive (inappropriate) behaviours learned through environmental experience. Treatments based on the model seek to replace maladaptive behaviours with adaptive (appropriate) ones. Behavioural treatments address the symptoms of disorders, though critics believe the symptoms are merely the 'tip of the iceberg' and underlying causes still remain and with time the symptoms will return or **symptom substitution** will occur, where other abnormal behaviours replace the ones removed.

Systematic desensitisation

Systematic desensitisation (SD) is a behavioural therapy developed by Wolpe (1958) to counteract phobias. A phobic experiences fear and anxiety as behavioural responses to phobic objects or situations, for instance being scared of snakes. SD uses classical conditioning to replace irrational fears and anxieties associated with phobic objects by use of the incompatible response of relaxation. The central idea is that it is impossible to experience two opposite emotions, fear and relaxation, simultaneously. Patients are taught deep muscle relaxation techniques and are instructed to use them when exposed, in stages of rising intensity (from weakest to strongest), to phobic objects or situations.

So at first a snake phobic merely looks at a photo of a snake, then at a snake in a tank and so on, until they are finally holding the snake. At each stage patients are instructed to use relaxation techniques and only move on to the next stage when they can maintain a relaxed state. Eventually, through repeated exposure to phobic objects with relaxation and no fear, the phobia is eliminated.

Key terms

Systematic desensitisation – a behavioural therapy used to modify phobias by constructing and working through a hierarchy of anxiety-producing stimuli

Contemporary research

The treatment of technophobia by systematic desensitisation – Mark Brosnan and Sue Thorpe, 2006

Technology pervades our occupational, educational and leisure lives and so technophobia, a fear of interacting with technology like computers, has a major negative impact on the life of sufferers. Indeed, technophobia is comparable in severity to more traditional phobias. The researchers investigated whether technophobia is treatable by psychological means.

Figure 6.16 Technophobia is a fear of interacting with modern technology

Aim: To see whether a fear of computers could be successfully treated by systematic desensitisation.

Procedure: In the first study, a sample of 16 participants was used: eight computer-anxious participants and a control group of eight non-anxious participants. A 10-week systematic desensitisation programme was delivered to the computer-anxious participants.

In the second study, 30 computer-anxious participants were assigned to a treatment group or a non-treatment group. There was also a non-anxious control group of 59 participants.

Findings: In the first study, computer anxiety and coping strategies were significantly improved in the computer-anxious group, becoming comparable to the non-anxious controls.

In the second study, testing established over the period of an academic year that the reduction in anxiety was three times greater in the treated group than the non-treated group. By the end of the year the treated group no longer differed from the control group, while the non-treated group remained significantly more anxious.

Conclusions: The behavioural therapy of systematic desensitisation is effective in reducing technophobia.

Evaluation: It is not known whether the therapy had a long-term benefit in reducing technophobia, nor whether it is effective against other forms of technophobia. The success of the therapy suggests a major benefit in allowing technophobes to participate in an increasingly technologically-orientated world.

Supplementary learning

Placebos

A placebo is a sham treatment, such as a pill containing no medicine. The placebo effect is a psychological phenomenon where patients given placebos improve in condition, due to believing the treatment is effective.

Kirsch *et al.* (2002) reviewed 38 studies of antidepressants and reported that those given placebos improved nearly as much as those given actual drugs.

Placebos demonstrate the importance of attitude, as well as treatment, in reducing mental disorders.

You are the researcher

Design a study assessing the effectiveness of systematic desensitisation in reducing a phobia of using mobile phones.

You will need an experimental group and a control group of participants, as well as a step-by-step hierarchy of gradual exposure to the feared object.

What experimental design would you use?

Write suitable experimental and null hypotheses for your study.

How would you assess the effectiveness of the therapy?

Figure 6.17 In 1924, Mary Jones used systematic densensitisation to remove Little Peter's fear of white fluffy objects

Key terms

Cognitive behavioural therapy – a cognitive therapy that challenges and restructures abnormal ways of thinking into useful, rational ones

Research into systematic desensitisation

- Jones (1924) used SD to eradicate 'Little Peter's' phobia of white fluffy objects. A white rabbit was presented at gradually closer distances each time his anxiety levels lessened. Eventually he developed affection for the rabbit, which generalised to similar white fluffy objects.
- Klosko *et al.* (1990) assessed various therapies for the treatment of panic attacks, finding that 87 per cent of patients were panic free after SD treatment, compared to 50 per cent taking the drug Alprazolam, 36 per cent receiving a placebo and 33 per cent receiving no treatment. This suggests SD to be highly effective.
- Rothbaum *et al.* (1998) reported on **virtual reality exposure therapy**, where patients are active participants within a computer-generated, three-dimensional world that changes naturally with head movements. SD-like treatment occurs, but without the patient ever leaving the therapist's office. Control was gained over the phobic stimuli, with less exposure to the patient of harm and embarrassment than with standard treatment.
- Gertz (1966) reported that 66 per cent of obsessive-compulsive disorder patients responded favourably to SD, suggesting the treatment is effective.

Cognitive therapies

Cognitive behavioural therapy (CBT) is based on the cognitive model, which sees abnormal behaviour resulting from disordered thought processes. CBT is an umbrella term for a number of different therapies, the two best known being rational emotive behaviour therapy and treatment of negative automatic thoughts. The central idea of both is to challenge and restructure maladaptive ways of thinking into adaptive, rational ones.

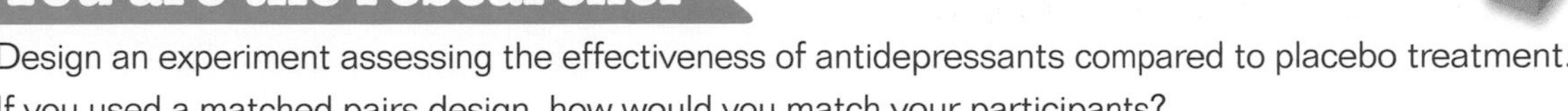

You are the researcher

Design an experiment assessing the effectiveness of antidepressants compared to placebo treatment.
If you used a matched pairs design, how would you match your participants?

Evaluation

Evaluation of systematic desensitisation

- SD is quick to administer and requires less input from the patient than other psychological therapies.
- SD is less traumatic than other behavioural treatments, like flooding, where patients have to confront phobias directly. SD is a more gentle step-by-step approach.
- SD can be modified successfully for use with different groups of patients with different needs, like the elderly or adolescents, emphasising its effectiveness.
- SD is considered more effective than drugs in treating anxiety disorders, as relapse rates are lower, suggesting the treatment brings long-term, lasting benefits.
- It is not always practical for individuals to be desensitised by confronting real situations. Real-life step-by-step situations are difficult to arrange and control. In addition, some patients' imaginations are not vivid enough to produce the desired effect.
- SD is only applicable to anxiety disorders, like phobias, meaning it is ineffective against the majority of mental disorders.
- It is claimed that relaxation techniques are not essential, but rather it is the exposure to the feared situation that is of paramount importance. Also, the step-by-step anxiety hierarchy merely helps patients build up to facing their fears, but is not an essential part of the therapy.
- SD is not effective in addressing phobias with an evolutionary origin. Such phobias have a survival value, have not developed through environmental experience and cannot be removed through counter-conditioning.

Rational emotive behaviour therapy

Rational emotive behaviour therapy (REMT) was developed by Albert Ellis in 1975. Ellis believes that irrational thoughts cause emotional distress and behaviour disorders. Irrational thoughts cause negative self-statements and therapy involves making patients' irrational and negative thoughts more rational and positive. Ellis (1990) identified eleven basic irrational **musturbatory beliefs** that are emotionally damaging and can lead to psychological problems. These include: 'I must be loved by everybody' and 'I must be excellent in all respects … otherwise I am worthless'. The therapist's aim is to challenge patients' thinking and show how irrational their thoughts are. Patients are told to practise positive and optimistic thinking. One method involves the 'ABC technique' of irrational beliefs, which comprises three steps to analyse the ways individuals develop irrational beliefs.

A = **Activating event**: patients record events leading to disordered thinking, such as exam failure.

B = **Beliefs**: patients record negative thoughts associated with the event, such as I'm useless and stupid.

C = **Consequence**: patients record negative thoughts or behaviours that follow, such as feeling upset and thinking about leaving college.

REBT involves reframing, in other words challenging negative thoughts by reinterpreting the ABC in a more positive, logical way. For example, the exam was difficult, or there was not enough time for revision. Basically REBT involves looking on the bright side and seeing things more optimistically.

Treatment of negative automatic thoughts

Treatment of negative automatic thoughts was developed in 1967 by Beck to treat depression. Beck proposed that people become depressed because of negative thoughts or schemas and see the world negatively. Depressives expect to fail, blame themselves and have negative self-views. Negative schemas contribute to the negative cognitive triad, where patients have negative thoughts about 1) themselves, 2) the environment and 3) the future. Beck identified several cognitive biases and distortions occurring in depressed individuals. Five of these are:

1. **Arbitrary inference** – the drawing of unjustified conclusions based on little or no evidence.
2. **Selective abstraction** – the focusing of attention on one detail without regard to other details.
3. **Over-generalisation** – the drawing of a general conclusion based upon limited events.
4. **Magnification** – making mountains out of molehills; small problems become magnified.
5. **Minimisation** – undervaluing positive attributes; minimising positive aspects in life.

Treatment of negative automatic thoughts is a collaborative process between patient and therapist. Firstly the problem and the desired goal are identified. Then negative thoughts associated with the depression are challenged. Patients are asked to undertake 'homework' between sessions to test these thoughts, for example, recording the number of times someone is rude. They may be surprised that people are not 'always nasty'. The final step involves patients monitoring perceptions realistically. Patients are taught to monitor negative automatic thoughts and examine evidence supporting them. Eventually they learn to see why they have distorted thoughts.

Research into CBT

- Tarrier (2005) reported CBT to be an effective treatment for schizophrenia, finding evidence of reduced symptoms and lower relapse rates.
- Flannaghan *et al.* (1997) found CBT effective in treating depressive stroke victims, suggesting that it is suitable for specific groups of depressives.
- Kvale *et al.* (2004) conducted a meta-analysis of treatment studies for people with dental phobias, finding that 77 per cent of CBT patients regularly visited a dentist four years after treatment.
- Spence *et al.* (2000) assessed the value of CBT in children with social phobias, finding child-focused CBT and CBT plus parental involvement effective in reducing social and general anxiety levels, with these improvements apparent at a one-year follow up. This suggests CBT has long-term effectiveness with phobic children.

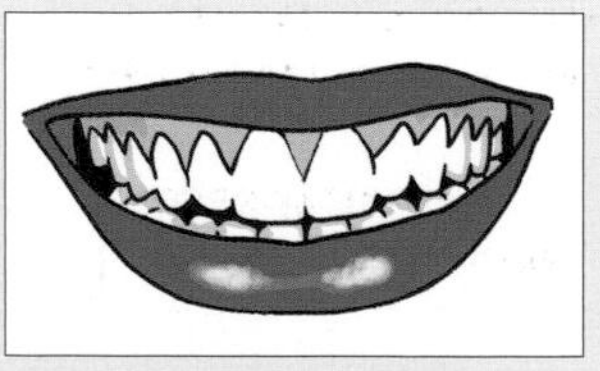

Figure 6.18 77 per cent of CBT patients regularly visit a dentist four years after treatment for dental phobia

You are the researcher

One problem with assessing the effectiveness of treatments is deciding whether improvements are merely short term.

Design a study assessing the effectiveness of three chosen treatments over a five-year period. What type of study would be used?

What would your IV and DV be?

Evaluation

Evaluation of CBT

- CBT has proven effective in over 400 studies in both children and adults. It is seen as effective for a wide range of disorders, including post-traumatic stress disorder, obsessive-compulsive disorder, depression and eating disorders. CBT is reputable enough to be available through the NHS.
- CBT is useful as it can be used not only with patients suffering from clinical mental disorders, but also with people with more moderate problems, like nervousness.
- The application of CBT occurs over relatively short time periods compared to other treatments and is more cost effective than such treatments.
- CBT has long-term benefits, as the techniques involved are used continually to stop symptoms returning.
- CBT is dependent on patients being able to talk about thought processes coherently, and so such therapies do not work for severe mental disorders, like schizophrenia.
- One problem with CBT is whether the theory behind it is correct. Is a depressed person's disordered thinking a cause or effect of depression? Many cognitive behavioural therapists believe the relationship works both ways.
- There are ethical concerns with CBT as it can be too directive. Therapists may abuse their power of control over patients, forcing them into certain modes of thinking and patients can become too dependent on therapists.
- CBT is difficult to evaluate. Senra and Polaino (1998) found the use of different measurement scales to assess CBT produced different measures of improvement among patients.

Strengthen your learning

1. How does psychoanalysis treat mental disorders?
2. Explain the difference between the *manifest* and the *latent* content of dreams.
3. Outline the process of free association.
4. Outline two pieces of research evidence suggesting that psychoanalysis is effective.
5. Explain two strengths and two weaknesses of psychoanalysis.
6. What is the aim of systematic desensitisation?
7. Outline two pieces of research evidence suggesting that systematic desensitisation is effective.
8. Explain two strengths and two weaknesses of systematic desensitisation.
9. What is the aim of cognitive behavioural therapy?
10. Outline either rational emotive behaviour therapy or treatment of negative automatic thoughts.
11. Outline two pieces of research evidence suggesting that cognitive behavioural therapy is effective.
12. Explain two strengths and two weaknesses of cognitive behavioural therapy.

Assessment Check

1 Each of the following statements relates to one of three psychological therapies. Copy and complete the table by placing a letter P for psychoanalysis, a letter C for cognitive behavioural therapy and a letter S for systematic desensitisation next to each statement to indicate which specific therapy they relate to. [6 marks]

Statement	Type of psychological therapy
The use of dream analysis to reveal inner conflicts	
The replacement of fear responses by relaxation responses	
Abnormal behaviour results from disordered thinking	
The replacement of irrational beliefs by more rational ones	
Bringing repressed thoughts and feelings into conscious awareness	
A step-by-step approach to a feared object or situation	

2 Yolanda believes that unless she writes down everything she knows she will fail her examinations. Her teacher constantly reassures her that this is not so, but Yolanda's negative thoughts persist and she finds it difficult to even start an essay, let alone finish one.
   a) Explain why cognitive behavioural therapy (CBT) may be appropriate for Yolanda. [3 marks]
   b) Outline what is involved in CBT. [3 marks]

3 Describe the use of systematic desensitisation (SD) in treating abnormality. [6 marks]

4 a) Outline one ethical issue in gaining informed consent to treat a patient with a psychological therapy. [2 marks]
   b) Explain how this issue could be overcome. [1 mark]

5 Outline and evaluate psychoanalysis as a treatment of psychological abnormality. [12 marks]

Examination guidance:

1 With this question you need to work out what type of psychological therapy each statement refers to and then place the correct letter in the box next to them.

2 Part a) requires you to refer to information in the scenario provided to explain why CBT is appropriate, while part b) requires a description of the technique.

3 This question requires a description of SD. Evaluation or description of other therapies would not gain credit.

4 Question 4 requires you to relate your knowledge of research methods, specifically ethical considerations, to the application of psychological therapies.

5 This is a long-answer question with six marks available for describing psychoanalysis and six marks for evaluation. This could be achieved by reference to the therapy's strengths and weaknesses.

End of chapter review

- Abnormality is a psychological or behavioural state leading to impairment of interpersonal functioning and/or distress to others.
- The deviation from social norms definition concerns behaviour violating accepted social rules, allowing distinction between desirable and undesirable behaviours.
- Social norms are not real, but are based on the opinions of elites within society used to maintain social order.
- Using social norms to define abnormality has limitations, like the fact they change over time, across situations, with age and between cultures.
- Social norms do not apply to individualistic persons and breaking social norms can be of benefit to society
- Rosenhan and Seligman (1989) suggest that failing to function adequately has seven features. The more someone has, the more they are classed as abnormal.
- There are limitations with this definition, like the subjective nature of the features of personal dysfunction and the fact that abnormality is not always accompanied by dysfunction.
- The deviation from ideal health definition sees abnormality as failing to meet the criteria for perfect psychological well-being.
- Jahoda identified six characteristics that individuals should exhibit to be normal. An absence of these characteristics indicates abnormality.
- The biological model perceives mental disorders as illnesses with physical causes.
- Studies involving viruses/infections, brain damage, biochemistry and genetics support this approach.
- The model has strengths, like being based on well-established scientific principles, but also has weaknesses, like its reliance on animal studies.
- The psychodynamic approach perceives mental disorders as arising from unresolved, unconscious childhood traumas. Traumatic experiences are repressed into the unconscious mind and affect adult behaviour.
- The model has strengths, like its pioneering influence, and some research support. However, the model has criticisms, like its unscientific nature.
- The behavioural model is a psychological approach perceiving mental disorders as abnormal behaviours learned through classical and operant conditioning and social learning.
- The cognitive model is a psychological approach perceiving mental disorders as due to negative thoughts and illogical beliefs.
- The model is supported by research evidence and is influential. However, it is not certain whether irrational thought processes are the cause or the effects of mental disorders.
- Drugs and ECT are the two main biological therapies.
- Drugs are cost effective and familiar, but have side effects.
- ECT does not damage the brain, but the mechanisms by which it works are not understood.
- Psychoanalysis, systematic desensitisation and CBT are the three main psychological therapies.
- Psychoanalysis is a psychodynamic treatment seeking to give patients insight into the origins of their disorders, by the use of techniques like dream analysis and free association. Importance is placed on childhood traumas and repressed impulses and memories.
- Psychoanalysis has proven useful, but there are difficulties in measuring its effectiveness.
- Systematic desensitisation is a behavioural therapy used to modify phobias by constructing and working through a hierarchy of anxiety-producing stimuli.
- Systematic desensitisation is quick to administer and requires less input from the patient than other psychological therapies, but is only applicable to anxiety disorders, meaning it is ineffective against most disorders.
- CBT is a cognitive therapy challenging and restructuring abnormal ways of thinking into useful, rational ones.
- Two well-known versions of CBT are rational emotive behaviour therapy and treatment of negative automatic thoughts.

Index

Page numbers in **bold** refer to keyword definitions.